MW00653445

THE EDUCATION MYTH

A volume in the series
Histories of American Education
Edited by Jonathan Zimmerman and Tracy L. Steffes

THE EDUCATION MYTH

How Human Capital Trumped
Social Democracy

Jon Shelton

CORNELL UNIVERSITY PRESS   **ITHACA AND LONDON**

First published 2023 by Cornell University Press

Library of Congress Cataloging-in-Publication Data

Names: Shelton, Jon, 1978– author.
Title: The education myth : how human capital trumped
    social democracy / Jon Shelton.
Description: Ithaca [New York] : Cornell University Press, 2023. |
    Includes bibliographical references and index.
Identifiers: LCCN 2022013532 (print) | LCCN 2022013533 (ebook) |
    ISBN 9781501768149 (hardcover) | ISBN 9781501768163 (pdf) |
    ISBN 9781501768156 (ebook)
Subjects: LCSH: Education—Economic aspects—United States—History. |
    Education—Political aspects—United States—History. | Education and
    state—United States—History. | Democracy and education—United States—
    History. | Human capital—United States—History. | Economic
    security—United States—History.
Classification: LCC LC66 .S54 2023 (print) | LCC LC66 (ebook) |
    DDC 379.73—dc23/eng/20220713
LC record available at https://lccn.loc.gov/2022013532
LC ebook record available at https://lccn.loc.gov/2022013533

For Lester and Erline Shelton,
who taught me love and kindness

Contents

Preface

This is a book about what has been politically possible in American history: specifically, the narrowing of political opportunity, over the past fifty years or so, toward the idea that only those who acquire the right human capital are worthy of economic security and social respect. I argue the path we've been on now threatens our very democracy, imperfect as it is. Indeed, in the recent past, Americans have seen our nation become increasingly unequal and our politics become increasingly divisive. It is not an exaggeration to say we face a political crisis on the scale of the American Revolution, the Civil War, and the Great Depression. Further, as I have studied our past, I have become convinced there is only one path forward that will save us: a dramatic recommitment to social democracy, or the idea that every citizen in our country deserves not just equality before the law and the right to political participation, but also a set of social and economic rights that guarantee a fundamental level of human dignity and equality. For a democracy to function, we all need economic security, which includes the right to a livelihood. Furthermore, everyone's contribution to our society through their work each day must be valued, no matter what their education level.

I want to begin by putting my cards on the table: my position, and the premise of this book's argument, stems from my perspective as an historian, as a union activist, and as a teacher, respectively. First, as an historian, I believe in the promise of American democracy. Embedded in the Declaration of Independence, our nation's political creed, is the idea that governments are instituted in order to secure every citizen's rights to life, liberty, and the pursuit of happiness. Of course, I recognize the limits to those rights—around race, gender, and social class—in the late eighteenth century. I also recognize that no one was talking about guaranteeing jobs in 1776. But, as an historian, I also understand that things change over time. The promise of American democracy is that we are all equals and we are all entitled, as the political theorist Danielle Allen puts it, to equal access to the machinery of American government.[1] In a modern world where one's livelihood is subject to a whole host of forces outside of one's control—from racism to macroeconomic conditions—ensuring life, liberty, and the pursuit of happiness requires the machinery of government to do much more than it did in an agricultural society that had accommodated chattel slavery. Most Americans, for much of the twentieth century, understood that reality, but unfortunately, a different narrative—one based on the idea that you only deserve an economic livelihood if you get yourself the right education—has dramatically lowered our expectations in our recent past.

Second, I am a proud member of my union (UWGB-United) and serve as vice president of higher education for the American Federation of Teachers-Wisconsin. As a labor activist, I understand the dignity of work. A crucial aspect of the American social democratic promise is the ideal of industrial democracy: that no matter where one works, every worker has the right to have a say in their working conditions and the means to make them better. Social democracy also means our society should value the important contributions every worker makes each day, and that no worker should be devalued for not having specific academic credentials. No job, no matter what level of training it requires, should be bereft of economic security, and no one should be excluded from having healthcare or a home because of the job they work.

Finally, I am a teacher. I began my career teaching high school, and for the past decade, I've been teaching at the University of Wisconsin-Green Bay, which is very much a nonelite institution. Most of my students come from working families, and many are the first in their family to go to college. They grow up in both urban and rural parts of Wisconsin, and though I've never systematically asked, there seems to be a rough level of parity between those who grew up in conservative environments and those who grew up in more liberal environments. Most of them, however, have internalized as common sense the idea that acquiring education constitutes their primary shot at a decent livelihood. Some of them appreciate this possibility, while others resent it and clearly come to college grudgingly. Others still object to any intrusion—like general education courses—on their pragmatic path to a specific career. But virtually every student understands that without more education, they seem to have a limited chance at long-term economic security. In this respect, they are like millions of millennials across the country who have internalized the notion that, above all, their lives should be devoted to acquiring "human capital." For this generation, the economic and political assumptions of the world in which they have come of age have been nothing short of catastrophic, causing them to live with heightened levels of economic insecurity, stress, and anxiety.[2]

In this regard, they view education differently than Americans in the past. Sure, generations that came before us have seen public education as important in acquiring skills to do well in the labor market, but Americans in the past half century are unique in seeing public education as being the primary—even the sole— avenue toward any chance at economic security. The reason for this prevailing view is because politicians, intellectuals, and others have pushed the notion that investing in "human capital" could replace social democratic alternatives that were once at the center of our political mainstream.

This book, then, explains how education—once a major piece of a broad vision for helping Americans gain economic security and facilitate democratic citizenship—was reduced, since the 1960s, to little more than a commodity through which to compete for a diminishing number of good economic opportunities. In the recent past, neither major party has offered much of a realistic vision to help working people enjoy more economic security or live better lives. The result has been growing political disaffection and division across the political spectrum. To restore and deepen American democracy at this critical time, we must think much more broadly about public education and its place in a nation that ensures all of us true life, liberty, and the pursuit of happiness.

THE EDUCATION MYTH

Introduction

In his State of the Union address on January 11, 1944, President Franklin D. Roosevelt proposed a Second Bill of Rights. While the original Bill of Rights appended to the Constitution in 1791 promised a core set of civil liberties, Roosevelt's proposal offered the guarantee of economic freedoms to all Americans. Following a decade of reforms that pulled the United States out of the Great Depression and refashioned the basic social contract, FDR pointed out that "in our day these economic truths have become accepted as self-evident. We have accepted, so to speak, a Second Bill of Rights under which a new basis of security and prosperity can be established for all regardless of station, race, or creed." The method with which Roosevelt ordered his proposed economic rights was highly significant.

Among these are:

The right to a useful and remunerative job in the industries or shops or farms or mines of the Nation;

The right to earn enough to provide adequate food and clothing and recreation;

The right of every farmer to raise and sell his products at a return which will give him and his family a decent living;

The right of every businessman, large and small, to trade in an atmosphere of freedom from unfair competition and domination by monopolies at home or abroad;

The right of every family to a decent home;

The right to adequate medical care and the opportunity to achieve and enjoy good health;

The right to adequate protection from the economic fears of old age, sickness, accident, and unemployment;

The right to a good education.

All of these rights spell security. And after this war is won we must be prepared to move forward, in the implementation of these rights, to new goals of human happiness and well-being.

Only after the rights to economic security had been established did FDR propose "the right to a good education." While Roosevelt clearly believed education was a necessary right (and in fact, the right to an education had been an expectation of many Americans since the nation's founding), education was not reducible to helping one succeed in the job market.[1]

Alternatives as bold as FDR's Second Bill of Rights continued to be at the center of the American political mainstream for decades after World War II. Indeed, policymakers—mostly Democrats but including some Republicans too—believed the government played a crucial role in ensuring access to economic security for working families. They believed labor unions played a major role in that trajectory and sometimes pushed for big alternatives: including a serious proposal in 1945–46 to create an economy that would guarantee every American breadwinner a job. In the years that followed, social democratic activists and policymakers persisted in pushing big alternatives to deepen the nation's commitment to social democracy. In 1966, for example, labor leaders A. Philip Randolph and Bayard Rustin proposed a Freedom Budget for all Americans they believed represented the next logical progression of the Civil Rights movement by ending poverty. A decade after that, Senator Hubert Humphrey (D-MN) and California Representative Augustus Hawkins (D-CA) proposed a bill that would once and for all guarantee every American the right to a job. Supported by Coretta Scott King as Martin Luther King's "legacy," and guaranteeing jobs to women workers too, a robust version of the Humphrey-Hawkins Act could have meant major strides toward a multiracial social democracy transcending the male breadwinner–centered version that had emerged during the New Deal.

Though the American social democratic promise never reached the heights FDR proposed in 1944, for the next three decades, there were important alternatives at the center of the American political mainstream. These alternatives coexisted, however, with another political narrative that grew exponentially during the same time: what I call the "education myth." Premised on the reality that education could in fact provide Americans new skills, this myth asserted that building human capital through education represented the best, and increasingly, the only way for Americans to access economic opportunity. As the twentieth century progressed, this myth choked off social democratic alternatives like the Freedom Budget or a robust version of the Humphrey-Hawkins Act, leaving the nation's political center bereft of any realistic ideas that would guarantee economic security and social dignity for the majority of Americans, particularly those without college degrees. The result, over the past four decades, has been the emergence of a deeply inequitable economy and a drastically divided political system.

The Education Myth tells this story. I'm certainly not the first historian to point out how Americans have sought to use the education system for socioeconomic gain. In the nineteenth century, as historians like Nancy Beadie and Michael Katz have pointed out, respectively, some Americans used the education system to develop social capital through economic networks, while others used it to discipline unruly workers.[2] By the twentieth century, Progressives sought to use education to solve the problems of economic inequality and poverty, and an entire "education gospel" emerged that saw education as an essential economic and social solvent.[3] Even many working people, as Cristina Groeger's important book shows us, saw the public education system as a vehicle to acquire new skills and to do better in the labor market.[4] I'm also not the first historian to show how problematic it is to expect the education system, by itself, to overcome economic inequality and create social mobility.[5] What my book adds to the exceptional work of other historians is to show how this unrealistic expectation about public education, which once coexisted with other mainstream alternatives about how to ensure economic independence, and later, economic security, has, in the recent past, utterly quashed those alternatives.

Though the Constitution only explicitly outlined civil and political rights, the document's preamble, through the notions of forming a "more perfect union" and "promot[ing] the general welfare," promised the growth of a nation that would facilitate new opportunities for its citizens. While most early architects of the political entity that became the United States, like slaveowner Thomas Jefferson, did not intend to fully (or at all) include women, Native Americans, or enslaved African Americans in this promise, they nonetheless sought to provide enabling freedoms such as access to land and public education that would make a wider circle of American citizens economically and politically independent.

From the Louisiana Purchase (1803) to the Homestead Act (1862), American policymakers sought to help individual citizens gain the economic independence that would make them good citizens. By the Civil War, most states outside the South guaranteed public education in their constitutions, and the Morrill Act (1862), signed into law during the war by President Abraham Lincoln, expanded access to both "liberal and practical" higher education through land grants to state colleges and universities. To be sure, these policies mostly targeted white Americans, and came at the expense of Native American sovereignty. Many of those who were excluded, however, such as the enslaved people who played a major role in the war to end slavery in the 1860s, leveraged this promise to fight for their own economic and political independence.

From the 1870s to the 1930s, as it became clear that most Americans would have to sell their labor each day to survive, working people stopped pushing for economic independence and started to demand security and industrial democracy. For the most part, working-class activists sought economic security through union recognition and collectively bargained agreements. Some workers did begin to seek increased economic opportunity through access to public education, but it was not the only, or even primary, way most Americans thought about attaining greater economic security. The New Deal actualized much of the call for this expansion of social democracy by ensuring labor rights through the Wagner Act (1935) and social programs like Social Security (1935), but despite the comprehensive vision FDR proposed in 1944, further efforts to expand social democratic gains mostly fell short during these years. Broader expansions of economic security, however, continued to appear on the horizon: a Democratic Congress sought to ensure a virtual guarantee of a job in 1945, and later, Roosevelt's successor Harry Truman (1945–53) proposed a program for universal healthcare, but conservatives stymied these possibilities. Though more Americans accessed good jobs and health insurance after World War II, these rights were never fully guaranteed, and benefits accrued disproportionately to white working men around a breadwinner model in which the labor of women was mostly invisible.

In the 1950s and 1960s, as the US economy became more complex and more jobs required greater skill, access to education became tied more closely to economic opportunity, continuing a process that had begun in the first half of the twentieth century. The GI Bill (1944), by providing, among other things, virtually tuition-free access to higher education for veterans, expanded expectations for both economic security and the idea that education could enhance one's opportunities in the labor market. States dramatically increased spending for public education, including both K-12 schools and state universities.

African Americans and other minorities protested against the gross inequities that existed in this postwar expansion of social democracy. Though many of these inequities were never fully rectified, there were meaningful efforts, such as the Civil Rights Act of 1964 and the Elementary and Secondary Education Act of 1965, to reduce the gap. At the same time, there were also enhancements in other enabling freedoms in the two decades after World War II, such as the expansion of Social Security and the introduction of Medicare and Medicaid. Still, for the most part, the period of reform under President Lyndon Johnson (1963–69) centered on the notion that the best way to alleviate poverty was to expand access to education and job training, not through broader efforts to ensure everyone had jobs, union rights, and healthcare.

The limitations of the reform agenda under Johnson, in fact, represented the beginning of an important trend. Over the past fifty years, the broader vision of American social democracy has been narrowed considerably: economists and other intellectuals, corporate interests, and politicians—most prominently Democrats but on both sides of the partisan aisle—have successfully pushed an erroneous narrative that access to the right education is all that is needed to give everyone an equal opportunity to secure a good life. This narrative is, in fact, a mythology, promising to bring good jobs and economic security, as if by magic, to all those who play by the rules. Indeed, much like the ancient study of alchemy, which sought to turn base metal into gold, this education myth promises to magically help the acquirer overcome any structural impediments—economic downturn, a geographic lack of jobs, and racial inequality, for instance—in order to find a job in an increasingly competitive marketplace that will provide a decent livelihood.[6] At the same time, efforts to enhance most other aspects of social democracy, such as guaranteeing the right to a job, a living wage, a union, childcare, healthcare, or housing, were either stopped in their tracks or rolled back.

This myth has increasingly relied on the fiction that the economy is a meritocracy: that those who succeed in getting the right education deserve economic security, while those who "fail" to get a good job deserve their fate. Philosopher Michael Sandel has referred to this way of thinking as the "tyranny of merit," pointing out that even if our society *could* be a true meritocracy (it isn't, and almost certainly never will be), neglecting the value of every citizen in our nation would still be disastrous. Indeed, those Americans who have not been "winners" in the human capital competition of the last fifty years, Sandel rightly argues, have lost the "social esteem" nonprofessional-class workers might have once enjoyed in past eras.[7]

Finally, the education myth has impoverished what political theorist Danielle Allen calls the "human potentiality" of civic and political engagement. By focusing only on economic opportunity, our education system over the past half century has mostly told every new cohort of students that learning to become good citizens in a democracy is no longer valuable.[8] The result is an American politics increasingly defined by the notion that our government primarily serves to facilitate marketable education and that citizenship is defined not by one's overall contributions to their community but by their ability to spin their education into economic prosperity.

The *Education Myth* explains how we got to this point. By the 1970s, a more complex economy required greater numbers of college-educated professionals, and for many of these workers, acquiring education had been a route to their relative success in the labor market. This transition occurred at the same time corporations went to war on nonprofessional workers, shifting production to areas where they could pay manufacturing workers less, making it more difficult for American workers to unionize, or investing in largely nonunion sectors like healthcare that leveraged existing racial and gender inequities.[9] Consequently, the growing professional class began to believe education—in a supposedly fair, meritocratic competition—was the key to success for everyone else too. In contrast to other explanations for the direction of the Democratic Party in the 1970s (some of these suggest Democrats were increasingly beholden to "special interests" such as unions, feminists, or civil rights activists), the reality was that over the course of the decade, more and more Democratic politicians saw themselves as representing this growing professional-class constituency. A new generation of officeholders—like Delaware senator Joe Biden—helped thwart a resurgent social movement to ensure the right to a job and universal healthcare in the 1970s.

Jimmy Carter (1977–81) was a driving force in this new Democratic Party, and while his administration helped elevate the status of public education, creating the federal Department of Education in 1979, it also diminished social democratic possibilities in other arenas of American life by declining to support a jobs guarantee and only lukewarmly fighting for workers' rights. The late 1970s, in particular, represented an important missed opportunity to create a truly multiracial democracy built on the foundation of economic security for all that no longer treated women as ancillary partners in a family dominated by a male breadwinner. Unfortunately, the failures of the Carter years narrowed future political possibilities. Later Democratic leaders Bill Clinton (1993–2001), elevated by the Democratic Leadership Council (DLC), and Barack Obama (2009–17) fervently advanced policies to tie education more closely to human capital as well as brokering trade deals (for Clinton, the North American Free Trade Agreement [NAFTA] and for Obama, the Trans-Pacific Partnership [TPP]) that put even more downward pressure on livelihoods for those without college degrees. Negotiating such deals undermined one of the fundamental premises of the American promise: that the nation exists to provide economic opportunities for average Americans, not workers elsewhere. In Clinton's case, he also collaborated with a Republican Congress to shred the social safety net for the poorest Americans while spending millions to incarcerate more working people, disproportionately Black and Latino, for lengthier prison sentences.

The education myth was driven primarily by Democrats, then: first in the 1960s by a Johnson administration that viewed education and job training as more important than broader social democratic interventions, then by "New Politics" Democrats representing professional-class constituencies in the 1970s, and finally, by the "neo-liberals" and the New Democrats of the DLC in the 1980s and 90s, respectively.[10]

Some Republicans, such as Education Secretary Terrel Bell, who commissioned the 1983 report *A Nation at Risk*, advanced a conservative version of the myth. By 2000, in fact, the education myth had become so consuming that even Republicans as prominent as President George W. Bush (2001–9) employed it, seeking political gain at the expense of Democrats, and touting school accountability through the No Child Left Behind Act as the way to provide Americans a shot at good jobs while liberalizing trade relations with China and undercutting manufacturing in the United States. Other Republicans, however, like President Ronald Reagan (1981–89), presidential candidate Pat Buchanan (1992 and 1996), and Wisconsin governor Scott Walker (2011–19), mobilized populist working-class resentments against the more educated professional class who had most strongly advanced the education myth. By 2010, political actors like Walker had established the playbook that the reactionary populist Donald Trump would use in 2016.

As this myth increasingly motivated policymakers' actions, inequality in the United States exploded and more and more Americans—about 65 percent of the population today lack college degrees—have struggled with long-term economic insecurity and disenchantment with the political process.[11] Especially since the economic crisis of 2008, even many college graduates have struggled to find the kinds of jobs the education myth says they should have been able to get, instead toiling in precarious conditions with low wages and massive student debt.[12]

And so, a primary—perhaps *the* primary—point of contention in American politics over the past decade has been between those who doubled down on this myth and those who are revolting against it. This conflict does not follow strict partisan lines, and because we tend to see so many political debates through a partisan lens, not enough Americans understand what is happening. But the education myth seems to be losing its salience. On the left, millennials and others shut out of the supposed meritocracy are in revolt against the Democratic Party: neoliberals like Hillary Clinton and Joe Biden had to muster the entire party establishment to suppress the social democrat Bernie Sanders in 2016 and 2020, for example, and as a result, Biden's agenda has already shifted toward a grudging embrace of a somewhat broader set of economic rights. Further, social movements in the past decade, led by teacher unions committed to racial justice and broad political economic change, have organized dozens of high-profile and successful actions in pursuit of a broader vision of social democracy.

Donald Trump's ascent on the right, capturing both the Republican Party and the presidency in 2016, and winning even more votes four years later, owes a heavy debt to those Americans who believe they are left out of an economy that has largely catered to well-educated elites. But Trump also speaks to the loss of social esteem among those outside the professional class because they have not measured up to the cultural values of the highly educated constituency at the center of the Democratic Party.[13] Though Trump especially mobilized white Americans without college degrees, his inroads with both African American and Latino voters in 2020 should give pause to Democrats who think a more demographically diverse America alone will eventually defeat Trumpism.[14]

The Education Myth tells this story, beginning by explaining how the expansion of public education in the United States was embedded in an expanding democratic promise. In the first three chapters of the book, which move swiftly from the nation's founding through the end of the 1960s, I show how this promise, limited as it was, set up a vision for a political system that would advance, first, economic independence for American citizens, and later, economic security. Public education played a growing role in these expectations, and developing Americans' civic and political capabilities (even as it sometimes sought to eliminate the distinct cultural practices of immigrants and other ethnic minorities) represented a major component of what American policymakers, intellectuals, and reformers thought public education should do.

I don't intend to romanticize these developments. At the beginning, most Americans were excluded from that promise. Over the course of the nineteenth and twentieth centuries, however, those left out—men without property, women, African Americans, and others—demanded the nation make good on its founding premise. In many cases, those whose basic civil and political rights had never been fully acknowledged, like African American union leader A. Philip Randolph, were the most visionary advocates for enhancing social democratic expectations for all Americans. These expectations also revolved around the gendered notion that men were primary breadwinners and economic security flowed through a hierarchical family. And, in fact, by the last great period of American reform, the Great Society, problematic views about the cultural deficiencies of African Americans and other poor Americans played a major role in narrowing the promise of social democracy toward the acquisition of human capital.

In the past half century, however, our political system has greatly diminished the limited social rights won by Randolph and others, and until very recently has successfully constricted even any serious consideration of more. Chapter 4 begins to tell that story, showing how some Democratic leaders, increasingly driven by professional-class notions of meritocracy in the 1970s, stifled important reforms like the right to a job while elevating public education to a greater level of symbolic significance. Conservative Republicans led by Ronald Reagan, as I show in chapter 5, cut federal education spending, but by the 1980s, even Reagan could not arrest the trajectory of the education myth. A growing consensus around the importance of education to ensure American economic competitiveness led even many moderate Republicans, like the president's own education secretary Terrel Bell, to push for greater investment. The report Bell commissioned, further propelled the myth by making exaggerated claims about the supposed problems with the American education system and why those problems were limiting the livelihoods of new generations of workers. At that point, even prominent Republicans like George H. W. Bush, as I show in chapter 6, sought to highlight their embrace of investment in human capital for political gain.

Bill Clinton, however, first as governor of Arkansas, then as chairperson of the Democratic Leadership Council, and finally as president, rode the crest of the education myth to the greatest political fortune. Indeed, as chapter 7 makes clear, investment in public education proved central to a much-reduced set of expectations at the core of the Democratic agenda—one that would make corporate America happy while stealing the political thunder of a new hard right group of conservative Republicans by the end of the 1990s. In chapter 8, I explore the high-water mark of the education myth: the bipartisan No Child Left Behind Act (2001) showed that there was little dissent in any mainstream political quarter, and Richard Florida's *Rise of the Creative Class*, published the same year, pointed to the growing cultural dominance of the professional class as well as the resentment from those left out of it. In chapter 9, I highlight the first significant political manifestations of the revolt against the education myth, showing how the failure of Barack Obama to make good on his promises on economic security helped empower a new wave of Republicans, like Governor Scott Walker in Wisconsin, who exploited the grievances of many voters with a Democratic Party that seemed only to cater to professionals.

Finally, in the last chapter, I document the growing cracks in the education myth. Trump's rise, following a similar playbook as Walker, capitalized on both economic and cultural resentments in winning a major upset over Hillary Clinton, who, like Obama, is a quintessential professional-class meritocrat. I also document the revolt against the myth on the left, as political figures such as Bernie Sanders and unions such as the Chicago Teacher Union (CTU) have pushed for a much more robust version of social democracy in which public education, as it was for FDR, is only one piece of a wider set of social and economic rights necessary for full citizenship.

Before moving on, I must clarify a few of my positions in this book. By social democracy, I mean the ideal that government should cultivate positive freedoms for all of its citizens by providing new economic and social rights. This terminology is important, and not a term Americans typically use to understand politics. Many Americans today think of politics along a continuum between conservatism and liberalism. They believe conservatism means the government plays a limited role in regulating the economy and liberalism means the government plays a bigger role. Conservatives caricature government intervention as "socialist," though socialism actually means that economic production is undertaken in a strictly democratic fashion (for instance, that workers elect their leaders in an enterprise and share more or less equally in the profits). Social democracy, however, is the notion that modern governments, within a capitalist framework, should actively work to ensure greater economic and social rights for ordinary citizens.[15] Regulation is a part of social democracy—higher taxes on the wealthy may be necessary to provide new freedoms to all those who work for a living—but it is not the primary way of understanding it.

Next, what do I mean by "human capital"? The notion of human capital stems from the work of neoclassical economists in the 1960s, led by Theodore Schultz and Gary Becker, who pointed out that acquiring new capabilities through education would advance one's long-term productivity. In turn, this productivity, they argued, was rewarded with the higher wages employers paid for the upgrade. Thus, the best way to ensure broad prosperity is for Americans to invest as much as possible in education and training. Becker believed this investment should mostly come from the individuals who benefit, though many other economists (including Schultz) have argued for greater social investment in individual human capital.

The concept of human capital has some validity, but its standard use in the field of economics obscures more than it clarifies, inverting the labor relationship that actually exists under capitalism. In reality, capital is a tool, such as a machine or a piece of infrastructure, used by a worker to produce something with market value. Those who own capital—like Jeff Bezos's Amazon, which owns the warehouses and sorting machines that distribute goods across the country—reap a large portion of the rewards, passing on a set wage to workers who sell their time to do the work machines cannot do. Workers with greater skill are often paid higher wages, but they are still selling their labor and almost never have the same power as those who own capital. With the exception of the highest echelons of the labor market (the best-paid professional athletes or hedge fund managers, for instance), most workers are only economically secure as long as they continue to have a job. Further, raising wages is never as simple as adding new skills: workers' pay is always related to factors completely outside of their control, such as the health of the broader economy, the number of other workers willing or able to sell the same skills, the political power of corporations to suppress labor markets, racial and gender discrimination, and many other variables. The concept of human capital, then, is an exercise in alchemy, suggesting workers have more control over their wages than they do, and implying that the labor market is a pure meritocracy in which one is rewarded for the prescience of their personal investment.

I also want to point out that this book does not comprehensively cover every quarter of American society. It is best thought of as the political history of an idea: how it is that the education myth became a dominant idea in our politics and how that idea is losing its salience. The political figures and thinkers I cite in this book were responsible for driving the changes I document, but as with all historical actors, they did so within the constraints of the existing system. Thus, when Carter and some other Democrats in the 1970s pushed public education instead of the right to a job, for example, they built—in new ways—on the assumptions of Democrats in the 1960s about the significance of public education as an anti-poverty tool. In the decades that followed, assumptions about the importance of education offered an increasingly well-worn path of least resistance when bigger political economic changes proved difficult or simply conflicted with officeholders' ideological agendas.

In the following pages, while I tell a national story, I often employ a granular lens to look at the state of Wisconsin. This is not a book about Wisconsin, but I use examples from my home state because it is broadly representative of the nation at large. It is deeply divided between a few liberal urban enclaves (Madison and Milwaukee, in particular) and the rest of the state, much of which is rural. Votes in statewide elections have been razor thin over the past few cycles and reflect our nation's divisions: Trump won by about 20,000 votes in 2016, Superintendent of Education Tony Evers beat Governor Scott Walker by about 30,000 in 2018, and Trump lost by a mere 20,000 in 2020.[16]

Finally, I want to make clear my view on education. I do not argue that expanding access to education is bad. Unlike some critics of mythological thinking, my argument is not that education is little more than an exercise in providing credentials or something we should strive to reduce.[17] Our public schools serve the valuable purpose of providing a common education and instructing future generations in democratic citizenship, and if they have gotten off-track, it is only because too many schools have been forced to focus too much on standardized testing and too many teachers have been deprofessionalized. Further, education does play an important role in preparing Americans for jobs: those students who want to work with their hands should be able to learn valuable vocational skills in our school system, and there should also be a place for any student who wants to go to college, no matter what they want to study. Indeed, I support a tuition-free future for public colleges, universities, and technical schools. What I oppose, however, is expecting education to do the impossible: ensuring, by itself, that our nation fulfills its historic promise to ensure all Americans have good lives. For that, we need to recommit to a broad social democratic vision of ensuring economic security and individual dignity for everyone.

FROM INDEPENDENCE TO SECURITY

Education and Democracy from
the Nation's Founding

In 1894, a committee formed by the University of Wisconsin Board of Regents issued a report exonerating Professor Richard T. Ely, under investigation for his support of the right of workers to unionize. The report proclaimed, "The great state University of Wisconsin should ever encourage that continual and fearless sifting and winnowing by which alone the truth can be found." Ely's work stemmed from an imperative, in Wisconsin, for public higher education to help solve the problems of the late nineteenth century. Indeed, prominent intellectuals in the state had begun to see the role such institutions could play in mitigating the economic inequality and labor turmoil brought on by industrial capitalism. John Bascom, as the president of the University of Wisconsin from 1874 to 1887, for instance, advocated the social gospel notion of Christian brotherhood. During his tenure, Bascom supported women's suffrage, labor unions (including workers' right to strike), democratic land distribution, and other social democratic reforms. Bascom believed the work of the faculty should reach beyond the confines of the university to shape political reforms. Legendary Progressive reformer Robert LaFollette, among others, credited Bascom's presidency with setting the groundwork for a university that helped make the state freer and more democratic.

In the twentieth century, the University of Wisconsin deepened its commitment to the notion that universities should help to further social democracy. Advocated by University of Wisconsin president Charles Van Hise (1903–18), the "Wisconsin Idea" asserted the university had an obligation to produce and disseminate knowledge to enhance the lives of every citizen in the state. Combined with the work of legislators like Governor (and later Senator) LaFollette and Charles McCarthy, the founder of the state's Legislative Research Bureau, the notion also meant that social democratic legislation to enhance economic and social rights should be informed by evidence-based research.[1] The state built on the Wisconsin Idea by implementing worker's compensation (1911) and in 1932 providing unemployment insurance (both firsts in the nation). Wisconsin intellectuals like the economists John Commons and Edwin Witte informed national policies, and the Social Security Act in 1935 was influenced by Wisconsin reforms.[2]

As the rise of the Wisconsin Idea illustrates, for much of the nation's history, prominent American intellectuals and policymakers saw public education as doing much more than preparing students for jobs. In the early years of American history, those who advocated for investment in public education—like Virginia's Thomas Jefferson—did so as part of a broader project of developing the capacity of American citizens by ensuring their political independence. As part of this effort, Jefferson and others also sought to facilitate the economic independence of more white American men. This project was far from perfect: it grossly violated the sovereignty of Native Americans and accommodated and even expanded chattel slavery, and the role of white women was limited to that of mothers who would instruct future male citizens.

Nevertheless, this imperative continued into the era of the market revolution, where the growth of wage labor began to diminish the potential of economic independence for a greater number of Americans. The impulse to develop capable American citizens, moreover, advanced a more egalitarian version of public education in the early years of the nineteenth century, even if it also sought sometimes to discipline those who toiled in an increasingly unforgiving market capitalism. In fact, the most prominent American champions of public education in the eighteenth and nineteenth centuries did not view it primarily, or at all, in terms of its ability to develop what economists would later call "human capital." Indeed, the United States became an early pioneer in advancing public education largely because political and intellectual leaders believed it was necessary to cultivate common American culture and political democracy.

By the late nineteenth century, industrialization and the proliferation of wage labor created the so-called labor problem: who would do the work driving American capitalism and under what terms. This was the problem to which Bascom, Ely, LaFollette, and others responded in constructing the Wisconsin Idea, and moving forward, this problem was arguably the most significant in American history until World War II. Indeed, as Americans sought social democratic solutions to the class conflict brought on by the Gilded Age, public education ended up as a key arena for social and economic intervention, particularly since employers resisted collective bargaining and social welfare laws that could have altered the balance of power between workers and their employers and offered more job security.[3]

Some reformers, like philosopher John Dewey and teacher union activist Margaret Haley, saw public education as the preeminent avenue for developing new generations of citizens capable of democratizing both the American economy and its political system. Not everyone viewed public education's role so broadly, however. In fact, other reformers sought to use public education for the purpose of social control, or aimed to reduce poverty by giving workers greater skills, which they believed were necessary to enhance wages and working conditions. During the first third of the twentieth century, therefore, the seeds of the education myth were planted, and more working people began to consciously seek greater access to public education as one path toward economic livelihood. Nevertheless, education did not represent the only, or even the primary, effort of working people to fight for economic security. Between the Civil War and the Great Depression, workers lost more often than they won. But they fought for various versions of broad social democracy—like collective bargaining, minimum wage and maximum hours laws, and other reforms—sometimes through unions and sometimes through the state. Indeed, the expectations of many reform-oriented workers, intellectuals, and other activists revolved around enhancing broader forms of social and economic rights, of which public education was only one part.

Education, Social Democracy, and the Early Republic

When the United States was forged from its rebellion against the British Empire, the nation's founding document of 1776 was structured around a promise that has transcended American history. "We hold these truths to be self-evident," the Declaration of Independence asserted, "that all men are created equal, that they are endowed by their creator with certain unalienable rights, that among these are life, liberty, and the pursuit of happiness. That to secure these rights, governments are instituted among men, deriving their just powers from the consent of the governed." Indeed, the Declaration did not simply call for a change in government; it promised a much more expansive vision of constructing a society that prioritized equality and human well-being.[4]

Some American political actors saw this promise more narrowly. Southern delegations to the Continental Congress and the Constitutional Convention, for example, were primarily concerned with maintaining their rights to own enslaved people. But other architects of the nation understood that securing the rights of life, liberty, and the pursuit of happiness meant state and federal governments would need to facilitate both economic independence and other qualities they believed necessary for Americans to act as citizens as a democracy. They certainly did not see enslaved people as independent, and women, the founders assumed, lacked full political agency too. Further, while Pennsylvania's constitution of 1776 allowed all men to vote without property qualifications, most state constitutions initially restricted the franchise to those who owned property. Property—whether land or an artisanal shop—allowed one to avoid depending on someone else for an economic livelihood, and by this logic, only an independent citizen could be trusted to make reasoned political decisions.

Some American thinkers and policymakers in the founding generation recognized that government could be used to facilitate economic independence, and therefore citizenship, by providing more Americans with land. There was also popular pressure to expand land ownership. In fact, opening land on the frontier was among the major reasons American colonists revolted against the British crown as King George III forbade them from acquiring land west of the Proclamation line of 1763. Of course, Americans repeatedly violated Native American sovereignty, often through military force, in their ruthless acquisition of these new lands, and the United States has still yet to come anywhere close to rectifying the consequences of that dispossession. Federal policies like the Land Ordinance of 1785, the Louisiana Purchase (1803), and the Homestead Act of 1862, nonetheless, were predicated on the notion that opening new opportunities for nonelite, white American citizens was paramount.[5] In fact, an early draft of Virginia's constitution authored by Thomas Jefferson proposed every citizen be entitled to fifty acres of land, and thus the right to vote.[6] For Jefferson, economic independence ensured enough citizens would have the political independence—not pressured from someone to whom one sold their labor—to ensure a thriving democracy.[7]

Thomas Paine, the revolution's most radical thinker, took the argument even further, envisioning a broad social democracy. In *Agrarian Justice* (1797), Paine argued for a 10 percent inheritance tax on those with estates, which would pay for a national fund to compensate everyone with a cash payment that would stake them when they turned twenty-one. Paine argued his plan would strengthen the nation, as it would "consolidate the interest of the Republic with that of the individual. To the numerous class dispossessed of their natural inheritance by the system of landed property it will be an act of national justice."[8] Though Paine's plan was never adopted in the United States, it inspired activists in the nineteenth century, particularly as working people began to assert the right to economic security after being forced by industrial capitalism into wage labor.[9]

Not only was facilitating economic independence important to the founding generation, but prominent political leaders also argued for public investment in education to provide Americans the knowledge and disposition for democratic citizenship. Indeed, many state constitutions highlighted the importance of an educated citizenry, and the founding generation developed plans to expand access.[10] As Jefferson put it in his 1778 proposal for public schools in Virginia, investment in education was essential in maintaining self-government by ensuring ordinary citizens knew "ambition under all its shapes, and [were] prompt[ed] to exert their natural powers to defeat its purposes." As the future president argued, not only would public education allow a more informed citizenry to learn from historical examples in which tyranny had threatened, but it would also ensure "those persons, whom nature hath endowed with genius and virtue" were educated "at the common expence of all."[11]

Jefferson proposed a school for every county in Virginia and all children, male and female, would be entitled to three years of tuition-free education that included reading, writing, arithmetic. He also envisioned that those male students who did especially well—"the best and most promising genius and disposition"—would receive additional public support, and some would even receive three years of study at the College of William and Mary. Clearly Jefferson hoped the education system would cultivate meritocracy, a fiction that would drive more and more American economic and social policies by the end of the twentieth century. Further, Jefferson, reflecting the views of most white Americans at the time, believed that only some people were able to rise to such heights, as he believed neither African Americans nor Native Americans were as intelligent as whites.[12] Nevertheless, Jefferson's proposal shows that the purpose of public education in the early republic had almost nothing to do with gaining new economic skills.

Though Jefferson's proposal for Virginia was rejected in 1779, he was able to push states to invest in public education through Congress's Land Ordinance of 1785, which he also authored. The ordinance provided that when western lands were divided and settled by Americans, every thirty-sixth section in a 640-acre township should be devoted to funding the construction of a public school. The Northwest Ordinance of 1787 further encouraged public education, asserting that "religion, morality, and knowledge, being necessary to good government and the happiness of mankind, schools and the means of education shall forever be encouraged."[13]

Writing around the same time, physician Benjamin Rush also advocated a system of publicly funded education in Pennsylvania. The imperative was "peculiarly necessary," Rush argued in 1798, because "our citizens are composed of the natives of so many different kingdoms in Europe. Our schools of learning, by producing one general, and uniform system of education, will render the mass of the people more homogeneous, and thereby fit them more easily for uniform and peaceable government." Though he was decidedly not making a feminist argument—Rush believed girls should be trained so they could grow up to instruct new generations of boys in republican values—he also argued for the public provision of education across gender lines.[14]

Horace Mann's Nation-Building Project

From the 1810s to 1830s, many American politicians promoted national investment in banking and infrastructure to connect disparate parts of the new nation, enhance the development of American manufacturing, and promote economic growth. This impulse was central to the political platform of the Whig Party, and it is thus not surprising that a Whig politician named Horace Mann became arguably the nation's most significant advocate for public investment in education. Indeed, Americans often consider the nineteenth century to be one of limited government involvement, but the expansion of public education over the course of the nineteenth century, even if at the state and local level, represented a key piece of a dramatic expansion of government programs.[15] Though Democrats sometimes opposed public education as a "Whig" project, the effort for common schools was not exclusively a partisan effort. Still, prodevelopment Whigs like Mann were its main proponents.

Examining Mann's logic for investing in public education is important. For Mann, as well as other proponents of public education, education was crucial, not to serve as job training, but to ensure that Americans had the knowledge and values to serve as bulwarks of a democratic republic under duress.[16] Many elite reformers like Mann sought to use the schools to counteract the growing class divisions, ethnic diversity, and anonymity brought on by market capitalism and urban life.[17] A Massachusetts state legislator, Mann took the position of secretary of the State Board of Education in 1837. Maintaining the position for twelve years, Mann not only compiled yearly reports to the legislature, but he also lectured at annual Massachusetts county education conventions in the late 1830s and 1840s. In these venues, Mann lobbied for expanding funding for new and better schoolhouses, textbooks, libraries, and teachers.

In 1837, for instance, Mann breathlessly asserted the importance of education both for preserving the American Revolution's legacy and for stanching social unrest. "Such an event as the French Revolution," he argued, "never would have happened with free schools; any more than the American Revolution would have happened without them. The mobs, the riots, the burnings, the lynchings, perpetrated by the *men* of the present day, are perpetrated, because of their vicious or defective education, when children." Expanding public education would ensure young people learned the proper republican virtue so they would respect order, act selflessly, and make rational decisions.[18] If they wished to sustain the nation, Mann lectured Americans in 1839, their political system would need much more conscious attention to public education: "If republican institutions do wake up unexampled energies in the whole mass of a people, and give them implements of unexamined power wherewith to work out their will, then these same institutions ought also to confer upon that people unexampled wisdom and rectitude."[19]

It wasn't until Mann's fifth annual report to the legislature, in 1842, that he even mentioned the economic benefits of education, and then only reluctantly. Chastising the Massachusetts towns that did not sufficiently invest in their schools, Mann pointed out that education brought economic benefits, pointing out that more knowledge could "raise more abundant harvests, and multiply the conveniences of domestic life . . . a single new idea is often worth more to an individual than a hundred workmen—and to a nation, than the addition of provinces to its territory."[20]

Mann's evidence included letters from a handful of employers showing that "other things being equal . . . those who have been blessed with a good Common School education, rise to a higher and a higher point, in the kinds of labor performed, and also in the rate of wages paid, while the ignorant sink, like dregs, and are always found at the bottom." Of course, Mann missed the reality that those who came from a family with the luxury of having their children attend school likely had other advantages, such as better nutrition and health, or simply the possibility of seeking higher wages elsewhere because their economic reality may have been less dire. Further, the educator's assumption in the exercise was that a large portion of the workers' greater economic benefit stemmed from their enhanced penchant for "punctuality and fidelity in the performance of their duties," which likely corresponded to those who had internalized docility toward their bosses. Even so, Mann concluded his report by pointing out that all these economic benefits were secondary, "dwindl[ing] into insignificance when compared with those loftier and more sacred attributes of the cause, which have the power of converting material wealth into spiritual well-being."[21]

While Mann's argument for investing in education clearly revolved around the national political project, by his final annual report, he had begun advancing the notion that access to education could unlock, by itself, economic opportunity. Mann's twelfth and final report, in fact, represented one of the earliest versions of what would become the education myth. Indeed, as increasing numbers of American working men lost access to their own farms and shops (and thus the political independence valued by the founding generation), Mann responded to the growing class divisions that penetrated American society by asserting the importance of education.

In 1849, Mann argued that if those without property were better educated, they would, almost magically, get along better with those who employed them, which would bring them prosperity. "If education be equally diffused," he supposed, "it will draw property after it, by the strongest of all attractions; for such a thing never did happen, and never can happen, as that an intelligent and practical body of men should be permanently poor." Indeed, Mann continued, in highly romantic language:

> Education, then, beyond all other devices of human origin, is the great equalizer of the conditions of men—the balance-wheel of the social machinery. . . . It does better than to disarm the poor of their hostility towards the rich; it prevents being poor. . . . The spread of education, by enlarging the cultivated class or caste, will open a wider area over which the social feelings will expand; and, if this education should be universal and complete, it would do more than all things else to obliterate factitious distinctions in society.

This wasn't quite an argument for human capital. Mann was not exactly arguing workers would acquire the skills that would bring them to par with capital; rather he was arguing, fancifully, that it would cultivate a disposition that would create common ground with those who employed them.

Still, in many ways Mann's assertion regarding the value of education sounds strikingly familiar to some of the modern mythologies based on the alchemical nature of "human capital" to overcome social and economic divisions. He clearly wasn't calling for a broader project to help working people maintain economic independence (or even a bigger share of what the economy produced) at the expense of capital. In fact, Mann feared the "creeds of some political reformers, or revolutionizers . . . that some people are poor because others are rich." He clearly rejected that explanation. Mann argued instead that "the greatest of all the arts in political economy is, to change a consumer into a producer; and the next greatest is to increase the producer's producing power;—an end to be directly attained, by increasing his intelligence."[22]

Mann, then, clearly sought to maintain the social order, a particular version of what the democratic republic should mean. In many ways, he was naïve and romantic, ignoring the stark realities brought on by market capitalism. The United States in 1849 was on the precipice of a sustained, and often bloody, conflict over the prospects for economic security for those Americans who were not enriched by the dramatic capital accumulation of the next century.

For the growing multitude of Americans who worked for wages as the country transitioned toward market capitalism in Mann's day, the relationship to public education was complicated. In some cases, workers and working-men's organizations supported public education, sometimes for the same reasons Jefferson had argued for it: the connection between knowledge and political democracy. In fact, the earliest working-class organizations in American history, forged in the 1820s, were built in part to advance universal public education. The growing market economy in the industrial Northeast impoverished wage laborers and forced children into the workforce. In addition to ensuring children would no longer compete with adults in the labor market, working-men's organizations demanded state and local governments provide free public education to all children. These calls were often explicitly linked to the impact education would play in ensuring political democracy for new generations of working people. As one working-men's association, pushing for a system of public education in Philadelphia put it in 1829, put it, "Real liberty and equality have no foundation but in universal and equal instruction."[23] Further, many workers also shared Mann's notion that education should cultivate republican citizenship, as "artisans" and "mechanics"—the terminology for workers at the time—read political and cultural magazines, belonged to subscription libraries, and attended lyceum lectures.[24]

On the other hand, some working people opposed the expansion of public education, particularly as reformers used it to push the ideology of the winners in the new market economy. Historian Michael Katz's classic work on nineteenth-century education reform, for instance, tells the story of Beverly, Massachusetts, whose citizens voted to abolish its high school in 1860. Katz shows that Beverly's working people led that charge to oppose it while the town's wealthy supported it, believing high school would provide social mobility. Working-class children, however, rarely attended secondary school, and their parents rejected it as just one facet of a new industrial social order that threatened their livelihoods with ever more precarious wage labor.[25]

Finally, because education served the purpose of constructing American citizenship, it is particularly significant that many white Americans intentionally excluded African Americans. Indeed, free African Americans sought enhanced access to education just as many white working people did during the mid-nineteenth century. Blacks, especially in the urban North, developed schools and sustained reading clubs and lyceums, and they did so with the anticipation of equal American citizenship. Many whites, however, fiercely opposed these efforts. Indeed, the growing expectation that white children should have access to schools in the North was fundamentally constructed on the premise of excluding African Americans. Just as the expansion of the franchise to nonproperty-holding whites in the 1820s, 1830s, and 1840s was accompanied by efforts to strip voting rights from African Americans, so in New Hampshire, Massachusetts, Pennsylvania, New York, and elsewhere the expansion of public education for whites was linked to limiting the education of Blacks.[26] It would take more than a century of activism for African Americans to successfully force their way into full exercise of citizenship in the United States, and it is no surprise that public education would represent an integral part of that fight.

Higher Education's Frontier: The Midwest

In the 1840s and 1850s, following the lead of their eastern counterparts, new states in the Midwest began to provide publicly funded grammar schools. For instance, Wisconsinites, many of whom were émigrés from New England, had accepted the notion that investing in public schools was important even before statehood, and when Wisconsin became a state in 1848, its constitution guaranteed a free public education. Indeed, the growth of public schools was dramatic. In 1836, the territory of Wisconsin only had about a dozen schools with about five hundred students; by 1849, there were thirty-two thousand students.[27] By pioneering broad access to public universities, Midwestern states went further than their peers on the East Coast. Chartered in 1848 by the new constitution, for instance, the University of Wisconsin began offering classes in 1850.

On the East Coast, colonial legislatures had subsidized private universities— such as Dartmouth, Yale, and Harvard—well before the Revolution. Founders Benjamin Rush, George Washington, Jefferson, and others had pushed for the creation of a national university as early as the 1780s. Though a national university was not forthcoming, state governments in the late eighteenth and early nineteenth centuries began founding public universities, establishing at least the ideal of greater accessibility to higher education if not always the funding to make it happen.[28]

In Midwestern states like Michigan and Wisconsin, these universities were founded explicitly on the principle that they serve all citizens, not just elites.[29] The future state's territorial legislature in Detroit founded the University of Michigan in 1817 as the culmination of a statewide system of public education, with free primary schools and a very low-tuition university, subsidized by the state. Though it would be a challenge to raise the funds to adequately support this system, the vision was capacious, driven by Jefferson's notion that education was necessary to develop a strong democratic society. The state's constitution, ratified in 1835, guaranteed every student access to a common school and obligated the legislature to allocate federal land grant funds to permanently support the university. Henry Tappan, a philosopher who authored a book envisioning higher education as an institution that would offer new generations of Americans a respite from "the excessive commercial spirit" of the market, served as an early and influential president from 1852 to 1863. Though continued resistance to raising taxes prevented Tappan's efforts to remake the university in this image, the University of Michigan by the 1860s prioritized a widely available, broad education that sought to do much more than empower individual earning potential.[30]

Similarly, when the Wisconsin legislature chartered its university, proponents of higher education aspired to offer a broad education that would reach as many students as possible. In 1849, the university's first chancellor, John Lathrop, proclaimed, in an address to about six hundred people in Madison that shut down the entire city, "The American mind has grasped the idea and will not let it go, that the whole property of the state, is holden subject to the sacred trust of providing for the education of every child in the state. Without the adoption of this system, as the most potent compensation of the aristocratic tendencies of hereditary wealth, the boasted political equality of which we dream, is but an illusion. Knowledge is the great leveler. It is the true democracy."[31]

Indeed, in the 1850s and 1860s, the university created a number of both liberal and practical offerings. As the Board of Regents pointed out while proposing a Department of the Practical Applications of Science in 1851, doing so would help the entire state by educating those "on whose intelligence and skill depend on the success of the industrial processes, the physical wealth, and the general prosperity of the community."[32] It is vital that we pay attention to this framing when we consider the origins of public education's imperative in American history. Though education today is seen as being mostly about nurturing individual opportunity, educational leaders in the nineteenth century believed that developing Americans' new skills opened the broader potential for the common good even when institutions offered "practical" training.

Independence versus the Slave Power

As states outside the South expanded public education in order to enhance both economic independence and citizenship (at least for whites), slaveowners in the southern states sought a much more hierarchical future. Contrary to various myths about our nation's history—that the conflict was primarily about state sovereignty or that it was a moral quandary over slavery—the sectional conflict arising between North and South before the Civil War was rooted in a fundamental political economic tension. Though important activists, most prominently Frederick Douglass, argued African Americans deserved to be fully fledged

American citizens, the growing rivalry between North and South in the 1840s and 1850s centered almost exclusively on the future of economic independence for white people. A good deal of this vision regarding independence revolved around public education.

One constituency—the southern "slave power," which had acquired unprecedented wealth by extracting labor from enslaved human beings—sought to use lands stolen from Mexico after President James K. Polk provoked a war in 1846 to expand slavery. The other constituency, led by Republicans like Abraham Lincoln, were motivated by the Jeffersonian notion of economic independence through access to land and the idea that economic value derived primarily from labor. They believed the slave power needed to be curtailed to ensure independence for a greater number of American citizens. For some the argument for economic independence took on a nakedly white supremacist premise, while for others like Lincoln, an alternative version offered space to include African Americans, too, even if on unequal terms.

Some northern Democrats, such as Pennsylvania representative David Wilmot, for instance, argued new American lands should not be open to slavery since they would close off opportunity for white men. He had no interest in liberating African Americans, however: "I have no squeamish sensitiveness upon the subject of slavery, nor morbid sympathy for the slave. I plead the cause of the rights of white freemen. I would preserve for free white labor a fair country, a rich inheritance, where the sons of toil, of my own race and own color, can live without the disgrace which association with negro slavery brings upon free labor."[33]

The notion that western lands should not be given over to the slave power was the fundamental tension that led to the growing sectional conflict of the 1850s. Although some Democrats like Wilmot could abide the existence of slavery so long as it didn't foreclose opportunities for whites, others—the founders of the GOP—understood slavery as an abomination to be eliminated. Still, though Lincoln and some other Republicans were unwilling to permanently accommodate the existence of slavery, they were also primarily concerned with what the expansion of slavery meant for the economic independence of white men squeezed out of landownership and into wage labor.

Lincoln's 1854 speech on the Kansas-Nebraska Act at Peoria, Illinois, highlights this argument. The bill had essentially invalidated the Missouri Compromise, which in 1820 had relegated slavery to areas south of Missouri as the nation acquired new land. Sponsored by Lincoln's rival, Illinois senator Stephen Douglas, the law allowed the citizens of the Kansas and Nebraska territories to vote on whether to permit slavery. As Lincoln explained, the law threatened the nation's promise of independence for free white citizens. Beginning with the Northwest Ordinance's restriction on slavery, Lincoln pointed out that those states "are now what Jefferson foresaw and intended—the happy home of teeming millions of free, white, prosperous people, and no slave amongst them." Denouncing the bill, the future president argued, "Slave States are places for poor white people to remove FROM; not to remove TO. New free States are the places for poor people to go to and better their condition. For this use, the nation needs these territories."[34]

Lincoln, therefore, opposed slavery and wished to abolish it at the beginning of the Civil War, but as president, he would move only gradually to eliminate it as the war ground on, although the momentum for abolition would pick up speed after African Americans troops became integral to the war effort. To Lincoln, the war was fundamentally about the trajectory of economic and political independence, predominately for whites. Perhaps the best statement of this reality is Lincoln's address to Congress in December 1861. In his speech Lincoln mainly gave an account of the war effort in its first year, but he concluded by laying out a vision, just as many of the founders had, in which political democracy relied on economic independence for ordinary citizens.

The Confederacy, Lincoln argued, was defined by its "war upon the first principle of popular government—the rights of the people." The new president obviously argued for political democracy, but more importantly, he raised a "warning voice against this approach of returning despotism" stemming from the premise that "capital" should be placed "on an equal footing with, if not above, labor in the structure of government." On the contrary, however, Lincoln asserted that "labor is prior to and independent of capital. Capital is only the fruit of labor, and could never have existed if labor had not first existed. Labor is the superior of capital, and deserves much the higher consideration." He then pointed out that the nation should serve to ensure working men access to economic independence: "No men living are more worthy to be trusted than those who toil up from poverty; none less inclined to take or touch aught which they have not honestly earned. Let them beware of surrendering a political power which . . . will surely be used to close the door of advancement against such as they and to fix new disabilities and burdens upon them till all of liberty shall be lost."[35] In an earlier iteration of these remarks in Wisconsin in 1859, Lincoln also linked free labor and economic independence to learning, arguing, "In one word free labor insists on universal education." And, importantly, the necessity of education transcended economic value: "Let us hope, rather, that by the best cultivation of the physical world, beneath and around us, and the intellectual and moral world within us, we shall secure an individual, social, and political prosperity and happiness."[36]

As Lincoln had pointed out on multiple occasions, including in his debates with Stephen Douglas in the 1858 US Senate race in Illinois, he did not see whites and Blacks as equals, but he nonetheless believed that African Americans deserved to enjoy the fruits of their labor. In fact, in 1860, he argued the US government should ensure their right to economic independence too: "I want every man to have a chance—and I believe a black man is entitled to it—in which he *can* better his condition—when he may look forward and hope to be hired laborer this year and the next, work for himself afterward, and finally to hire men to work for him!"[37]

Lincoln envisioned a world in which those who labored could earn their way to independence, that public education could facilitate citizenship, and that government could facilitate that journey. It is thus not surprising that a crucial piece of the Republican agenda was the Homestead Act, signed into law by the president in 1862 after secession removed southern Democratic obstructionists from Congress. Providing 160-acre plots for an inexpensive fee, the law settled, once and for all, the question of whether the West should serve to advance slavery or to facilitate the economic independence of American citizens. Though the vast majority of the millions of acres of land (1.5 million acres by 1864 alone) distributed would go to white families, African Americans were not excluded from its promise, and thousands were able to access land under those terms.[38] Further, although the Homestead Act was woefully insufficient in arresting the trajectory of a capitalism that subordinated more and more Americans to the whims of large corporations, it is nonetheless significant that the effort, at least in theory, prioritized the economic independence of individual Americans.

Support for public education also played a significant role in the Republican vision: in the legislative session of 1861–63, after passing the Homestead Act, Congress also enacted the Morrill Act (1862), a concerted effort to build public higher education in the United States. The law provided thirty thousand acres of federal land to every state for each of its representatives in Congress, the proceeds of which would allow each to "promote the liberal and practical education of the industrial classes in the several pursuits and professions in life." After passing the Morrill Act, as one historian has pointed out, the United States thus became "the first nation in the world, whether in peace or in war, systematically to commit its resources for the support of higher education."[39] Congressional action clearly meant to advance the total education of Americans, and while such development could certainly benefit an individual's human capital, the language of the law tells us that the goal was the broad development of each state's working population.[40]

Just as had been the case with the Morrill Act, the secession of southern Democrats, who put their own interests in exploiting human property above all else, allowed Congress to establish a federal office of education. A congressional resolution of support for the bill in December 1865 stressed "the universal intelligence of the people" in vouchsafing the country's future "republican inter-ests." Further, policymakers clearly envisioned the education office as part of a nationalist project, one that would, at least in theory, include freedmen and freedwomen. Not only was the office designed to "enforce education without regard to color," but proponents of the bill also contended that "the great disasters which have afflicted the Nation and desolated one-half its territory are trace-able, in a great degree, to the absence of common schools and general education among the people of the lately rebellious States."[41]

When the Civil War ended, and the new battle for African American rights began in the South, the success of Reconstruction hinged on whether African Americans would be included as full American citizens, and two of the most significant elements of this struggle involved economic independence and edu-cation. Indeed, as early as 1863, Lincoln had moved beyond touting earlier, now historically embarrassing, colonization schemes to send free African Ameri-cans to Africa, and by 1865 called for those states that had seceded to educate Blacks.[42]

In 1865, William Tecumseh Sherman, as a wartime expedient, issued Field Order No. 15, providing African Americans in South Carolina and Georgia forty-acre plots of land that had been abandoned by plantation owners and raising African Americans' expectations for permanent land ownership. Blacks expected the Reconstruction project after the war to compensate their years of unpaid labor and loyalty to the union in the form of independence through land ownership.[43] Tragically, a combination of outright white supremacy from Presi-dent Andrew Johnson and the ideology of the northern Republicans who ran the Freedman's Bureau privileged the property rights of treasonous southern planta-tion owners, leaving most Blacks without land and dependent on sharecropping, a form of labor exploitation bordering on outright theft.[44]

Just as was the case for white Americans, African Americans defined equality through both economic independence and education, and the federal govern-ment's lack of commitment to either would prevent Blacks from exercising full citizenship. For a time—and not coincidentally that time coexisted with federal guarantees of Black political rights—African Americans successfully pushed toward an expanded education system in the South capable of providing education on par with that of whites. Ensuring political and economic "self-sufficiency" in the postwar order represented the primary motivation for Blacks in the South seeking education. After the federal government pulled out and white suprem-acists "redeemed" the southern states, however, Black children went to school in segregated, subpar institutions, and though African American communities heroically paid twice for their schools (once for the taxes that disproportion-ately subsidized white schools, and another time, voluntarily, to give their kids some semblance of what they lacked from public funds), Blacks continued to be excluded from the broader promise of American democracy.[45]

The End of Independence

As Reconstruction came to its tragic conclusion, the "labor problem" emerged as the nation's most important political issue. Indeed, the very year the US Army pulled its remaining troops out of the South (1877), a labor conflict of epic proportions underscored just how woefully insufficient was the Lincoln Republicans' vision of facilitating economic and political independence through land and education. The Great Railroad Strike of 1877—precipitated by four years of economic downturn—highlighted the anger of the growing number of wage laborers who, to use Lincoln's words in 1861, would be "fixed to that condition for life." As more workers faced a lifetime of wage labor, they increasingly fought for social democracy: new economic and social rights that would protect them from the predations of a marketplace dominated by industrial capital. The battles lines drawn from the 1870s on no longer revolved around the potential of economic independence, but instead on the means through which workers could secure an economic livelihood.[46]

The forms the conflict over the "labor problem" took were many, and they have been amply documented by historians.[47] For skilled workers, the effort hinged on control of the shopfloor. Employers sought to de-skill this work and make (mostly male) workers either interchangeable or to break their ability to organize. Perhaps the most spectacular example of this conflict is the Carnegie Steel Works' violent efforts to break the Amalgamated Association of Iron and Steel Workers in Homestead, Pennsylvania, in 1892. Other workers' organizations, such as the Knights of Labor in the 1880s, the American Railway Union in the 1890s, and the Industrial Workers of the World in the early twentieth century sought broader, industrywide organization. Sometimes, workers brought the fight, as the Knights (and some of their remnants) did, into the broader terrain of urban politics. The high-water mark of the Knights' power, in fact, coincided with a coordinated effort in 1886 to force employers in Chicago, Milwaukee, and elsewhere to agree to an eight-hour day for all workers.

After the crippling depression of 1893, Jacob Coxey's march on Washington, DC, stands out at as an important example of early, radical calls for social democracy. In 1894, Coxey, unemployed workers, and others marched from Ohio to Washington, DC, to compel the federal government to create jobs through public works. Though the police crushed the protest, it highlighted a protean demand for the federal government to take a role in providing economic security for working people.[48] Farmers, through the populist movement, sought an array of social democratic interventions to protect their economic livelihoods: a "sub-treasury system" that would pool small farmers' selling power so they would receive higher prices for their crops, a graduated income tax, and public ownership of the railroads and the telegraph so private companies couldn't exploit farmers who relied on that knowledge and transportation infrastructure.[49]

Political reformers, from both the working classes and the growing middle class, during the Progressive Era sought policies to improve workers' economic security through maximum hour laws, worker safety laws, or social insurance like workman's compensation and unemployment insurance (all of these aspects of the New Deal were developed through various state laws first). In part, middle-class reformers participated in these efforts because they understood their moral necessity. But, reformers also sought these social democratic interventions because they feared overt class war and instead sought to suppress class conflict by engaging in reform movements in which moderate government interventions could alleviate some of the most glaring inequalities.[50]

Rethinking Schools, Remaking Society

There were two major efforts—from two very different directions—to remake education during the Progressive Era, and both sought to use education to solve some of the major problems brought on by the rise of industrial capitalism. First, some reformers sought to make the school system more vocational. In fact, the vocationalism movement of the early twentieth century was the first concerted effort in American history to push schools to serve the primary purpose of providing young people the skills they supposedly needed to succeed in the workplace. At best, these efforts responded to the legitimate demands of some working people for skills that would allow them access to better jobs in an increasingly complex economy. At worst, vocationalism sought to remake the American school system into one that was explicitly tiered, replicating the class inequalities in the rest of society. The second set of efforts sought to democratize the education system in order to strengthen American democracy. At best, these efforts sought to train American citizens to take political action against the antidemocratic political economy of the Gilded Age. At worst, these efforts perpetuated negative caricatures of immigrant working people, employing public education for the purpose of social control.

Neither of these reform movements fully remade American education. The vocationalist ideal gained traction, but the nationalist imperative of education for the sake of democracy persisted beyond the 1930s too. Further, while public education as a broad democratic response to the problems of industrialization grew in prominence during the early twentieth century, it comprised just one part of a growing social democratic argument for economic security.

It is important to examine both movements in more detail, beginning with the push by reformers to make education more responsive to the needs of employers. In Chicago, in the 1890s and early 1900s, for example, some Progressive reformers, in alliance with business interests, attempted to create a two-tiered public education system in which the city's working-class children would receive a stripped-down "practical" curriculum, while middle-class and elite children would continue with a liberal education. Labor unions in Chicago, including the Chicago Teachers' Federation, the nation's first teacher union, successfully resisted this effort. The opposition of unions to this plan didn't mean workers necessarily opposed using schools to impart job skills, however. Whereas employers often sought to narrow the curriculum toward training for a specific job, unions in Chicago, Boston, and elsewhere supported certain kinds of vocational education as long as it was broadly applicable to a lot of different jobs and didn't undermine efforts by unions to have some control over the job market.[51]

In Boston, school reformers in the late nineteenth century increasingly sought to use education to alleviate the economic inequalities brought on by Gilded Age capitalism. As late as the 1880s, aside from a few specific professions, public education was not connected to job training. In the years after, however, reformers assumed workers' low wages were related to their lack of skills and sought to change the system in a purportedly meritocratic direction. Though many workers, especially immigrants, did benefit from English-language instruction and some, especially women workers, found new job opportunities from public school investments in practical white-collar courses in bookkeeping and type-writing, the new emphasis on gearing public education toward job training failed to significantly alter the economic hierarchy.[52]

Importantly, however, a growing number of working people who went to school longer in the early twentieth century did so because they sought access to better and more sustainable jobs. For women workers, in particular, high barriers to gain a livelihood in manual labor and the relative weakness of unions in women's work made education for white-collar labor a rational choice. Indeed, even though reformers failed to turn the US system into one exclusively focused on vocationalism, Americans—especially the increasing number of white-collar workers—were beginning to connect public education to economic opportunity in important ways by the 1920s and 1930s.[53]

The clear limits, however, to education's ability to democratize American society on economic terms nonetheless illustrated the necessity of other important social democratic interventions. On a national level, the most important victory for the vocationalist drive during this period was the passage of the Smith-Hughes Act in 1917. With support from both business and organized labor, Smith-Hughes provided funding to states for vocational education. Funding was limited, however, and the law failed to help many students gain higher-paying jobs.[54]

The most important shift that resulted from the effort to connect workers with better skills was the massive expansion of public high schools from the 1910s to the 1940s. In 1890, less than 10 percent of Americans ages fourteen to seventeen were enrolled in high school. By 1920, that number jumped to 38 percent, and by 1936, it had skyrocketed to 65 percent. More students went to high school in part because of new limits on child labor, and during the Depression more stayed in school simply because there were few jobs available.[55] But many students clearly also went to school because their families supposed it would provide greater economic opportunities.

While some economists have argued that more education blunted radical social movements in the early twentieth century, public education did very little to decrease economic inequality.[56] For one thing, the expansion of high schools in the early twentieth century initiated a race for even more credentials. Thus, when more students went to high school in the first third of the twentieth century, students from wealthier families sought greater advantage in the job market by accessing the higher tracks comprehensive high schools now offered, which in turn put them on the path to college.[57] Further, labor conflict in the 1910s, 1920s, and 1930s was immense, and employers fought tooth and nail to prevent working people, whether they had a high school degree or not, from attaining economic security.

During this era, another group of Progressives sought to democratize American politics through citizenship education and, even more broadly, by reforming public schools to help students develop greater civic and political capabilities. Progressive intellectual and educator John Dewey was the most important proponent of this effort.[58] In Dewey's most significant work, *Democracy and Education* (1916), he explained that a "democratically constituted society" required an essential interest in education, as common schools could teach students to be active social agents in an interdependent world. In fact, Dewey believed work would be "reduced to a mechanical routine unless workers see the technical, intellectual, and social relationships involved in what they do, and engage in their work because of the motivation furnished by such perceptions."[59] Indeed, Dewey believed more educated workers could build agency in the workplace (elsewhere he also wrote about the importance of unions in this endeavor) to forestall employers' efforts to reduce their workday to mindless drudgery.

There were a number of other American thinkers who subscribed to Dewey's vision for reforming American education, but perhaps the best example of his reach can be found in the thought of Margaret Haley, an early leader of the nation's first teacher union, the Chicago Teachers Federation (CTF, founded in 1897). Though the union was initially formed to fight for teachers' economic security, Haley's rise to prominence in the union occurred, not coincidentally, as teachers and other working-class people fought off reformers' efforts to tier the public school system.[60]

Haley's thought is illuminating, particularly in her memorable articulation of what public education should do in "Why Teachers Should Organize" at the annual meeting of the National Education Association (NEA) in 1904.[61] In the speech, Haley cited both Mann and Dewey. She began by pointing out the American people, even a half century after Mann sought common schools, were not fully prepared for democracy. Teachers needed to organize, she argued, so they could ensure they did their part to prepare future citizens. Citing Dewey next, Haley argued American public education would only adequately prepare future citizens for democracy when teachers were treated as experts worthy of leading a democratic school system. Haley's argument for why teachers should organize, then, showed that teachers were workers like any other, but their work was also to teach other Americans to be citizens in a democracy, a stance that was in opposition to probusiness reformers.[62]

Public Education, Citizenship, and Immigration

Other American reformers, decidedly less radically democratic than Dewey or Haley, continued to value public education for its use in facilitating citizenship, though some of these efforts explicitly sought social control. The massive increase in immigration to the United States from the 1890s to the 1910s rapidly expanded public school systems, leading to bureaucratic reforms and new efforts to "Americanize" immigrant children in the schools.[63] Many American policymakers felt significant anxiety about the impact of the millions of immigrants who came to the United States from eastern and southern Europe in the years around World War I. As a result Congress passed laws that severely restricted immigration.[64] Education reformers sought to use the schools of the early twentieth century to assimilate the children of immigrants, just as Mann envisioned the purpose of common schools in the 1840s. As with Mann, these early twentieth-century reformers sought to teach literacy and citizenship, not job training.[65]

Examining calls for enhanced federal support for public education helps to illustrate this trend. In 1910, a bill to establish a federal executive level department was the subject of congressional hearings, and in the 1910s and 1920s, a number of similar proposals were introduced into Congress. The Towner-Sterling bill, sponsored by the aptly named Iowa congressional representative Horace Mann Towner, was introduced in 1921. The bill had five primary purposes, as a National Education Association (NEA) publication from 1923 pointed out:

A. Removing illiteracy
B. Americanizing the foreign-born
C. Establishing effective programs of physical education
D. Providing well-qualified teachers for all public schools, and
E. Equalizing educational opportunities within the States.

Expanding public education, the NEA argued, was especially important at that time because World War I had highlighted a fundamental deficiency in the education of Americans. Asserting the importance of facilitating citizenship, the publication pointed out that "the effective exercise of every sovereign power of our National Government is dependent on intelligent, right-minded citizenship. An educated citizenry is the first great need of today, just as it was the first great need of the new Republic in 1789."[66]

The NEA believed a greater federal role was necessary because American democracy was threatened by the number of foreign-born "illiterates" entering the country. In language that would make most Americans today cringe, the NEA pointed out that "now that the war is over, hundreds of thousands of aliens are once again entering our country each year." The publication also highlighted the problem of "illiteracy" among native born Americans, arguing that "the problem is more clearly revealed as principally one of improving our schools."[67] Further, the NEA argued schools in every state must ensure adequate "Americanization" through education, and the bill proposed $7.5 million to states to teach immigrants fourteen years and older about American citizenship and the English language. Indeed, though this law never passed, the debate in Congress, combined with the NEA's vigorous support, shows that, even in this nativist guise, many American educators viewed public education more for its purpose in developing citizenship than augmenting job skills.[68]

New Deal Rising

While reformers like Dewey and Haley viewed education in terms of its promise in democratizing society, other Americans, including an increasing number of working people by the 1930s, had begun to view public education's potential for individual economic *opportunity*. While schools continued to serve the function of educating citizens for democracy, particularly as educators and other policy-makers feared what immigration would do to the polity, education began to more clearly serve the purpose of advancing economic opportunity too. And yet, this increase in education did little to arrest the war on workers in the 1920s, or the overall lack of rights and economic security for working people, a problem only magnified during the Great Depression. The 1930s changed everything, as new reforms established the ideal that broad economic security would be a driving consideration of American policymakers moving forward.

2

TO SECURE THESE RIGHTS

Education and the Unfinished Project of
American Social Democracy

On June 22, 1944, President Franklin D. Roosevelt signed into law the Servicemen's Readjustment Act, more colloquially known as the GI Bill. The policy that most comprehensively reflected FDR's social democratic vision during World War II, the GI Bill became law just six months after Roosevelt's State of the Union address that January calling for an Economic Bill of Rights. The expansion of social democracy in the GI Bill, which went well beyond the cash payments of previous veterans' programs, is illuminating. The law was passed in part to navigate the massive problem of integrating sixteen million veterans into a demobilizing economy in which there would be serious competition for jobs and housing. The intention, however, was also clearly to provide both economic security and additional economic opportunity for veterans.[1] As the name suggests, the Servicemen's Readjustment Act was premised on expanding security for male breadwinners, who in turn would provide for the women and children in their families. Further, the implementation of the GI Bill, which allowed southern white supremacists the discretion to deny full benefits to Black veterans, was also racially discriminatory, and the benefits accrued disproportionately to white families. Nonetheless, the social democracy of the New Deal and the two decades after World War II ushered in a time of rising expectations of greater social and economic rights for most working Americans. Policymakers, union leaders, and civil rights activists all sought new, sweeping possibilities: the right to a job, broad access to healthcare, and high-quality, truly universal public education.

35

After World War II, indeed, the expansion of the social safety net continued. These efforts included an expansive investment in housing in 1949 and an expansion of social security in several different amendments to the law in the 1950s. The overall project of American social democracy, however, was left unfinished. Despite the very real possibility of a meaningful jobs guarantee at the conclusion of World War II—what Senator Robert Wagner (New York) and other social democrats hoped could be Roosevelt's final legacy—the full employment guarantee was stymied by Republicans and southern Democrats who would only consent to a watered-down version of the law.

This chapter highlights the place of education in this story. From its subordinate position in FDR's Second Bill of Rights, public education would grow in the postwar years into an increasingly prominent aspect of the social democratic project. When policymakers from the state to the federal level talked about education in this era, they increasingly connected it to the idea of economic "opportunity." The use of the word *opportunity* to describe education has a long history in the United States. Advocates of enhanced state funding to smooth over unequal local spending invoked the terminology of "equal educational opportunity" in the 1910s and 1920s, for instance. But "opportunity" in that language referred to a broader view that included both greater economic reward and greater democratic citizenship.[2]

The GI Bill represented the harbinger of a policy shift toward a more conscious embrace of the link between education and economic opportunity. Though the law included many economic guarantees—all as compensation for servicemen's contribution to the war effort—we mainly remember the GI Bill as the first major federal foray into public education in the post–New Deal era. In addition to preventing returning GI's from flooding the labor market (a reminder that the federal government's focus on economic security prominently featured jobs), the authors of the bill also recognized the growing complexity of American society and workers' needs for more education.[3] The GI Bill, importantly, was also constructed to fund veterans' higher education or job training just about anywhere they chose, ensuring a wide range of economic opportunity through access to new capabilities.

Still, as the ideals set forth by Harry Truman's President's Commission on Higher Education (1949) show, support for the civic and political capability of public education played a major role in policymakers' arguments for expanding access to education too. The advance of this notion continued in the 1950s. Indeed, it is illuminating that *Brown v. Board of Education* (1954), the Supreme Court decision that gave the death blow to the notion of "separate but equal," revolved around both political capability and equal economic "opportunity" in public education. The robust set of economic rights FDR envisioned in 1944, especially the right to a job and the right to healthcare, were not to be. This failure, occurring at the same time Americans increasingly viewed education in terms of economic opportunity, set an important precondition for the rise of the education myth. Later, reform-oriented political figures, especially Democrats, could argue that opportunity through education would do what the unfinished project of New Deal–era social democracy had failed to do: ensure all Americans had a chance at economic security.

Self-Evident Economic Truths

In his State of the Union address on January 11, 1944, President Franklin D. Roosevelt proposed a "Second Bill of Rights," representing the culminating moment of the administration's vision for a robust social democracy. There has been so much written about the legacy of the New Deal and the Roosevelt administration at this point that it can be difficult to grasp just how revolutionary the years from 1933 to 1945 were. But the New Deal represented the political ascent of decades of efforts by working people and middle-class reformers to deal with the class conflict and widespread poverty brought on by industrial capitalism. Indeed, in the 1920s and 1930s, and especially after the onset of the Great Depression, the key efforts to expand American social democracy revolved around industrial democracy and economic security. These were driven by the efforts of working people to organize, and workers fought for these aspirations more than they sought increased opportunity through access to education.[4]

Though the early years of Roosevelt's presidency focused on an assortment of measures to stop the nation's economic chaos, by 1935, the New Deal found a firm and coherent reform footing, seeking to discipline the power of the wealthy, using Keynesian stimulus to build broad consumer demand in the economy, and empowering workers to build democracy in the workplace.[5] FDR signed into law numerous policies ensuring meaningful economic rights: for working people to form unions and collectively bargain, a guaranteed minimum wage, and provisions for old age and poverty. Examining the Wagner Act (1935) shows just how dramatic the departure was. In fact, the law pointed out that collective bargaining rights were essential for the nation's economic security:

> The inequality of bargaining power between employees who do not possess full freedom of association or actual liberty of contract and employers who are organized in the corporate or other forms of ownership association substantially burdens and affects the flow of commerce, and tends to aggravate recurrent business depressions, by depressing wage rates and the purchasing power of wage earners in industry and

by preventing the stabilization of competitive wage rates and working conditions within and between industries.

Further, by deeming it an "unfair labor practice" to fire a worker who was involved in organizing a union, the law tacitly asserted that workers had a right to their job.[6]

Finally, if not a consensus, powerful forces in the Roosevelt administration advanced the idea that every American should enjoy the right a job: the Federal Emergency Relief Administration (FERA) under Harry Hopkins as early as 1934 sought to directly create jobs for the unemployed and worked from the assumption that every American deserved a job. The Works Progress Administration (WPA), created in 1935 and also administered by Hopkins, dramatically reduced unemployment and created a growing bloc of congressional representatives who supported the notion that government take an active role in ensuring Americans had jobs.[7] By the early 1940s, the National Resources Planning Board (NRPB), an institution within the executive branch, articulated perhaps the single most coherent call for a postwar social democracy that would guarantee full employment, economic prosperity, and a generous social safety net.[8]

The version of social democracy advanced in the 1930s and 1940s had its limits. To push legislation through a Congress in which southern Democrats held key committees, the administration had to accommodate Jim Crow, leaving out domestic and agricultural workers from the Social Security Act, for instance, and implementing housing programs through New Deal agencies like the Federal Housing Administration (FHA) in ways that severely disadvantaged African American workers. It is also the case, however, that most African American voters enthusiastically supported the New Deal, as the programs offered direct employment to Black workers and from the election of 1936 on, African Americans overwhelmingly voted Democrat.[9]

Indeed, the social democratic achievements of the 1930s widened the expectations of many policymakers, union leaders, and civil rights activists for broader economic rights. By 1944, Roosevelt, under attack from reactionary Republicans and southern Democrats, sought to deepen the state's commitment to economic security for all Americans by connecting it to national service during wartime. This second—economic—bill of rights, he hoped, would build on earlier advances to reinvigorate the social democratic trajectory of the United States.

Why were these new rights necessary? Because, FDR argued, as "our industrial economy expanded," the original constitutional rights alone "proved inadequate to assure us equality in the pursuit of happiness. We have come to a clear realization of the fact that true individual freedom cannot exist without economic security and independence. Necessitous men are not free men. People who are hungry and out of a job are the stuff of which dictatorships are made." After a decade of reforms to make working Americans more economically secure, the president argued that "these economic truths have become accepted as self-evident."[10]

As FDR's call for a Second Bill of Rights indicates, the New Deal was a project designed to strengthen the fabric of American democracy. As had been Jefferson's vision of a nation in which every white family enjoyed economic independence, and as Lincoln sought a nation in which slavery was eradicated so all Americans could enjoy the fruits of their labor, so too did Roosevelt project a stronger nation of American citizens who could, having their needs met, pursue happiness.

FDR clearly saw public education as part of the project of strengthening American democracy. As he put it in an address to the NEA in 1938, "The only real capital of a nation is its natural resources and its human beings. So long as we take care of and make the most of both of them, we shall survive as a strong nation, a successful nation and a progressive nation—whether or not the bookkeepers say other kinds of budgets are from time to time out of balance." Though he invoked the words *human capital*, he used this term in a very different form than it would be used later by economists like Theodore Schultz and Gary Becker: "No nation can meet this changing world unless its people, individually and collectively, grow in ability to understand and handle the new knowledge as applied to increasingly intricate human relationships. That is why the teachers of America are the ultimate guardians of the human capital of America, the assets which must be made to pay social dividends if democracy is to survive."[11]

The GI Bill: Security and Opportunity

Roosevelt, as early as December 1941, called for vocational education for returning veterans, and the administration had authored a modest version of a bill to provide employment and education to returning veterans in 1943. The version was limited, however, because FDR sought to expand economic security for everyone, not just GIs. His call for the right to a job, universal healthcare, and other rights in the January 1944 speech was accompanied by the call to make every worker part of the war effort by drafting them into national service.

Roosevelt's broader push for economic democracy was stymied by conservative opposition, however, and Congress instead passed a comprehensive GI Bill that would only serve military veterans. This push came from the American Legion, which had been publicizing the struggles of veterans returning from combat.[12] The legion, a historically conservative force in the United States opposed to radicalism, got to work drafting for Congress a capacious set of benefits in late 1943.[13] Conferring with representatives from the Federal Housing Administration (FHA), Association of Land Grant Colleges, the NEA, and the American Council of Education (ACE), a committee led by the legion's former national commander, Harry Colmery, put together a bill by the end of the year. The legion sought primarily to compensate GI's for the interruption of their livelihoods by service in the war.

Thus, while FDR's comprehensive call for social democracy did not gain traction in Congress, a more robust version of his veterans' policy—what historian Harvey Kaye has called "history-making"—garnered support even from Republicans and southern Democrats, particularly after the legion's grassroots efforts to push legislators in both houses to pass the bill, and Roosevelt signed it into law.[14] The GI Bill ultimately provided veterans the right to reemployment if they gave up a job to serve, unemployment compensation, education, and loan guarantees for homes and farms. In its provisions, one can clearly see a more limited version of the Second Bill of Rights. Indeed, the bill was popularly understood as a set of rights, too. As a 1944 Veteran's Guide to the GI Bill put it, veterans were "entitled" to loans for housing, farms, and business; reemployment; education; life insurance; and tax relief.[15]

And, in fact, the new guarantees reached a massive number of Americans. Within a decade, about four million Americans had used the home loan provisions either under the GI Bill or other housing programs that survived, likely because of the GI Bill, to serve nonveterans.[16] Further, just as it had been in FDR's proposed Second Bill of Rights, the GI Bill's provision of education was only one aspect of a broader program to help servicemen. The rationale for providing it stemmed in part from the idea that education could help soldiers adjust psychologically both to the military and to life after the military, as well as strengthen the civic and political capability of veterans.[17] The public provision of education, then, was widely understood as helping veterans to return to secure lives, not simply as vocational training.

Much of the congressional floor debate in 1944, in fact, revolved around jobs and pay for veterans as the legislature's most important priorities, not education or training. In January 1944, for example, Representative Philip Philbin (D-MA) pointed to the broad intervention necessary to ensure returning veterans didn't face economic insecurity: "The best repayment we can give to these boys is to arrange our national economy so that when this war is over they will return to a nation . . . where they can obtain jobs at decent wages under the same system of free enterprise they left behind, which will permit them to enjoy in a fair, just and generous measure the benefits of democracy and freedom."[18] When Representative Marion Bennett, a Republican from the World War Veterans' Legislation Committee, reported the bill to the floor on June 15, a short paragraph on education was buried between descriptions of the GI Bill's sections on medical care; insurance; mustering out pay; burial allowance; farm, home and business ownership; and unemployment compensation.[19] Representative Dean Gillespie, highlighting the broad system of social supports for veterans, framed the GI Bill around both security and opportunity: "[Our veterans] will come home with a sense of security and the right to life, liberty, and the pursuit of happiness in a Nation of opportunity and private enterprise."[20] Given the wider purchase of social democracy at the time, it was fitting that Gillespie was a Republican.

Congressional proponents believed supporting higher education was important, but, clearly, they viewed it as an opportunity—for both the individual and perhaps for the nation—that represented something extra, but not required for a job. For example, a statement from Representative Joseph O'Hara (R-MN) in January 1944, cited his own experience to point out that "I was one of these who had to finish college training after the last war. I had a year of college left to complete my course, and if someone had come along and offered me a good job at $1000 a month the chances are I would have taken than job and never finished my professional education."[21] The implication was that if veterans legislation only ensured jobs, many GI's would not seek opportunities beyond that. Representative Samuel Weiss (D-PA) spoke in support of the GI Bill just as it came out of conference committee, "The major concern and the principal thought of all our gallant fighting sons is. . . . Will I get my job back? Will the country soon forget me and fail to get me employment? While looking for work, will my Government tide me over so that I will not be required to sell apples or seek relief?" Weiss did mention education, but he argued it was an additional opportunity, not necessary for the expectation of an economic livelihood.[22]

The massive funding for higher education in the GI Bill was not the primary locus for veterans to access economic security, but it nonetheless provided millions of new opportunities, both in economic and civic life. Modeled loosely on a Wisconsin law passed in 1919 that provided World War I veterans thirty dollars a month to attend any nonprofit high school, college, or university in the state, the education component of the GI Bill was more robust than competing bills. The GI Bill guaranteed up to four years of education for most returning veterans, while the initial White House proposal would have guaranteed most veterans only a year's worth of vocational training.[23]

The expansion of access to higher education under the GI Bill was profound. Eight million American veterans (of either WWII or the Korean War) accessed higher education with funding provided by the bill. Though the benefits went to some men who would have gone to college regardless, the new funds played a major role in expanding access to higher education for those from working-class families who would likely not have been able to afford to go.[24] As political scientist Suzanne Mettler puts it: "To appreciate the scope of the GI Bill's influence, we must consider that among men born in the United States in the 1920s . . . fully 80 percent were military veterans. And unlike veterans of the Vietnam War and today's all-volunteer force, they were broadly representative of the general male population."[25]

Funding higher education through the choices of individual GIs, rather than by only allowing access to specific institutions, opened up more space for the argument that education facilitated individual opportunity. A competing bill debated in Congress in May 1944, for instance, proposed to provide higher education only to those who, with the consent of university educators, had concrete plans that met the greater needs of American society. Though unemployment and reemployment provisions and housing spoke to security, the push to allow veterans to decide where to access their education, in contrast, enhanced the notion that education equated to an opportunity that veterans were best able to determine how to use. And, this structure of paying for higher education became the model for later expansions of access with the Higher Education Act of 1965 and its amendments, which would also build consent for the notion of education as economic opportunity. Further, the generous benefits of the GI Bill (including up to five hundred dollars a year in tuition and living stipends that increased if the veteran had a family) and the relatively low tuition at most universities meant that GI's, practically speaking, could go to just about any college or university.[26] Finally, the GI Bill's partial focus on vocation—the VA also pushed campuses to engage students in vocational counseling, and millions accessed vocational training—forced campus administrators and students to think more carefully about the link between postsecondary education and job training.[27]

There were clear limits to this expansion of higher education, however. Most obviously, the fact that the GI Bill was framed around military service limited the benefits, mostly, to men, though the 2 percent of those who served who were women were eligible.[28] In this respect, the GI Bill represented the preeminent manifestation of that fact that New Deal era social democracy had been built on a model that put male breadwinners at its center. Building on the broader sweep of American history that had put men at the center of public life and viewed women's economic contributions as invisible, women, whether they worked or not, were characterized as dependent. The majority of workers forming unions in the wake of the Wagner Act were men, and the construction of Social Security—which allowed single women to claim benefits for "dependent" children but not single men—reinforced gender roles that privileged men as the focal point for growing economic security.[29] The GI Bill did the same, as one historian has argued, forcing women in postwar America "into new dependencies that limited their life options."[30]

Further, the color-blind nature of the GI Bill allowed African American veterans to benefit from its education provisions, but profoundly less so than white GIs. Forty-nine percent of nonwhite veterans, compared to 43 percent of white veterans, used the education and training benefits of the GI Bill by 1950, including 56 percent of nonwhite veterans in the South. Black GIs were less likely to attend college, however (just 12 percent compared to 28 percent for white GIs).[31] Part of this discrepancy resulted from the fact that African Americans had disproportionately been unable to complete high school; more important, however, was the construction of the GI Bill. Essential to garnering the support of powerful southern racists like Mississippi Democrat John Rankin, the final version of the bill allowed local centers of the VA to administer education benefits. Racist administrators kept Blacks in the South from accessing the better resourced, all-white institutions.[32] Though African Americans outside the South could, theoretically, attend integrated institutions, Blacks in the South (the vast majority of Blacks who used GI Bill funds), could only access segregated institutions, and these institutions were hampered by extremely low budgets and even more overcrowding than white institutions that had expanded access after World War II.[33] As sociologist Ira Katznelson has persuasively argued, "On balance, despite the assistance that black soldiers received, there was no greater instrument for widening an already huge racial gap in postwar America than the GI Bill."[34]

The Right to a Job?

Although there were many who were against it, the idea that all Americans had the right to an economic livelihood assumed wide purchase during the Roosevelt years. While it is often forgotten in discussions about the GI Bill, veterans' publications made clear that the law gave them the right to return to their job after service.[35] Economic planners, both in the Roosevelt and Truman administrations, pushed for meaningful policy changes that would guarantee good jobs for everyone, not just GIs. So too did social democrats in Congress. Indeed, throughout 1945 and into 1946, Congress debated a proposed full employment bill that would have effectively established the right to a job for all Americans.

Led by Keynesian New Dealers, the push for full employment came from several different directions. In addition to Harry Hopkins, the WPA, and the National Resources Planning Board, proponents included economists such as

Alvin Hansen (who collaborated with the NRPB), the Congress of Industrial Organizations (CIO), and the National Farmers Union (NFU), whose leadership saw the interests of farmers as intertwined with the overall fate of the national economy. Even some prominent Republicans supported the idea. As GOP presidential candidate Thomas Dewey put it in September 1944: "If at any time there are not sufficient jobs in private enterprise to go around, the government can and must create job opportunities, because there must be jobs for all in this country of ours."[36]

Based on a proposal by the NFU and introduced by Senator James Murray (D-MT), the original draft of the Full Employment Act of 1945 established the right to a livelihood for every adult. Indeed, the bill introduced in 1945 mobilized FDR's language in the Economic Bill of Rights, asserting in its opening paragraph "that every American able to work and willing to work has the right to a useful and remunerative job in the industries, or shops, or offices, or farms, or mines of the nation."

Unfortunately, the bill was heavily influenced by Leon Keyserling, a Keynesian cool on the idea of the federal government directly employing workers in need of a job. Keyserling, an economist on the staff of Senator Robert Wagner who played a major role in drafting both the Social Security Act and the Wagner Act, turned away from the popular legacy of the WPA, as did other social democrats involved in drafting the bill who believed directly guaranteeing a job would make it more difficult to circumvent conservative opposition. This turn of events was unfortunate, since more than 75 percent of Americans at the time believed the government should function as employer of last resort.[37] Instead, the 1945 Senate bill charged the president with ensuring the federal government filled whatever gaps were left by the private sector in job creation: not literally guaranteeing everyone a job, but, even so, making certain the state would ensure everyone's right to a livelihood through economic planning.

Twelve days of committee hearings sandwiched around the Japanese surrender to the Allied forces in the summer of 1945 brought a forceful case for ensuring full employment. Senator Wagner led congressional hearings on the bill in 1945 for the Committee on Banking and Currency. Wagner, who had authored the National Labor Relations Act and been integrally involved with the construction of the Social Security Act, introduced discussion of the bill by remarking, without hyperbole, "We meet to consider what I profoundly believe to be as important a proposal as any before the Congress within my memory." While some policymakers quibbled about the definition of "full employment," Wagner asserted it could be defined easily: "The right to work is synonymous with the inalienable right to live. . . . Society was organized to enlarge the scope of that right and to increase the fruits of its exercise. . . . Whomever believes in this right to work, believes in it for every adult who is looking for an honest job at decent pay, must believe in full employment." Drawing on the experience of the nation during the Depression, Wagner believed the government was responsible for ensuring jobs for everyone.[38]

Though not without opposition,[39] the bill attracted a broad array of constituencies who supported a government guarantee of full employment in the Senate hearings. Bishop Bernard Sheil, director of the Catholic Youth Organization in Chicago, pointed out: "It is not enough to say that all men are created equal, with equal rights to life, liberty, and the pursuit of happiness." Citing Pope Leo XIII, Sheil stated, "[If] private industry is unable to afford men the opportunity of a decent and honorable living, government is bound by its very nature to employ all its resources to secure all citizens this essential right to work."[40]

While pointing to some of the dramatic inequalities that still existed in the labor market, NAACP secretary Walter White testified that the wartime economy and federal nondiscrimination policy had already brought much more economic security for African Americans. "It is tragic," White asserted, "that it took the catastrophe of war to give the Negro for the first time in his more than three centuries in America an opportunity to earn a decent living." But White urged the Full Employment Act to be passed, arguing it would "clearly establish the responsibility of the Federal Government for guaranteeing an economic bill of rights to all Americans." Indeed, White also urged the government to pass other planks of FDR's bill of rights such as a national housing guarantee and an expansion of social security.[41]

Paul Hoffman, president of the Studebaker Corporation and chairman of the Committee for Economic Development, also argued for the right to a job. The Keynesian businessman made the logical argument that "the recognition that the principal role of the Federal Government in our free economy is that of a policy maker takes us only a short distance toward the answer to our question of the responsibility of the Federal Government for employment."[42] Francis Brown, a representative from ACE, also testified in the Senate. He pointed out that "the problems of youth and youth employment and the problems of higher education are inextricably involved in the solution of the problem of full employment." Full employment would require "training at all levels," according to Brown, which meant universities could both provide that training and advance the state of knowledge in the nation. Finally, he argued, there was a clear link between full employment and funding for higher education: "Economic crises and unemployment mean the diversion of public funds from education to meet more urgent immediate demands for relief and unemployment compensation."[43] Brown thus argued that the right to a job would augment the nation's human capital stock, even if the term *human capital* was not yet in employ. But the causal relationship in Brown's logic is important: broad economic security would facilitate the development of new skills for working people, not the other way around.

Senator Murray, the NFU, and others embarked on an immense public relations campaign in support of the Senate's version of an employment guarantee. The Union for Democratic Action (later the Americans for Democratic Action) led the charge, receiving support from a range of constituencies, including the AFL, CIO, Businessmen of America Inc. (a liberal small business association), the YWCA, the NAACP, and the National Women's Trade Union League.[44] President Truman also forcefully supported the bill. In an address to Congress in September 1945, for example, the new president outlined his notion of a "fair deal" which centrally included "a national reassertion of the right to work for every American citizen able and willing to work—a declaration of the ultimate duty of Government to use its resources if all other measures should fail to prevent sustained unemployment."[45]

Despite some minor amendments, the bill sailed through the Senate in late September 1945 by the overwhelming margin of 71–10. Conservative forces like the National Association of Manufacturers and the American Farm Bureau mobilized against the bill, however, as it made its way to the House, where they sought to eviscerate it of any meaningful obligation on the part of the federal government to ensure full employment. The bill's opponents feared the growth of labor's bargaining power if there were no longer a reserve army of unemployed workers, and they also feared the growth of the state, which they believed might someday develop industries to compete with the private sector in order to fulfill a jobs promise.[46] In the House hearings, for instance, one key spokesperson for business argued that "the Bill should be purged of its remaining vestiges of the right-to-a-job idea, its qualified but still persistent reliance on Government spending as a panacea, and the surviving remnants of its mandate for long-range fiscal-year forecasting."[47]

Ultimately, the critics succeeded in watering it down significantly. Though the more robust bill had made it through the Senate without many modifications, it was critically weakened in the House Committee on Expenditures in Executive Departments. President Truman vigorously pushed for the guarantees of the Senate when the two bills were in conference reconciliation, but the House version won out. The name change—from the Full Employment Act of 1945 to the Employment Act of 1946—evoked the much weaker version of the law's jobs promise.

The Employment Act of 1946 left the federal government with the highly qualified responsibility to "to promote maximum employment, production, and purchasing power." The law basically created a process for establishing macroeconomic goals: The Council of Economic Advisors (CEA), to be appointed by the president, was responsible for developing an annual report, on which Congress would hold hearings. The CEA would publish a final revised report, and Congress and the president could then use the material to legislate.[48] The fight for the right to a job was by no means dead, but the limited nature of the Employment Act of 1946 significantly constricted future social democratic possibilities.[49]

Though the right to a job was not to be, the dramatic growth of unions in this era encouraged workers to use collective bargaining to carve out something resembling FDR's Second Bill of Rights. The Wagner Act ushered in the expectation that workers enjoyed the right, or even obligation, to organize, and wartime policy—in which workers were automatically enrolled in their union in exchange for unions' agreement not to strike—expanded membership even more. The number of workers in unions exploded in the 1930s and 1940s, from three million members in 1935 to ten million by the end of 1941 and to fourteen million, more than one-third of the nonagricultural workforce, by the end of the war.[50]

Unions sought a secure share for workers of what the abundant American economy produced. The best example of this effort is the militance of Walter Reuther and the United Auto Workers (UAW), one of the most social democratic unions in the United States at the time. Soon to be president of the union, Reuther in 1945 had vigorously supported the full employment bill. In a letter to Wagner, he asserted that "the Government must coordinate and direct the overall basic planning which is necessary to successfully convert our war economy to peace production with a minimum of unemployment, and it must continue in this role once conversion takes place." While Reuther also asked that more labor standards be included in the bill, he enthusiastically endorsed the notion of a "right to useful, remunerative, regular, and full-time employment."[51]

In a strike of General Motors in 1945–46, in fact, Reuther and the auto workers sought similar guarantees through collective bargaining. In the walkout, the UAW asked for a 30 percent wage increase while pushing GM to maintain the sale price of their cars, thus arguing for an even greater share of what was being produced. Though the UAW was unable to win these conditions (they won a modest pay increase instead) the union went on to negotiate what observers called the "Treaty of Detroit" in 1950: a collective bargaining agreement in which workers automatically received wage increases to cover rising cost of living and for increases in productivity over the life of the contract in addition to health insurance and a pension in exchange for labor peace. As one historian explains it: "Quickly spreading to much of unionized heavy industry, the Treaty of Detroit proved a milestone from which there was no turning back."[52] Over the course of the 1950s and 1960s, organized workers built on the growing power of labor to negotiate much of the economic security FDR called for in the Second Bill of Rights: health insurance, retirement, job security (through seniority policies), and increased time for leisure. Nonunionized employers were forced to offer workers similar benefits to limit worker attrition or to avoid unions in their workplace.

It is true that these benefits accrued disproportionately to white, male, blue-collar workers, and that they privileged male breadwinners in what Gabriel Winant calls the "insulated pools of economic security" created in unionized heavy industry in the 1950s.[53] The incremental increases, nonetheless, revolutionized the lives of millions of working people. As Jack Metzgar argues in his powerful meditation on how his father's more secure livelihood changed his family's future, *Striking Steel*:

> The perception of remembrance of the 1950s as a time of repressive conformism and spiritless materialism . . . did not relate to us. . . . All the discretion that the foremen and the company were losing was flowing right into our home. There were choices. There were prospects. There were possibilities. Few of these had been there before. Now they were. And because they came slowly, year by year, contract by contract, strike by bitter strike, they gave a lilting, liberating feeling to life—a sense that no matter what was wrong today, it could be changed it could get better—in fact, by the late 1950s, that it was quite likely that it *would* get better. . . . If what we lived through in the 1950s was not liberation, then liberation never happens in real human lives.[54]

Wisconsin represented an exemplar of these trends. The state had been a pioneer in social democracy in the early twentieth century. Built on the Wisconsin Idea—that expert knowledge could inform a more democratic politics and Progressive government programs—the state was the first in the nation to pass worker's compensation (1911) and, in 1932, was the first to provide unemployment insurance. Wisconsin intellectuals like the economists John Commons and Edwin Witte informed national policies, and the Social Security Act in 1935 was influenced by the Wisconsin law.[55] Further, the state passed a jobs program for unemployed workers under Governor Phillip La Follette in 1931, as well as labor legislation in 1937 (the Wisconsin Labor Relations Act, also known as Wisconsin's "Little Wagner Act") that established the Wisconsin Labor Relations Board, limited employers' efforts to break unions, and compelled employers to bargain with certified unions. New organizing efforts flowered across the state, such as at the General Motors plant in Janesville, and workers flocked into unions. Though a conservative legislature set new restrictions on workers' rights in 1939, workers joined unions in huge numbers in Wisconsin in the 1940s. Union membership exploded from under 20,000 in 1935 to over 250,000 by 1960. In 1959, Wisconsin was the first state to ensure public employees had collective bargaining rights, and by 1974, Wisconsin was fifteenth out of the fifty states in unionization rate, with about 32 percent of its workers covered by collectively bargained contracts.[56]

The Expansion of Educational Opportunity—for Democracy and Citizenship

The rising standard of living, the overall prosperity of the postwar era, and the growth of more white-collar professions (including a tremendous increase in teachers), led more and more young Americans to continue their education longer than previous generations. Public investment in schooling, at all levels, exploded in the 1950s and beyond, and the average level of education increased dramatically. American attendance in high school, already on the increase before World War II, continued its ascent. The national high school enrollment rate grew from around 50 percent in the 1930s to 80 percent by 1955 and the graduation rate rose from about 40 percent to about 65 percent over the same period.[57]

College enrollments similarly grew. In addition to the GI Bill funds that expanded access, states significantly expanded funding for higher education too.[58] Outside the South, state governments had already begun investing more money on higher education before World War II: state and local spending on higher education, as a percentage of total budgets, doubled in the first four decades of the twentieth century.[59] These increases continued into the postwar era: total spending on higher education by state and local governments exploded from about $250 million in 1945 to over $500 million just five years later and to $3.2 billion by 1965. Though federal investment in public education, in part the result of the Cold War competition for technological supremacy, accounted for a sizable portion of the increase, the vast majority came from state governments. As a percentage of total funding on higher education in the United States, state spending climbed from 19 percent to almost 21 percent and then 23 percent over the same time period.[60] Though GI Bill investment had disproportionately offered education to men (college graduation rates for males born in the mid-1920s were double those for women in the same cohort), broader investment in higher education brought many more women into higher education by the 1950s with huge increases in access to college beginning with the generation of women born in the mid-1930s.[61]

It is important to point out that this expansion occurred simultaneously with the growth of blue-collar livelihoods. While the lives of Jack Metzgar's parents were getting better, for example, so were the educational opportunities for both their son and daughter, the former who went on to college and became a history professor. Thus, while American social democracy persisted in a much more limited manner than what FDR had envisioned in its most comprehensive form, the dramatic increase in public support for education continued as one aspect in a broader program of facilitating both economic security and opportunity.

Further, many policymakers understood education as doing more than serving the purpose of developing skills for the job market, and in fact, yoked the expansion of postsecondary study to the development of the civic capabilities of Americans. The quintessential example of this vision is the President's Commission on Higher Education created by President Truman in 1947. In the late 1940s, as Truman's charge to the commission made clear, the nation's higher education system was at a crossroads. Indeed, the GI Bill and the dramatic expansion of access had begun to strain the resources of universities. Appointing George Zook, president of ACE, as chairperson,[62] Truman suggested the commission study the questions of how to expand educational opportunity "for all able young people," the "adequacy of curriculum, particularly in the fields of international affairs and social understanding," the possibility of more technical institutes in the United States, and the expansion of funding for new facilities.[63] In fact, at the very time Truman called for economic security in the form of a jobs guarantee and national health insurance, he also clearly viewed education as both a social and economic opportunity to be layered on top of the security blanket.

After months of analyzing American higher education, the commission ultimately made the case that colleges and universities were most important for their role in building a strong democracy in the tumultuous international Cold War climate in which the United States had emerged as a leader. The complexity of American political economy, the report asserted, "has made a broader understanding of social processes and problems essential for effective living." Philosopher Horace Kallen, famous for his work on cultural pluralism, served on the commission. Therefore, it was not surprising that the report also included a call for higher education to help build national unity. "We undertake to effect democratic reconciliation," the report argued, "so as to make the national life one continuous process of interpersonal, intervocational, and intercultural cooperation." In addition, the heightened role of the United States in international politics required "a knowledge of other peoples—of their political and economic systems, their social and cultural institutions—as has not been hitherto so urgent." Finally, growing fears of nuclear annihilation had "deepened and broadened the responsibilities of higher education for anticipating and preparing for the social and economic changes that will come with the application of atomic energy to industrial uses."[64]

In sum, the report eschewed the argument that public education served to enhance the skills of workers in any narrow sense. Instead, the new skills to come from higher education would help ensure a more secure workforce that could make sense of their rapidly changing nation and its place in the world. Indeed, the ultimate goal, moving forward, for US higher education was to advance

> Education for a fuller realization of democracy in every phase of living.
>
> Education directly and explicitly for international understanding and cooperation.
>
> Education for the application of creative imagination and trained intelligence to the solution of social problems and to the administration of public affairs.

Not only did the report argue that college students must study democracy, but that the very way universities were administered should be restructured because "democracy must be lived to be thoroughly understood."[65]

The commission called for substantial investment—in materials, research, and instructors—to achieve these goals. Pointing out that total investment in education in 1947 (even with the GI Bill) was only 0.5 percent of gross national product, the report asserted the nation's failure to fund education was "indefensible in a society so richly endowed with material resources as our own. We cannot allow so many of our people to remain so ill equipped either as human beings or as citizens of a democracy." In fact, the report even took issue with the argument that individual economic opportunity represented education's purpose: "All too often the benefits of education have been sought and used for personal and private profit, to the neglect of public and social service. . . . The democratic way of life can endure only as private careers and social obligations are made to mesh, as personal ambition is reconciled with public responsibility."[66]

Pointing to the number of Americans, who because of race, region, or rural upbringing lacked education, the report asserted that "these conditions mean that millions of youth are being denied their just right to an adequate education. The accident of being born in one place rather than another ought not to affect so profoundly a young person's chance of getting an education commensurate with his native capacities." In addition to calling for a minimum high school degree for all Americans, the report also recommended two years of tuition-free education at all public universities in order to double the number of Americans in higher education within just a few years.[67] This argument took as its the premise, though certainly in a much more inclusive version, Jefferson's notion that the government should use public education to ensure Americans had every opportunity to develop their own social capacities.

In fact, Truman's Higher Education Commission, combined with the president's Commission on Civil Rights (which also released its report in 1947), helped to elevate the century-long efforts of civil rights activists to ensure equality in higher education for African Americans. The Civil Rights Commission, like the Higher Education Commission, forcefully argued that all citizens—not just those who had contributed military service, as in the GI Bill—deserved the right to higher education.[68]

It is no surprise, then, given the significant increase in the importance policymakers placed on education in the 1940s and 1950s, that one of the most important federal landmarks in the struggle against segregation occurred in that realm. The *Brown vs. Board of Education* (1954) decision clearly addressed racial inequality in schools in the United States after World War II. As the Truman Commission on Higher Education pointed to the necessity of using the higher education system to enhance American democracy, the antidemocratic nature of American apartheid was glaring. *Brown v. Board* represented the culmination of decades of efforts by the NAACP Legal Defense Fund attorneys (most prominently Thurgood Marshall) to highlight the unequal nature of segregation. Particularly important had been *Sweatt v. Painter* (1946), a lawsuit that sought redress of the stark disparity between the educational opportunity at the University of Texas's all-white law school and the inferior all-Black law school the state created to maintain segregation. Further, the provisions of the GI Bill accessed by African Americans directly impacted the demand to eliminate segregation, as GI Bill recipients were disproportionately active in confrontational civil rights activism in the 1950s and 1960s.[69]

The *Brown* decision ruled that "in the field of public education, the doctrine of 'separate but equal' has no place. Separate educational facilities are inherently unequal." It is worth pointing out why an education case represented the Warren court's primary avenue for dismantling the doctrine of "separate but equal." Indeed, the relatively short decision commenced by highlighting the state of public education in 1954. When the Fourteenth Amendment had been ratified in 1868, the court pointed out, public education, even in the North, was "rudimentary." But conditions had changed by the 1950s, and the court argued it must "consider public education in the light of its full development and its present place in American life throughout the Nation." And, clearly, education had grown in the postwar era to a place of utmost importance. In fact, it was integral to American democracy itself. "Today," the decision argued,

> education is perhaps the most important function of state and local governments. Compulsory school attendance laws and the great expenditures for education both demonstrate our recognition of the importance of education to our democratic society. It is required in the performance of our most basic public responsibilities, even service in the armed forces. It is the very foundation of good citizenship. Today it is a principal instrument in awakening the child to cultural values, in preparing him for later professional training, and in helping him to adjust normally to his environment. In these days, it is doubtful that any child may reasonably be expected to succeed in life if he is denied the opportunity of an education. Such an opportunity, where the state has undertaken to provide it, is a right which must be made available to all on equal terms.[70]

The message could not have been clearer in its argument for why a good education was essential, and as had been the case with the Truman Commission on Higher Education report, facilitating human capital was not primarily why education was important. On the contrary, the court mostly zeroed in on why education was crucial in teaching democratic citizenship in a more complicated postwar environment. When *Brown v. Board* mentioned professional training, the court talked about opportunity in a broader sense than merely the economic.

Still, in its focus on individual adjustment and opportunity—particularly the notion that "it is doubtful that any child may reasonably be expected to succeed in life if he is denied the opportunity of an education"—the court decision did highlight a transition. Whereas the GI Bill and FDR's Second Bill of Rights had framed education in the context of a broader expanse of economic security, the Brown decision had begun to assert the growing necessity of education in access to economic mobility, even if the discussion of the labor market was implied more than expressed.[71]

Great Expectations

In the 1930s and 1940s, the New Deal brought nation-changing advances in social democracy. Though labor rights, social security, and other government supports allowed greater numbers of Americans to access good jobs, healthcare, and decent housing, none of these were fully institutionalized as "rights." Only public education reached even that rhetorical level, as civil rights activists successfully pushed the nation to guarantee, at least in theory, a comparable education for every American child. In the 1960s, Lyndon Johnson's Great Society would usher in the last important expansion of American social democracy. Though the Democrat's agenda in the 1960s prioritized limited expansions of economic security, it also advanced a greater argument for economic opportunity that sowed the seeds of the education myth. Many of the assumptions around government interventions like the Elementary and Secondary Education Act, for example, focused on the notion that poor people, particularly African Americans, needed to overcome their individual deficiencies. Schools would thus give them the "equal educational opportunity" to succeed on their own, in spite of other structural limitations they might face in accessing good jobs.

EDUCATION'S WAR ON POVERTY IN THE 1960s

In 1964, Gary Becker published the first edition of his seminal work *Human Capital: A Theoretical and Empirical Analysis with Special Reference to Education*. Becker began his work on the book in 1957, right in the middle of an era in which American policymakers were dramatically expanding access to public education at every level.[1] As Becker noted, the very notion of human capital, though more widely accepted than a decade before, was still controversial because many thinkers still connected the concept to chattel slavery. Slaveowners in the US South, for example, had functionally treated human property—enslaved African Americans—as capital to be used for everything from the production of goods to collateral for loans, dramatically enriching themselves in the process.[2]

Nevertheless, Becker and other economists, especially from the University of Chicago, persevered, arguing that wages should best be thought of as the profit from workers' "human capital." Though Becker would go on to become the most prominent economist associated with the concept, in its formative period Becker's colleague Theodore Schultz represented its most important advocate, and he was the thinker who most influenced American policymakers during the period of reform called the Great Society in the 1960s. Schultz and Becker were both part of the University of Chicago economics department, the site of a movement after World War II in which academics like Becker studied the microeconomic decisions of individual, supposedly rational, actors in order to understand society and chart policy. While both economists advocated for investment in human capital, there were key differences in their thought, particularly around who should finance the investment. Schultz, a neo-Keynesian rather than a libertarian like Becker, believed public education and other investments in human capital could make the entire society more prosperous and even maximize everyone's noneconomic happiness. He advocated for the government to pay for it, even if the benefits accrued to individuals. In contrast, Becker believed individuals should finance as much of their own education as possible, either with help from their family or through loans, preferably in the private marketplace.[3]

Both Schultz and Becker agreed, however, that after World War II, economists had misunderstood the huge productivity growth in the United States. By focusing only on physical capital, corporate investment, and labor, most economists, they argued, had failed to understand that advances in human capital—including healthcare, migration in pursuit of better employment, and most prominently, education and job training—were instrumental in the broad postwar economic affluence of the United States. Schultz argued, for example, in his Presidential Address to the American Economic Association in 1960, "that such investment in human capital accounts for most of the impressive rise in the real earnings of the worker."[4]

More and more working people, even before World War II, consciously viewed education and job training as an investment in economic opportunity, a trend that certainly continued after the war. The GI Bill's focus on providing individual opportunity through education also helped to illustrate the growth of this idea. Given this context, it is unsurprising that a focus on education as human capital began to make inroads in the field of economics. As early as the 1960s, as Becker argued, the field had shown a "tremendous amount of circumstantial evidence testifying to the economic importance of human capital, especially of education. Probably the most impressive piece of evidence is that more highly educated and skilled persons almost always tend to earn more than others. . . . Inequality in the distribution of earnings and income" he concluded, "is generally positively related to inequality in education and other training."[5] Schultz, even more sanguinely, gushed that, in 1960, "laborers have become capitalists not for a diffusion of the ownership of corporation stocks, as folklore would have it, but from the acquisition of knowledge and skill that have economic value."[6]

In one sense, Schultz and Becker were correct. Americans were attaining greater levels of education and workers were more productive. But denying the greater context of racism, the geography of jobs, and the sexism of the breadwinner model of the American workplace in crafting a monocausal explanation for how to reduce income inequality was deeply problematic. Furthermore, considering human capital as equivalent to other kinds of capital represented a major contradiction. In the 1989 edition of the book, Becker pointed out that human capital was different from "physical or financial" capital because "you cannot separate a person from his or her knowledge, skills, health, or values the way it is possible to move financial and physical assets while the owner stays put."[7] But the distinction between these different kinds of "capital," both at the time and now, is even more basic, and equating human capital to physical and financial capital represented a monumental sleight of hand. In reality, increased skills for workers, as had always been the case, didn't allow them to profit in the same way capitalists profited: by reaping rewards from the labor of others. Rather, human capital merely increased the uniqueness of the labor workers would be selling.

Empirically, more education or training *could* certainly increase one's earning power. But there are a number of assumptions embedded in this notion. First, it assumes that workers figure out how to acquire a skill that will allow them to add value to a product or service that can be either sold in the marketplace or that a government would pay for. Second, it assumes the worker has acquired skills than can't easily be acquired elsewhere. Third, it assumes groups of employers don't engage in anticompetitive practices to keep wages down. And finally, it assumes that racism or sexism (what Becker referred to as "tastes") won't allow employers to arbitrarily refuse to pay a premium for more skilled work. If all these conditions are met, employers are likely to recognize those skills with higher wages or risk losing them to higher-paying employers. Even in this case, however, employers would not reduce their profits by sharing with the more productive worker; rather they would either extract more value from other less skilled workers or raise the price of their products to meet the cost of skilled labor. But by analyzing the increase in education as human capital, Schultz and Becker elided the broader power dynamics that existed in society and fantasized that every worker was not working on someone else's terms but was an entrepreneur who invested in him- or herself. Workers, no matter how great their skills, could never act as "capital" as long as all they had to sell was their labor.

Nevertheless, this general economic perspective, which was that investment in human capital would make working people more prosperous, made major inroads in the 1960s. The rise of this thought, both in academia and in politics, signified an important aspect of the Great Society: that helping workers to overcome their own supposed deficiencies was at least as important as expanding access to a broader set of economic rights. Schultz's version, indeed, which envisioned that investment in public education at all levels could "reduce the unequal distribution of personal income among individuals and families" found a welcome audience in the Johnson administration.[8]

In contrast to our highly partisan political times, not only did Johnson and other Democrats support investment in human capital as a primary antipoverty solution, but so too did a number of moderate and liberal Republicans. The suite of policies that made up the Great Society package—the Elementary and Secondary Education Act (ESEA) and Higher Education Act (HEA), in particular—not only put the federal government squarely into the realm of public education, but also put education at the center of the argument that facilitating economic opportunity could provide the mobility necessary to eliminate poverty.

The Great Society thus signified the foundational moment in the rise of the education myth in American politics. The rise of the myth did not go uncontested, however. Social democrats, particularly civil rights activists like A. Philip Randolph and Bayard Rustin, fought for the kind of bold plan that could have actually achieved political equality and economic security for all. Their "freedom budget" was not enacted into law, but its premise represented the core of an important alternative in competition with the education myth over the course of the 1960s and 1970s.

The Great Society

On November 22, 1963, Vice President Lyndon Johnson took the presidential oath of office, hours after the assassination of John F. Kennedy. A New Dealer who saw his work as continuing the legacy of Roosevelt, Johnson leveraged his mastery of the legislative process to usher through an era of social democratic expansion unrivaled by any other in American history except the New Deal. Johnson also had important social winds propelling him: the growing realization of widespread poverty in the midst of American prosperity made clear by popular political works like Michael Harrington's *The Other America* (1962), and, more important, the civil rights movement at its peak influence. Just months before Kennedy's assassination, for instance, the March on Washington for Jobs and Freedom highlighted both the power of the movement as well as the extensiveness of its economic and social demands.

In his January 1964 State of the Union address, the new president declared an "unconditional war on poverty." The Johnson administration debated how to fight such a war, and some voices, such as Labor Secretary William Wirtz, argued for public-sector jobs and income redistribution. Others, like CEA chair Walter Heller, believed the less politically controversial tactic of increasing "opportunity" would be more successful.[9] Heller, Melinda Cooper has shown, was an "enthusiastic" acolyte of Schultz's human capital arguments, and successfully pushed the administration to implement them in Johnson's "war" mobilization.[10]

Therefore, Johnson's vision for political action did not focus very much on jobs, instead offering a strategy predicated on strengthening the capacity of the poor.[11] One can easily see how Schultz's ideas were translated into the administration's vision. As Schultz argued in 1960, "No small part of the low earnings of many Negroes, Puerto Ricans, Mexican nationals, indigenous migratory workers, poor farm people, and some of our older workers, reflects the failure to have invested in their health and education."[12] Four years later, in his State of the Union address, President Johnson argued, "Very often a lack of jobs and money is not the cause of poverty, but the symptom. The cause may lie deeper in our failure to give our fellow citizens a fair chance to develop their own capacities, in a lack of education and training, in a lack of medical care and housing, in a lack of decent communities in which to live and bring up their children."[13] While Johnson mentioned medical care and housing in his diagnosis of the problem, it was evident that by focusing on skill acquisition rather than more broadly on the economic structure, there would be clear limits to what the so-called War on Poverty could do.[14]

Just a few months later, Johnson outlined a sweeping vision for developing Americans' capabilities in his call for a "Great Society," a vision that started with "an abundance and liberty for all. It demands an end to poverty and racial injustice, to which we are totally committed in our time." But that was just the beginning. Among other things, it was "a place where every child can find knowledge to enrich his mind and to enlarge his talents." Thus, the Great Society would be developed in three places: in the city, in the countryside, and "in our classrooms." "Our society will not be great until every young mind is set free to scan the farthest reaches of thought and imagination," asserted Johnson. The president highlighted the fact that 25 percent of Americans did not complete high school, and 100,000 high school graduates did not go to college because they couldn't afford it. Overcrowded classrooms, outdated curricula, and underpaid teachers plagued the school system. Importantly, though Johnson did not reduce education to job training, he went on to argue that "poverty must not be a bar to learning, and learning must offer an escape from poverty."[15]

In a little over a year (sandwiched around Johnson's reelection campaign), the administration worked with Congress to pass a series of laws driven by a vision of social democracy, civil rights, and opportunity through education: the Civil Rights Act (July 1964), the Economic Opportunity Act (EOA, August 1964), the Food Stamp Act (August 1964), the Elementary and Secondary Education Act (April 1965), amendments to the Social Security Act establishing Medicare and Medicaid (July 1965), the Voting Rights Act (August 1965), and the Higher Education Act (November 1965). It is clear from the wide-ranging nature of the legislation that Johnson and other social democrats sought to expand enabling freedoms in a holistic effort to eradicate poverty and ensure everyone a basic degree of economic security. Still, in comparison with the New Deal, the notion of assisting Americans through education to overcome supposed individual insufficiencies played a much larger role in the Great Society. Created by the EOA, the Office of Economic Opportunity (OEO) piloted Head Start and funded job-training programs in the inner cities, for instance. And, ESEA and HEA were explicitly premised on the notion that expanding access to education would reduce poverty by helping individuals acquire the right skills to meet the needs of the job market rather than ensuring jobs existed with sufficient wages and guarantees of long-term security.

The Elementary and Secondary Education Act

With the possible exception of the GI Bill, no single federal policy has altered the position of education more in the United States than the Elementary and Secondary Education Act of 1965. With one piece of legislation, the federal government began a sustained presence in funding K-12 education, and the assumptions embedded in the law were instrumental in how Americans thought about the purpose of education moving forward. Much like the dramatic shift around race and education brought on by *Brown v. Board*, however, ESEA was both a turning point and the culmination of a decades-long push for more federal funding for public education. The Smith-Hughes Act (1917), for instance, had provided funding earmarked for vocational education. In addition, the NEA and other groups had lobbied for increased federal funding for education—in addition to a cabinet-level department—since the 1920s.[16]

Further, the National Defense Education Act (NDEA), signed into law by President Dwight Eisenhower in 1958, had played an important role in establishing a sizable federal presence in local education. Before that, opponents of federal support for education in the 1950s believed it threatened the autonomy of state and local governments, and Catholics fought to fund private schools in any federally supported programs. Resistance from conservatives and Catholics limited the scope of NDEA, but the law nonetheless provided an important precursor to ESEA.

The Soviet Union's launch of the satellite Sputnik in 1957 helped overcome some of the objections about the federal role of education as more policymakers, hoping to win the Cold War, supported greater federal investment. As the law's introduction put it: "The Congress hereby finds and declares that the security of the Nation requires the fullest development of the mental resources and technical skills of its young men and women. . . . It is therefore the purpose of this Act to . . . insure trained manpower of sufficient quality and quantity to meet the national defense needs of the United States."[17]

Here the trajectory of federal education policy built on efforts by college administrators, led by Harvard University's president James Conant, to win the Cold War by making the nation's system of higher education more meritocratic. Before World War II, the nation's elite universities mostly catered to the sons of wealthy and powerful families. Conant argued that ensuring the nation's best universities instead served its most capable students was necessary for the United States to build the most intellectually capable new generations of leaders. Though this version of meritocracy had broader national goals in mind, it did set in motion an important ideal: that the education system, particularly higher education, should represent a competition in which the winners deserved the reward of a degree from an elite institution.[18]

The Space Race further stimulated the impulse to use public education to maximize the talents of the nation's best and brightest students in the competition. Thus, the aid in NDEA was categorical. Earmarked to support math, science, and foreign language instruction through laboratory equipment purchases and professional development, the federal funding for education was much more limited than it would be under ESEA, and disproportionately helped students in affluent districts.[19] The NDEA also included federal loans for higher education, based on need and with preference for math, science, and foreign language, establishing a funding model that served substantially more Americans when Congress passed the Higher Education Act seven years later.

Both the stated goals of the legislation and the remarks of representatives in congressional hearings made clear the intent of the law was to develop a more internationally competitive stock of human capital. In contrast to future efforts to use education to make the nation more competitive, however, such as Goals 2000 (1994), NDEA did not frame the need for funding public education in terms of individual economic opportunity. Further, some of the bill's critics in Congress—such as Representative George McGovern (D-SD)—pushed for even more extensive investment in education so the education system would do *more* than develop technical skills. "Accepting the Soviet challenge in education," he argued, "we must never forget the basic principles of democracy that we are seeking to defend. . . . There is a desperate need for scientific and technical training, but we seek above all the well-balanced, educated citizen, who is aware also of his cultural, social, and moral responsibilities in a democratic society."[20]

Less than a decade later, however, the Johnson administration justified the expansion of federal aid for education by arguing it would increase the economic opportunity of individuals. Much of the Great Society agenda, indeed, revolved around the notion that job training and the acquisition of new skills and habits would allow Americans living in poverty to find jobs, even if economic structures such as the geography of jobs, racism, and lack of childcare, particularly for single women without a place in an economy built on the centrality of male breadwinners, provided significant impediments.

Further, a growing consensus of experts believed that economic inequality, especially for African Americans, was entwined with a "culture of poverty" or "cultural deprivation," and they buttressed this narrative in the late 1950s and 1960s. These arguments included works such as psychologist Frank Riessman's *The Culturally Deprived Child* (1962), and more infamously, Daniel Patrick Moynihan's report, *The Negro Family*, which asserted that matrilineal African American families, stemming from slavery, had left Black men unable to compete in the labor market.[21] In short, the War on Poverty included a clear pedagogy designed to help the poor (with a disproportionate focus on African Americans) overcome their supposed individual inadequacy.[22] This pedagogy stood in contrast to other alternatives such as A. Philip Randolph and Bayard Rustin's proposal for a Freedom Budget, which sought to make the structure of American society much more equal and working Americans' lives more broadly secure.

Indeed, the EOA, which emphasized the necessity of the state in altering the behavior of the poor, represented the centerpiece of the Johnson agenda, asserting "it is the policy of the United States to eliminate the paradox of poverty in the midst of plenty in this nation by opening, to everyone, the opportunity for education and training, the opportunity to work, and the opportunity to live in decency and dignity." The narrowing of the aspirations of the New Deal vision in this language was important, implying that those willing to work should only have the "opportunity"—not the right—to "live in decency and dignity." It is true the Johnson administration's shift toward "opportunity" was intended to be more than economic and, at least on some level, defined by the aspiration of empowering the poor. Influenced by the opportunity theory of sociologists Richard Cloward and Lloyd Ohlin, the EOA funded the Community Action Program, which created over a thousand local agencies designed to provide the impoverished the "opportunity" to better their communities while ostensibly pulling themselves out of poverty.[23] Nevertheless, the limits of opportunity theory were clear, as no one in the Johnson administration seems to have ever seriously asked whether the poor could actually find jobs or where exactly they should find them.[24]

Following similar assumptions about opportunity, political efforts to win enormous investment for public education in the Great Society culminated with the ESEA in 1965. Though President Kennedy had proposed a major federal aid package for teacher salaries and school construction, the proposal got hung up on calls from Catholics to include parochial schools and the perception that federal funding would threaten state and local control of public education. Wrapping ESEA in the cloak of the civil rights movement and the War on Poverty allowed Johnson to finally overcome these objections.[25] Further, to circumvent the thorny problem of funding private schools, Commissioner of Education Francis Keppel proposed that federal support for education be distributed as "categorical aid" (the part of the law we now know as Title I) so that schools would receive funds in proportion to the number of poor families they served. Doing so stifled opposition from proponents of parochial schools, which could also get funding under the bill's provisions.[26] Finally, by providing funds that were meant to help all poor students, virtually every congressional district in the nation would see federal funding.[27]

Drafted and sent to Congress in January 1965, the bill made its way through both houses nearly unamended. Though the vast majority of support for the bill's 263–153 margin in the House came from Democrats, 35 Republicans also supported it, and 57 Democrats, mostly from the South, joined 96 Republicans in opposition. In the Senate, the bill passed with a commanding majority of 73–18; only 4 Democrats and 14 Republicans opposed it. The bill invested in public education in several ways, the most important of which was Title I, which increased federal education funding from under 5 percent of total national spending in 1964 to almost 9 percent by 1968.[28] Titles II and III provided funding for libraries, textbooks and other instructional materials, science, music, and physical education, while Title IV included appropriations for educational research and training and Title V funded grants to strengthen state departments of education.

The history of the bill illustrates the widespread political calculus—even from the most liberal American policymakers—that broadening opportunity through education and altering the behavior of the poor represented the essential path to greater economic security. In his State of the Union address in January 1965, for example, President Johnson outlined the goals of this tremendous investment in public education in the program he called the Great Society. Though providing skills for workers would assist with a growing economy, significantly, Johnson believed federal support for education would primarily serve the function of "improving the quality of American life." Specifically linking Thomas Jefferson's call for education's role in facilitating democracy, Johnson called for an investment of $1.5 billion to "help at every stage along the road to learning."[29]

The rationale for ESEA, then, was not reducible to economic opportunity, but in the congressional trajectory that followed, the growing connection between individual economic opportunity and education was evident. In a message to

Congress a week later to accompany the education proposal, the president elaborated on the need for federal investment. After pointing to the high school dropout rate—about one in three—Johnson immediately pivoted to the impact of education on economic opportunities. "Unemployment of young people with an eighth-grade education or less is four times the national average. Jobs filled by high school graduates rose by 40 percent in the last 10 years. Jobs for those with less schooling decreased by nearly 10 percent."[30]

When Johnson got into the details of aid for K-12 schools, he connected lack of education directly to poverty, because he believed poor people lacked both skills and character. "Today, lack of formal education is likely to mean low wages, frequent unemployment, and a home in an urban or rural slum. Poverty has many roots, but the taproot is ignorance." Just as Horace Mann's survey of business owners in his fifth annual report had ignored the role the economic success of a family surely played in accessing education, Johnson ignored the possibility that an economic infrastructure in which the poor lacked access to jobs might make success in education more difficult. "Just as ignorance breeds poverty," he concluded, "poverty all too often breeds ignorance in the next generation."[31]

House hearings, held in January and February 1965, also began with the premise that the economy was strong enough that Americans in both urban and rural areas (disproportionately African American) simply needed to be made ready for jobs. The House Committee on Education and Labor Report was submitted on March 8, 1965, by Representative Adam Clayton Powell (D-NY), who had fought for years to prevent federal funding for segregated schooling. The report began by unequivocally connecting education to jobs, highlighting the unemployment rate of young adults and pointing out that high school dropout rates were inversely related to income levels. The implication was clear: more education would reduce poverty, and more funding was needed to provide more education for the poor. "The Federal concern with poverty as a national problem," Powell's report concluded, "is evidenced in recent major legislation passed by the Congress. Title I can be considered as another very potent instrument to be used in the eradication of poverty and its effects."[32]

In the Senate hearings, Commissioner Keppel also pointed to the connection between education and poverty: "The Nation's job market relentlessly discards those with a poor education. . . . If we fail to spend enough for good education today—and spend where it counts most, we will . . . spend many times more in social services tomorrow. We cannot tolerate the drag of unemployment, nor should we content ourselves by covering it with welfare funds."[33] Here was a significant departure indeed from the debates of 1945 around guaranteeing jobs. Keppel may not have argued against a safety net, but he clearly concluded there would only be jobs for those with the right education.

The arguments from dissidents in the Senate are illuminating because they spoke to the support for investing in human capital even by many prominent members of the Republican caucus. In fact, the minority report of the Labor and Public Welfare committee, while voting to report out the bill, pointed to the long history of GOP support for education—from the Morrill Act to NDEA—and asserted the bill didn't do enough to actually help poor students. Republicans Peter Dominick (CO), George Murphy (CT), and Paul Fannin (AZ) pointed out that the Title I formula, which rewarded school districts for what they already paid for education, meant the ten wealthiest counties in the United States would receive twice as much funding as the ten poorest. "In other words, the majority says that we should help the children of these poorer counties—but not too much."[34] The bipartisan nature of ESEA, passed without any debate over whether education could dramatically shape economic opportunity but over how to do it, underscored the fact that education's role in developing individual human capital was becoming a key premise of how American policymakers viewed the scope of social democracy.[35]

New Opportunities in Higher Education

After Johnson signed ESEA into law, the nation's colleges and universities, bursting with students by the mid-1960s, represented the final piece of the Great Society education agenda. GI Bill funds, NDEA, and state appropriations combined to dramatically expand access to higher education in the 1950s and 1960s. Particularly in states with strong economies, large public investment in K-12 education, and a substantial portion of prosperous union workers, the demand for expanding higher education was profound.

In the 1960s, state spending on higher education continued the increase that began in the 1940s and 1950s. In California the 1960 Donahoe Act, more popularly known as the "master plan," provided highly affordable access to college for everyone in the state, with the University of California at the top of a hierarchy based, at least in theory, on merit: the top 12.5 percent of the state's high school students were guaranteed entry at the flagship, while the next tier of students were guaranteed a spot at one of the state universities, and everyone else could go to the numerous community colleges.[36] University of California president Clark Kerr, an advocate for Schultz's version of human capital investment, enthusiastically endorsed the plan, seeking to ensure broad access to higher education in the state.[37] State spending and broader access to higher education occurred elsewhere too. In Wisconsin, for instance, state support for higher education rose from $4.32 per $1,000 of personal income in fiscal year 1961 to $11.39 by 1968.

Ohio increased spending from $2.02 to $5.02 over the same time, and spending in Michigan jumped from $5.42 to $8.76. New York and Pennsylvania, two states that had traditionally not spent as much on higher ed, increased from $1.60 to $6.65, and from $1.79 to $6.89, respectively.[38]

The increased demand for access to higher education came both from students and from community leaders and reached every corner of the country. There are numerous ways to demonstrate the demand, but looking at the history of my home institution, the University of Wisconsin-Green Bay, provides a paradigmatic case study. In Wisconsin, the University of Wisconsin had long meant the institution in Madison. The legislature also chartered the University of Wisconsin-Milwaukee (previously a state college that merged with the UW's Milwaukee extension) in 1956. State universities, many of which had begun as teachers' colleges, provided other alternatives. Following the trends in other states, university attendance in Wisconsin more than doubled from just under 50,000 in 1955 to about 110,000 less than a decade later.[39] By the end of the 1950s, the University of Wisconsin had opened regional centers run by the university's extension program. Demand for higher education in Green Bay, a small city known for the NFL Packers and paper mills, had begun to grow dramatically. By 1961, the downtown campus was the second largest of the two-year extension centers and growing faster than any other.[40]

In 1963, the Green Bay Area Chamber of Commerce and community leaders from other cities in the region established the Northeastern Wisconsin Education Committee to lobby the state's Coordinating Committee for Higher Education (CCHE) for a university. Ultimately, the CCHE concluded there should be an additional four-year university, recommending it be built by 1969. Indeed, the CCHE, constituted in 1956 to coordinate and expand higher education in Wisconsin, in 1964 sought its own "master plan" to meet citizens' demand to bring higher education within commuting distance of virtually every part of the state by the early 1970s.[41] The UW Board of Regents not only supported a campus in northeastern Wisconsin, but also an additional university south of Milwaukee, which would end up becoming present-day UW-Parkside in Kenosha. In January 1965, the CCHE published a "Comprehensive Plan for Higher Education in Wisconsin." Explicitly connecting to Johnson's War on Poverty, the report called for greater state expansion of quality higher education in order to combat poverty and unemployment: "Automation, the computers, chemicals and the new methods and machinery they have made possible have diminished the nation's employment opportunities at the untrained level, and have increased them heavily at the technical and professional levels. Recent national studies have indicated that 'pockets of poverty' actually are 'pockets of the untrained,' not only the high school dropout but the graduate who hasn't the skills the employment market requires."[42]

The plan pointed to California, whose investment of "unprecedented sums" in "universal opportunity for higher education for its people" had yielded substantial "economic and social benefits." Not only, the plan argued, did investing in higher education give individuals higher salaries (and the state more tax revenues), it gave them more spending power, and more importantly, provided "an atmosphere that attracts research-oriented business and industry, and enables these private enterprises to attract and hold employees of the highest caliber." Still, the report's recommendations heavily emphasized the point that higher education could not be simply vocational, asserting that "liberal arts work is central to collegiate education." Echoing the call of Truman's Commission on Higher Education, the Coordinating Committee also sought a higher education system that would allow workers to meet the demand for "trained and skilled specialists" but also gave them the broader skills to adapt to "changing world conditions and the growing complexity of national and international affairs." The latter required "competent judgment of economic, civic, and political problems and a broadened citizen interest in and understanding of foreign peoples." In addition to recommending the campuses that would eventually become Green Bay and Parkside, the committee also proposed a system of two-year colleges out of the remaining extension centers, which would eventually become a thirteen-campus UW college system.[43]

By 1964, there were many other Green Bays in the country, as community and student demand had pushed for much greater access to higher education. Johnson wanted to expand access to even more students, expanding federal support beyond the loans established through NDEA.[44] Stemming from the recommendations of a 1964 Presidential Task Force on Education chaired by future Health, Education, and Welfare (HEW) secretary John W. Gardner, Johnson on January 12, 1965, called on Congress to expand funding for higher education through direct means-tested support:

> Each year an estimated 100,000 young people of demonstrated ability fail to go on to college because of lack of money. . . . Only one of three young people from *low*-income families attend college compared with four out of five from *high*-income families. For many young people from poor families loans are not enough to open the way to higher education. Under this program, a special effort will be made to identify needy students of promise early in their high school careers. The scholarship will serve as a building block, to be augmented by work-study and other support, so that the needy student can chart his own course in higher studies.[45]

The growing importance of the notion of human capital was just as important for expanding access to postsecondary education in the 1960s as it was for elementary and secondary. As Becker argued in *Human Capital*, expanding affordable access to higher education was a major part of the way Americans thought about how to reduce inequality:

> Currently, many persons in the United States argue that most persons are intrinsically equally capable of benefiting from a college education: only poverty, ignorance, and prejudice prevent some from acquiring one. Generally the most important causes of differences in opportunities is differences in the availability of funds. . . . For a variety of reasons cheaper funds are more accessible to some persons than to others, and the former then have more favorable supply conditions. Some may live in areas providing liberal government and other subsidies to investment in human capital, or receive special scholarships because of luck or political contacts. Others may be born into wealthy families, have generous parents, borrow on favorable terms, or willingly forego consumption while investing.[46]

Sponsored by Representative Edith Green (D-OR) in the House and by Senator Wayne Morse (D-OR), the bill that was introduced into Congress in early 1965 (Senate hearings began in March) would put into practice several policies designed to eliminate what Becker had called "supply curve" inequality by expanding inexpensive access to higher education. In addition to funding university extension and continuing education programs, libraries, and books, HEA created a student aid system including grants (which later would be expanded and named for Senator Claiborne Pell), an expansion of the EOA's funds for work-study programs, and an expansion of federal backing for loans begun by NDEA to means-tested students.[47]

Hearings on the bill followed a path similar to that of ESEA, as there was little disagreement about whether higher education could help eliminate poverty and increase individual economic opportunity. The Senate Committee on Labor and Public Welfare, for example, held twelve days of hearings, and heard from dozens of witnesses, including university faculty and administrators and other supportive organizations like the AFL-CIO and the ACLU. The committee also received hundreds of letters of support. Arguments for the bill stressed the importance of higher education both for the good of the nation (echoing the arguments made all the way back in the nineteenth century's Morrill Act) and for individual opportunity. Put in historical context, however, it was clear legislators now connected individual opportunity much more closely to education. Vermont senator Winston Prouty (R)—who had been a key voice in ushering ESEA through the same committee—summed up this line of thinking: "A new program to strengthen our colleges and universities to expand individual opportunities for higher education should be given high priority on the list of necessary legislation. The primary center of American life, no longer either agrarian or industrial, is shifting to learning. . . . Today, higher education is becoming essential in helping individuals and societies realize even their most fundamental aspirations."[48]

Without much controversy, the bill passed with huge bipartisan majorities in the Senate (79–3) and the House (368–22), highlighting the consensus around the significance of expanding education for the purpose of broadening individual economic opportunity, a key foundation for the construction of the education myth. There were some important limits to the promise of higher education in HEA, however. While the intent of ESEA was to give all children access to a quality education through twelfth grade, HEA was set up in a way that acceded to rationing access to higher education. The contrast with the GI Bill's promise is striking. Though in practice, many eligible African Americans and women were not able to access the GI Bill's full benefits, funds were available, at least in theory, to all veterans. Further, the funds would cover tuition and expenses, thus making college a virtually expenseless endeavor beyond the opportunity cost of not working. The provisions of the HEA, however, would provide colleges and universities a limited number of grants ($70 million worth in total, distributed based on need) and students who did not get scholarships would need loans. Though the creation of Pell grants in the 1972 Higher Education Amendments enhanced access for more students (and the elimination of admission discrimination against women did so along gender lines), by making some students pay back loans rather than simply funding all tuition as the GI Bill had, the HEA contributed to the notion that education was an investment in one's own human capital and not a right.

The Freedom Budget: Path Not Taken

By the end of 1966, transformative legislation tapered off as the American escalation of Vietnam began to torpedo Johnson's presidency. By then, however, the Great Society had firmly implanted the notion that education would play a major, perhaps the primary, role in providing economic opportunity moving forward. Before moving on, however, it is useful to examine a path not taken. After the monumental legislative achievements of 1964–65, civil rights and labor activists A. Philip Randolph and Bayard Rustin revisited the idea of guaranteeing the right to a sustainable livelihood through jobs. Following the clear limits of the War on Poverty, their program for guaranteeing economic security centered on full employment seemed particularly necessary. Randolph and Rustin, who had, along with Martin Luther King Jr. and other civil rights activists, been arguing for years that mere formal equality under the law could not ensure economic security for African Americans, advanced a bold vision for a "Freedom Budget" that would have done what the Employment Act of 1946 failed to do.

Asa Philip Randolph was one of the most important labor leaders in US history. As president of the all-Black Brotherhood of Sleeping Car Porters, Randolph led the dramatic growth of that union in the 1930s. A fierce organizer for both civil rights and labor rights, Randolph formed the Negro American Labor Council in 1959 to fight the discrimination African Americans faced within the labor movement.[49] Bayard Rustin was a socialist, peace activist, and labor activist who played an instrumental role in helping King and in the fight against segregation in the South (indeed, it was Rustin who seems to have convinced King of the tactical importance of nonviolent resistance).[50] Randolph, who first proposed a March on Washington in 1941, conceived of the more famous march twenty-two years later, while Rustin was the architect of the immense undertaking.

By 1963, Randolph was making the prescient argument that just as African Americans had begun to get access to decent jobs in manufacturing, automation was threating to eliminate the entry level positions that would allow Blacks to gain economic security. Though King's speech at the March on Washington is typically what Americans remember about August 28, 1963, Randolph's speech more fully captured the challenges facing African Americans. While supporting the demand of desegregation, the core of Randolph's speech centered on economic security: "It falls to [African Americans]," he argued, "to demand new forms of social planning, to create full employment, and to put automation at the service of human needs, not at the service of profits—for we are the worst victims of unemployment."[51]

In 1965, the AFL-CIO honored the union leader's career by creating the A. Philip Randolph Institute, which Rustin headed. Rustin got to work putting Randolph's call for guaranteeing employment into action. In a powerful essay in *Commentary* in February 1965, Rustin had reflected on the next phase of the civil rights movement following the Civil Rights Act and Johnson's electoral landslide the previous November. Though the economy was booming in the mid-1960s, Rustin pointed out that "more Negroes are unemployed today than in 1954, and the unemployment gap between the races is wider. . . . A higher percentage of Negro workers is now concentrated in jobs vulnerable to automation than was the case ten years ago." Though Rustin might have added that Blacks in urban areas faced such inequities because employers had begun to move jobs either to suburbs (to pay lower property taxes) or, seeking cheaper labor, to areas in which unions were weaker, he pointed to a serious deficiency with the War on Poverty policies.[52] They did very little to ensure there were jobs for African Americans, no matter how much money the OEO poured into job training or ESEA and HEA into education.

Rustin pointed out that while the Civil Rights Act had removed legal barriers to good jobs, in contrast to other times in American history when other ethnic groups had been able to build economic security, "we are moving into an era in which the natural functioning of the market does not by itself ensure every man with will and ambition a place in the production process." Presciently, Rustin argued that "this means that an individual will no longer be able to start at the bottom and work his way up; he will have to start in the middle or on top, and hold on tight. It will not even be enough to have certain specific skills, for many skilled jobs are also vulnerable to automation. A broad educational background, permitting vocational adaptability and flexibility, seems more imperative than ever." But simply providing education and job training would not be enough. Rustin concluded that the civil rights movement must fight for a "great expansion of the public sector of the economy. . . . as it looks at the number of jobs being generated by the private economy."[53]

That is exactly what Rustin, working with Randolph, called for with the Freedom Budget. Originally discussed in a White House conference on civil rights chaired by Randolph in June 1966, the full proposal came out in October. Resurrecting FDR's social democratic promise during World War II, the Freedom Budget proposed massive spending to provide all Americans access to a job and a living wage and good education, housing, and healthcare at the cost of $185 billion over ten years.[54] In Rustin's definition of true freedom in the United States, "for the first time, everyone in America who is fit and able to work will have a job. For the first time, everyone who can't work, or shouldn't be working, will have an income adequate to live in comfort and dignity. And that is freedom. For freedom from want is the basic freedom from which all others flow."[55]

Indeed, the Freedom Budget represents an important alternative to the American human capital trajectory since it rejected the notion that job training and education would be enough to overcome the impediments many Americans faced in attaining economic security. As Rustin argued for the proposal in December 1966, the move to integrate and enhance public education had failed to overcome the structural inequalities evidenced by recent urban uprisings: "One sees that 12 years after the Supreme Court decision of 1954, Negro people are almost twice as crippled with unemployment as whites, that Negro teenagers have an unemployment rate three times that of whites . . . that there are now more Negro youngsters in segregated schools than there were in 1954, and that the ghettos have remained the same size but with more people, more rats, more roaches, and therefore more despair."[56]

The Freedom Budget received support from the social democratic wing of the Democratic Party. Michael Harrington and the League for Industrial Democracy promoted it. So did the Industrial Union Department of the AFL-CIO (effectively run by Walther Reuther, who through the UAW had been a prominent supporter of the March on Washington), and United Farm Workers leader Cesar Chavez. King, who began working on the Poor People's Campaign in 1967, continued to support the Freedom Budget into 1968. The bill met predictable responses from conservatives, however, and despite support from some quarters of the left, it was not enough to overcome the opposition, as the supporters failed to galvanize the kind of mass movement that would have been necessary to force Congress to act on it. Further, the plan's accommodation with military spending as the Vietnam War had become increasingly unpopular limited its allies on the left. The Freedom Budget was never taken up by the Johnson administration or in Congress.[57]

Kerner Commission: The Limits of the Great Society

The failures of the Great Society to eradicate poverty were glaringly evident following a series of urban insurrections in American cities in the mid-1960s. Indeed, the situation had become so severe—particularly after the brutal police suppression of Black communities led to urban insurrections in Detroit and Newark in 1967—that President Johnson chartered a national commission, led by Illinois governor Otto Kerner (D), to study the problem.[58]

The commission, reporting its findings only a month before the murder of King in 1968, concluded that the United States was quickly "moving toward two societies, one black, one white—separate and unequal."[59] Johnson disavowed the commission's findings, which went well beyond his assumptions about what was responsible for poverty. The findings of the Kerner Commission spoke not just to the impoverishing conditions in American cities, but to the failure of national policy—even after several years of federal investment in compensatory education—to create the conditions for fulfilling lives for the next generation of African Americans. Indeed, the commission noted that the "typical rioter was a teenager or young adult . . . somewhat better educated than his nonrioting Negro neighbor, and was usually underemployed or employed in a menial job." In fact, one could conclude from the commission report, as Bayard Rustin did, that the Great Society's efforts to raise expectations were in large part responsible for the simmering resentment in American cities when the programs proved insufficient.[60] The report argued, in fact, that the rioters sought "fuller participation in the social order and the material benefits enjoyed by the majority of American citizens. Rather than rejecting the American system, they were anxious to obtain a place for themselves in it."[61]

The commission pointed to the grievances of African Americans, who, two years into the Great Society, still sought stable employment and good housing. Instead of pushing to double down on repressive police tactics, however, the report argued that finally making good on the American promise of social democracy represented the only way to stanch the gross inequalities that had led to the violence. While the report concluded with a number of options for police reforms—more Black police officers, new training and other programs to develop community support for police, for instance—the most significant recommendations hinged on facilitating economic democracy.

The report clearly stated that "pervasive unemployment and underemployment are the most persistent and serious grievances in minority areas. They are inextricably linked to the problem of civil disorder." Even so, the commission still exhibited the human capital assumptions that were crowding out other alternatives in American politics. Though it did call for the direct creation of jobs (as many as two million over the three years to come), the Kerner Commission's recommendations for economic security largely revolved around the idea that young (male) African Americans were ill-equipped for employment and needed to be made ready for the labor market. Comparing Blacks to earlier waves of immigrants to the United States, the report asserted that the economy had changed to one in which it was more difficult to acquire good jobs in unskilled positions. "When the European immigrants arrived, they gained an economic foothold by providing the unskilled labor needed by industry. Unlike the immigrant, the Negro migrant found little opportunity in the city. The economy, by then matured, had little use for the unskilled labor he had to offer."[62]

While the economy was certainly more complex than in the early twentieth century, the lack of historical context is glaring. The masses of "unskilled" immigrant workers who came to the United States in the early twentieth century hardly gained a "foothold" in the American economy. The examples of immigrant workers toiling in dangerous, degrading, and deadly working conditions, with virtually limitless working hours and low wages that were cut whenever there was an economic downturn has been well documented by both historians and observers at the time.[63] Indeed, it was the support for workers to unionize, which in turn allowed them the power to bargain for healthcare and retirement, and other economic supports like social security and subsidies for housing through the FHA and GI Bill that truly gave immigrant workers and their progeny their permanent "foothold" in American society.

The bigger problem, then, in the 1960s, was that the partial social democracy as it had been built by the United States had disproportionately excluded

African Americans. The report, however, proceeded from the premise that education and job training would ultimately allow Blacks to achieve economic prosperity in the US: "The 500,000 'hard-core' unemployed in the central cities who lack a basic education and are unable to hold a steady job arc made up in large part of Negro males between the ages of 18 and 25. In the riot cities which we surveyed, Negroes were three times as likely as whites to hold unskilled jobs, which are often part time, seasonal, low paying and 'dead end.'" The commission recommended, in addition to eliminating outright discrimination, the federal government should "provide on-the-job training by both public and private employers with reimbursement to private employers for the extra costs of training the hard-core unemployed, by contract or by tax credits."[64]

Education was also crucial. The Kerner report did not reduce education to job training, pointing out that "education in a democratic society must equip children to develop their potential and to participate fully in American life." Nevertheless, unequal education, according to the commission, played a major role in the lack of economic security for African Americans: "In the critical skills—verbal and reading ability—Negro students are falling further behind whites with each year of school completed. The high unemployment and underemployment rate for Negro youth is evidence, in part, of the growing educational crisis." To improve education in the urban areas, the report called for the investment of "substantial federal aid to schools" to assist with desegregation (including a call, rightly, for efforts among suburban school systems to cooperate in this effort) and doubling down on the Great Society investment in compensatory spending.[65]

In sum, the Kerner Commission report, which addressed some of the structural limitations of the labor market, still focused too much on education and job training, downplaying the extent of the investment in economic democracy necessary to fully end racial inequality in America. As Rustin assessed it, the plan was too slow and too limited, and "the Report failed to declare unequivocally that the government must be the employer of first and last resort for the hard-core poor."[66] Even with its much more limited version of Randolph and Rustin's Freedom Budget, however, the Kerner Commission recommendations were largely a nonstarter. As it had for the Freedom Budget, the growing conflict over Vietnam sucked up oxygen that could have gone into a fuller discussion about the course of American social democracy. Further, characterizing jobs policy as an African American problem during the 1960s (in contrast with, say, the debate on full employment in 1945–46), racialized interventions like a jobs guarantee that would have actually helped all poor Americans.[67] Considering the association of these efforts with the uprisings in American cities, which many whites connected to the breakdown of "law and order," one can understand the difficulties in building political momentum by the end of the Johnson administration.[68] In fact, Johnson himself by that point had little appetite for a program on the scale of the Freedom Budget or even the more limited actions suggested by the Kerner Commission, arguing that do so meant "rewarding riots."[69]

In spite of both the tactical failures of Randolph and Rustin and their allies as well as the poor timing of the plan, the failure for the Freedom Budget, or even the recommendations of Kerner to be seriously considered highlights the narrowing of American social democracy and the rising education myth. But, in the 1970s, there would be one last chance for a big, bold alternative.

4

NEW POLITICS

Democrats and Opportunity
in a Postindustrial Society

As the United States celebrated its bicentennial in 1976, political economic tur-
bulence suggested the third hundred years in American history would be very
different than the second hundred. Stuck in the doldrums of an economy marked
by both sluggish growth and inflation, American industries faced a profit crunch,
and employers' efforts to increase profits by curtailing workers' rights and send-
ing capital elsewhere was undermining the family-based economic security
many blue-collar workers had grown to expect just at the time that advances in
civil rights and feminism meant women and people of color were getting greater
access to those jobs. In both major parties, there were existential debates about
the nation's political future. On the Republican side, conservative Ronald Reagan, pushing tax cuts, fiscal responsibility, and less government as the response
to the crisis, sought to challenge the moderate wing of the party. More and more
Democrats, increasingly adhering to professional-class notions of meritocracy,
responded ambivalently to the nation's economic problems. While some Democrats sought new advances in social democracy, including resurrecting the right
to a job, other, recently elected, Democrats represented a growing professional-
class constituency, and instead sought to advance public education and limit big
social interventions, even at a time of massive economic crisis.

It is fitting that sociologist Daniel Bell's widely influential book *The Coming of
Post-Industrial Society* was published in a new edition that presidential election
year. Based on a series of essays written over the course of the 1960s and 70s (the
earliest was written in 1962), Bell first brought them together in book form in

76

1973. In the foreword to the 1976 edition, Bell pointed out that he was forecasting a future, "an *as if* based on emergent features," in which American society would be largely organized around service work, information, and the production of knowledge. What was "emergent" in the 1970s, Bell argued, were "the foundations of a vastly different kind of social structure than we have previously known." The sociologist described a society in which a "knowledge class" was growing more powerful. Charting the shift beyond a society whose economy and ethics were driven by manufacturing, Bell pointed out that 65 percent of workers in the United States toiled in the service sector and 70 percent were projected to do so by 1980. As opposed to the service sectors of other societies in history (highly unequal societies with large numbers of poorly paid domestic workers, for instance), these services in the postindustrial society were increasingly built around knowledge construction (such as education) and other human services like healthcare. Importantly, this also meant an increased role for women workers, who disproportionately did service-sector work, and of course, constituted the majority of workers in the biggest single knowledge sector occupation in the United States: teachers.[1]

Finally, Bell, putting his finger on the transition within the Democratic Party, poignantly asserted that this society would be one built around, in theory, the principle of meritocracy: "A post-industrial society, being primarily a technical society, awards place less on the basis of inheritance of property (though these can command wealth or cultural advantage) than on education and skill."[2] Certainly one can see here why so many of the architects of the Great Society—especially Johnson, who clearly believed in the alchemical powers of education—had valued education's ability to help the poor overcome their supposed deficiencies. Following this premise, a meritocratic society built on equal access to education and reward for skill-building would ensure every American was responsible for their own success or failure in acquiring a good job.

The Coming of Post-Industrial Society also made clear another problem that seems especially obvious today. This new order brought with it a growing political resistance to those left out of the knowledge economy: "Any new emerging system creates hostility among those who feel threatened by it," Bell concluded. "The chief problem of the emerging post-industrial society is the conflict generated by a meritocracy principle which is central to the allocation of position in the knowledge society. Thus, the tension between populism and elitism, which is already apparent, becomes a political issue in the communities."[3] Some Republicans understood this: Kevin Phillips, writing in the *New Republican Majority* in 1969 had already highlighted how Republican populists were counterposing the GOP to a new establishment professional class emergent in the 1950s and 1960s.[4]

This chapter documents the political shifts of the 1970s, a decade that was perhaps more crucial than any other in the rise of the education myth. At the same time that blue-collar workers faced downward pressure on their liveli-hoods and more working people, especially women, joined the already low-wage service sector, increased access to higher education continued to produce more and more professional-class workers, who did comparatively better than those without college degrees. As this demographic became central in the party's New Politics in the 1970s, Democrats' commitment to broad political economic inter-ventions, even in a time of dire economic crisis, wavered.

Social democrats did not simply capitulate, however. Indeed, senator and presidential candidate Hubert Humphrey, California representative Augustus Hawkins, activist Coretta Scott King, and others fought hard to reinvigorate the social democratic premise of the New Deal during the economic crises of the 1970s. By the end of the decade, however, the once robust promise of economic security had been critically diminished. In particular, the failure in Congress in 1978 of both labor law reform and, for the last time, a meaningful jobs guarantee represented crucial, resounding defeats.

President Jimmy Carter, a technocrat more responsive to the nation's grow-ing professional class, only ambivalently supported these reforms. Perhaps his most important achievement, in fact, was to elevate education to its own cabinet-level department in the federal bureaucracy. By itself, establishing a stand-alone Department of Education could have augured well for an expansion of American social democracy—had it been one important piece of advancing a vision of enabling freedoms that included a jobs guarantee, healthcare, and labor reform. In contrast to the promise of the Great Society, however, which envisioned some basic, though insufficient, level of security combined with additional educational opportunity, by the end of the 1970s, education was increasingly left alone to facilitate a mere chance at economic security. Indeed, by the decade's conclusion, the myth that human capital was singularly responsible for economic opportu-nity had emerged at the center of American politics.

New Politics and the Rise of the Professional Class

The Democratic primary of 1972 represented a watershed for the party. Though the GOP had not achieved unified control of government since Roosevelt and the New Deal order shifted the trajectory of American politics in the 1930s, the Democratic Party coalition—middle-class liberals and working-class people—had been tenuous since the fractures that became evident in the election of 1968. With the Democratic Party facing both the brunt of the New Left's anger over the Vietnam War and the anger of racial minorities against a color-blind liberalism that seemed incapable of ending institutional racism in the United States, Richard Nixon emerged to show how the GOP (mobilizing the nascent right-wing populism Phillips referenced in the *Emerging Republican Majority*) could feed off the resentment of the "great silent majority."[5] In response to the calls of young people, antiwar activists, feminists, and civil rights activists, the Democratic Party underwent a series of reforms in the years between the disastrous 1968 election and the election of 1972 to make the party more inclusive.

Some have argued that in the 1970s Democrats shifted toward the politics of radical "special interests," losing white working- and middle-class voters who believed the GOP could better represent the "center."[6] It is true that the reforms leading up to the 1972 campaign empowered what was called the New Politics, and these reforms disempowered the traditional brokers, particularly labor leaders, who had been important in selecting Democratic nominees since World War II. The most important interest directing the shift in the party, however, was the growing class of white-collar professionals thriving in what Bell argued was becoming a postindustrial society. With the American economy increasingly relying on human services and technical knowledge, the locus of power in the Democratic Party was shifting toward a growing professional class. There are a number of different metrics we could use to highlight this shift, but perhaps the simplest is to examine the number of Americans with a postsecondary education. In 1940, about 7.5 million Americans aged twenty-five and above had attended at least one year of college (about 10 percent of the total population), and about 3.4 million were graduates. By 1965, those numbers had increased to 18.8 million (18 percent of the total population) and 9.7 million, respectively. By 1972, the respective numbers were 25.5 million (23 percent) and 13.4 million. And by 1976, 33 million Americans over the age of twenty-five had attended college (28 percent) and about 17.5 million had graduated.[7] Further, in just the first six years of the 1970s, the number of white-collar workers increased by 3 percent each year, while blue-collar workers decreased by about the same percentage.[8] Amendments to the HEA, first in 1972, which expanded grants to low-income students and barred institutions of higher education from discriminating against women, and in 1978, which expanded access to grants and federally subsidized loans, further increased access to college.[9]

It wasn't only that more Americans were going to college. By the early 1970s, a greater percentage of college students were thinking about postsecondary education as a specific avenue toward a profession, and thus identifying as a "professional." In 1973, for instance, *New York Times* reporter Iver Peterson recounted a trend called the "new vocationalism." A "survey of campus correspondents," he reported, showed "college students around the country are changing their tastes in studies away from many of the abstract and theoretical courses that were popular during the 1960's and toward studies that teach 'hard knowledge' or that lead to professional training and a comfortable career." Academic advisers pointed out that programs in "premed, prelaw, business, nursing, agriculture and the newly developing health-sciences and handicapped-training courses" were "swelling." As Peterson pointed out, more students were consciously seeking out a professional path, as the "security" it offered "was a greater consideration today than it was five years ago." The piece also suggested that as budgets got stretched in state legislatures during economic downturn, many lawmakers wanted students to "be devoted to studies that turn out men and women able to do the jobs that most need to be done."[10]

It was in this context that Patrick Lucey, Democratic candidate for governor in Wisconsin in 1970, ran on the prospect of merging the UW campuses and the state college system. Appropriations on a per-student basis for the state university system had been much lower than for the four UW schools (Madison, Milwaukee, and the recently created Green Bay and Parkside), and both Lucey and other stakeholders argued that creating one streamlined system would be the best way to mitigate the pressure on the budgets of both systems in the 1970s. Recognizing the growing importance of higher education in the state, Lucey, as governor-elect, held a series of one-day hearings in December 1970 on important priorities for his agenda. "Creating a Responsive Higher Education System" was the first. And the way the Lucey administration described the hearings is illuminating: the new governor believed there was a "need to maintain, develop, and expand a higher educational system that prepares Wisconsin people for professional careers and allows for individual advancement," including "the suitability of University and State University graduates for the Wisconsin and national job markets."[11]

The state was facing both a major budget shortfall due to the 1970 recession and a continued demand to expand the university system, and Lucey sought to merge the state universities and the UW campuses. The governor proposed a bill to merge them in March, and on October 6, 1971, the state legislature approved it. Lucey signed it into law a week later. The new system included thirteen campuses and fourteen freshman-sophomore "centers," and it was now the third largest in the nation. In large part the merger was about economizing (projecting to save $4 million in administrative costs), but Lucey also sought a common educational vision for the state. Clearly, the consolidation of the system occurred in the context of a demand from business for a more skilled workforce, though the Lucey administration did not view that as the only reason for the university system.[12] The system's new mission, which still guides the UW today, emphasized first and foremost, "the development of human resources" in a broad effort, with employment at its center, to develop citizens capable of operating in a complicated world:

> The mission of the University of Wisconsin System is to develop human resources, to discover and disseminate knowledge, to extend knowledge and its application beyond the boundaries of its campuses, and to serve and stimulate society by developing in students heightened intellectual, cultural, and humane sensitivities, scientific, professional and techno-logical expertise, and a sense of purpose. Inherent in this broad mission are methods of instruction, research, extended training, and public service designed to educate people and improve the human condition. Basic to every purpose of the UW System is the search for truth.[13]

The growing number of college-educated professionals, as historian Lily Geismer convincingly argues in her study of suburban Boston, believed that American society was a meritocracy in which they had succeeded. Since they had been able to access a professional career and individual success through the education system, so should everyone else. These professionals enthusiastically backed McGovern in 1972, and though their economic success in the job market had stemmed from federal support for roads, housing, and military-industrial development, they had no problem with efforts to shift away from the security-oriented politics of the New Deal order and toward market reform. Indeed, Geismer examines a program in Massachusetts called the Metropolitan Council for Educational Opportunity (METCO), which in the late 1960s and early 1970s bused a select number of African American children to mostly white suburban schools. The premise of the program hinged on the notion that better education was the key to alleviating the inequality that existed between whites and Blacks. Far from equalizing education on a systemic level, the gains of the limited number of children who could access METCO helped to give suburban professional-class liberals "a means to distinguish themselves as more open-minded than whites in the south or South Boston [and] made them even less willing to consider more comprehensive solutions to the interrelated issues of residential segregation and educational inequity."[14]

Though progress on equalizing the quality of public education moved slowly but steadily from the Supreme Court's modest push for "all deliberate speed" in *Brown v. Board of Education II* (1955) through the late 1960s, a series of conservative Supreme Court decisions in the 1970s sharply delimited the notion that the US education system was a real meritocracy or that it was likely to become more meritocratic. With four Supreme Court appointments during his five years as president, Nixon shifted the court in a much more conservative direction. In 1973, for instance, the court's decision in *San Antonio Independent School District v. Rodriguez* determined states did not have any obligation to ensure poor school districts were funded at the same level as wealthy districts. The next year, in *Milliken v. Bradley*, the court struck down a metropolitan remedy to segregation in Detroit, arguing suburban school districts could not be forced to participate in a desegregation plan unless there was both an "interdistrict violation and interdistrict effect." Since there was no evidence suburban school districts had committed discriminatory actions, the court argued, Detroit and other cities were therefore left on their own to redistribute resources within the district while excluding the much-better-resourced suburbs.[15]

Democrats gained a large congressional majority in 1974 as a result of Watergate and Nixon's resignation, but some of the most important New Politics Democrats ushered in by that midterm election were committed to the meritocratic promise of education and particularly the optimism that new technology would bring new jobs.[16] Well-educated professionals themselves, many of the Democrats elected that year shared the same ideology of the nation's growing number of knowledge workers. For instance, it was 1974 when McGovern's former national campaign director Gary Hart won a Senate seat in Colorado from an incumbent Republican.

Sociologists Barbara and John Ehrenreich characterized the problem of this growing professional class in critical terms. As they argued in a now famous article in *Radical America* in 1977, the educated professionals who represented the vanguard of the postindustrial society—what they called the Professional-Managerial Class (PMC)—did not have the same interests as the blue-collar manufacturing workers (and low-paid service sectors) whose livelihoods were under duress in the 1970s. The Ehrenreichs pointed out that as early as the beginning of the twentieth century, the class structure in the United States and other capitalist countries was not being divided, as Marx and Engels predicted in the *Communist Manifesto*, into a small number of capitalists and a large immiserated working class, but into an increasingly complex society in which "new, educated and salaried middle-class strata had appeared and were growing rapidly."[17]

The Ehrenreichs argued that, rather than an aberration to be worked around, middle-class "technical workers, managerial workers, 'culture' producers, etc.— must be understood as comprising a distinct class in monopoly capitalist society." The labor of these workers was built on knowledge (as Bell had argued), they were paid salaries instead of hourly wages, and most importantly, they were marked by the contradiction that while they did not "own the means of production, [their] major function in the social division of labor may be described broadly as the reproduction of capitalist culture and capitalist class relations." Middle-class professionals thus shared a common economic interest as well as a "coherent social and culture existence" including "a common lifestyle, educational background, kinship networks, consumption patterns, work habits, beliefs." This group increasingly served to mediate the class conflict that existed in American society: they were the social workers, psychologists, and teachers who served as "a force for regulation and management of civil society." The Ehrenreichs concluded, in fact, that that the relationship between the PMC and working-class people was "objectively antagonistic."[18] Thus while the PMC might resent the greed of the capitalist class, they also often acted with "elitism toward the working class."[19] As Barbara and John Ehrenreich readily acknowledged, there were members of the PMC who consciously sought not to serve the interests of capital and to ally with workers. Broadly speaking, however, the growing number of professional-class Americans did appear to be pushing for interests different than many working people, connecting education specifically to a professional career and building their lives around the dubious principle that individual effort in the education system led to just economic and social rewards.

Noncollege-educated workers were clearly on a downward trajectory in the 1970s. Over the course of the decade, two million American manufacturing jobs were lost, and entire industries—like textiles and steel—shrank as national policymakers in both parties failed either to protect them from international competition or use microeconomic planning to reinvigorate them.[20] As the historian Lane Windham has shown, workers tried hard to form new unions in blue-collar and nonprofessional service work but saw renewed resistance from employers at every turn, and were not as successful in their efforts to organize as workers in previous decades had been.[21] The struggle in the Democratic Party in the 1970s, then, was about more than radical rights-based special interests versus labor power brokers. Instead, the competition was a fundamental struggle about whether the party and its leaders were going to advocate for policies that would prioritize technological development and the supposed meritocracy of education or, as Bell had argued for in his conclusion of *The Coming of Post-Industrial Society*, for a "just meritocracy" that would also include strong union rights, sustainable blue-collar livelihoods, the right to a job for every person who wanted one, and other social guarantees.

From Job Training to Jobs Guarantee

In 1968, Richard Nixon ran as a conservative alternative to liberal Nelson Rockefeller, successfully wresting away the Republican nomination by mobilizing the growing populist wing of the party. Though chaos in the Democratic Party over the Vietnam War redounded to Nixon's benefit that year, his win also clearly represented a rightward shift in American politics. The Nixon administration helped advance a conservative version of the education myth by pushing for job training for workers, though without extending any of the already limited advances in economic security Democrats had sought in the Great Society.

Here the Nixon administration built on liberal support for direct federal investment in adult job-training programs that began in the 1960s. As early as the late 1950s many American politicians and labor leaders had grown to fear the impact of automation on jobs. In 1960, for instance, the US Senate established a permanent subcommittee—the Subcommittee on Employment and Manpower—to study the issue and recommend possibilities. Two years later, Kennedy signed into law the Manpower and Training Development Act (MDTA), which provided federal funds to retrain workers who lost jobs due to automation.[22]

Political interest in the problem of automation continued well into the 1960s. A. Philip Randolph, for example, worried about the impact of automation on African Americans, who often worked on the lowest rungs of the employment ladder, referencing the problem in his speech at the March on Washington in 1963. A little less than a year later, Congress established the National Commission on Technology, Automation, and Economic Progress. Chaired by Howard Bowen, economist and president of the University of Iowa, the commission also included Daniel Bell, UAW president Walter Reuther, and president of the National Urban League Whitney Young. The commission recommendations, reported to President Johnson in 1965 (and published in 1966), connected the relationship between technology, productivity, and the "substantial and persistent unemployment during the period 1954–65." The commission was careful to point out that the overall impact of technology was positive, but it also unequivocally stated that automation reduced jobs. "It is the continuous obligation of economic policy," the commission argued, "to match increases in productive potential with increases in purchasing power and demand."[23]

How did the commission recommend doing so? Unsurprisingly, a commission in which social democrat Reuther played a major part called for the federal government to provide employment as a "last resort" in addition to a "family income" floor. But the report also helped advance a narrative of the importance of job training, arguing that lack of education, not technology, provided the biggest threat to the future: "Unemployment tends to be concentrated among workers with little education, not primarily because technological developments are changing the nature of jobs, but because the uneducated are at the 'back of the line' in the competition for jobs." In addition to calling for direct job creation, then, the report also called for robust investment in compensatory education (then underway, of course, as ESEA had just been introduced by the administration), increased access to higher education, and "lifetime opportunities for education, training, and retraining, and special attention to handicaps of adults with deficient basic education."[24]

The Great Society's emphasis on job training and education were instituted with the notion that they could solve the deficiencies of the poor to help them overcome poverty, and the reality was a much thinner investment in economic security than Reuther, Young, and others called for in the commission. So while the Johnson administration pushed for policies around job training for the poor, just as had been the case with its investment in public education, the failure to ensure there were actually jobs available gave credence to the idea that since the federal government provided funding for education and job training, the poor only had themselves to blame if they could not find work.

As a conservative, Nixon had little appetite for major expansions of government programs, but he was more than willing to support job training. As was the case for his predecessor, focusing on the skills of workers was a palatable way to show evidence his administration sought to increase possible avenues toward economic security without altering the nation's social structure. Under the influence of libertarian economist Milton Friedman (a contemporary of Theodore Schultz and Gary Becker), Nixon's secretary of labor (another Chicago school economist named George Schultz) pushed to lower the minimum wage for younger workers and for a law that would automatically increase federal funding for job training when national unemployment moved above a certain threshold. The administration's Philadelphia Plan also sought to broaden access to skilled work by forcing all-white building trades unions to hire a certain number of minorities in order to be eligible for federal contracts. Nixon did not want to create jobs outright, however: in 1970, he vetoed a bill that would have created forty thousand public service-sector jobs.[25]

A recession in 1969–70 gave Democrats, like New Jersey representative Dominick Daniels, space to push direct job creation back onto the political agenda. By December 1970, unemployment had reached 6.1 percent and persisted around that level through 1971.[26] Under pressure from Democrats, Nixon reluctantly signed into law an emergency jobs bill in 1971. Two years later, Nixon and Congress compromised on another bill that reorganized the MDTA and OEO and decentralized job-training responsibilities from the federal government to local governments, called "prime sponsors." In exchange, the Comprehensive Employment and Training Act (CETA) of 1973 also fulfilled Democrats' growing calls for public service jobs.[27]

CETA was far from the jobs guarantee Rustin, Randolph, Reuther, and others argued for in the late 1960s. But as unemployment remained high—it increased from 5.1 percent in January 1974 to 7.2 percent by the end of the year—Congress was able to amend the law, now titled the Emergency Jobs Act of 1974, to include a reservoir of public service jobs and put direct job creation back in the political mainstream.[28] Introduced by Representative Daniels in October, the bill was passed after the election of 1974, the post-Watergate election that had given Democrats a huge congressional majority. Signed into law on New Year's Eve by Republican president Gerald Ford, the Emergency Jobs Act ultimately provided $2.5 billion for the direct creation of public employment.

More important, the bill rekindled an argument for the central role of a jobs guarantee and, thus, a dramatic expansion of American social democracy. Eli Ginzberg, chair of the National Committee for Manpower Policy, connected the bill to past efforts to ensure full employment in his testimony to Congress that October. The economist argued, "We have never seriously implemented the Employment Act of 1946. . . . I see the growing stress on public service employment as one of the critical areas by which Congress over a period of years can come closer to delivering on its 1946 promise." Ginzberg criticized the direction of American politics in the 1960s, asserting that focusing on training "avoided the job issue" of ensuring everyone who wanted to work could do so.[29] Similarly, the AFL-CIO's representative at the hearings, Research Director Nathaniel Goldfinger, pointed to the necessity of public service jobs. Goldfinger, in fact, acknowledged that investment in job training "while important and necessary . . . must be followed by a job if it is to have any value. It compounds the problem to give training and hope to the disadvantaged and then throw them back into the morass from which they came."[30]

Although the Emergency Jobs Act put direct job creation squarely back on the map, its impact on employment was minimal. By not establishing employment as a right for everyone, it allowed many "prime sponsors" to use federal funding to defray the costs of jobs they would have filled anyway instead of bringing new workers into the labor market.[31] Compared to the Full Employment Act promise of 1945, the Emergency Jobs Act was quite limited. Still, recommitting to the principle that the government could create a reservoir of public service jobs helped to rekindle a bigger conversation about the future of social democracy in the United States.

No Guarantees

In 1976, the Democratic field for president was wide open. Social democratic Senator Hubert Humphrey (MN) was an early favorite but withdrew because of health concerns. With a slew of liberal candidates like Representative Morris Udall (Arizona), labor's first choice Henry "Scoop" Jackson (Washington), and white supremacist George Wallace (Alabama), Georgia governor Jimmy Carter faced a crowded field. Carter ran as a Washington outsider who would restore honesty and dignity to the federal government. Indeed, the peanut farmer won the primary in part because of a national mood opposing Washington insiders (stemming from Watergate), and the fact that not enough voters coalesced around any other competitor in a crowded field.

Many unions did not see Carter as a candidate capable of reinvigorating the labor movement or social democracy in the United States. Once the primary was over, however, labor joined forces behind Carter.[32] Though the AFL-CIO did not endorse McGovern in 1972, they came back around to supporting the Democratic candidate in 1976. The federation's public endorsements, however, are telling in their lukewarm embrace of Carter himself. A late August statement from the AFL-CIO's general board focused on the poor record of Gerald Ford and centered their endorsement around the Democratic Party platform. That platform sought a recommitment to social democratic programs, including economic planning and eliminating unemployment, extending collective bargaining rights to public employees, and repealing section 14(b) of the Taft-Hartley Act, which allowed states like Carter's Georgia to pass its antiunion "right-to-work" policy. Although the AFL-CIO praised Carter's commitment to racial justice, much of the argument for supporting him came down to his character and leadership abilities, not a record of social democratic vision or policy achievement.[33]

The National Education Association (NEA) and its members, however, embraced Carter and played a major role in helping him win both the nomination and a closely contested general election against Ford. For the vast majority of its existence the NEA had been primarily devoted to advancing the cause of education and lobbying for better salaries for teachers and other school personnel (including administrators). Only in the late 1960s did the NEA fully embrace the notion of its locals collectively bargaining. It did not expel administrators from its ranks until the early 1970s, and it never affiliated with the AFL-CIO.[34] In fact, after the NEA established a Political Action Committee in 1972, Carter was the first presidential candidate the union ever endorsed. Having sought to elevate education in the federal bureaucracy since before the Civil War, the NEA and its members saw in Carter a candidate finally willing to place education on par with other cabinet-level priorities. The NEA and its locals were instrumental in turning out the vote for Carter in November.[35]

Doing so, both NEA leaders and rank-and-file members believed, would once and for all establish the professionalism of the teaching occupation. Indeed, since the onset of common schools in the nineteenth century, teachers had been expected by administrators and parents to act like professionals, but they were rarely treated accordingly.[36] In the late nineteenth century, teaching provided, at least for women, both a status and salary that was higher than that for most other women workers. The price, however, was foregoing a family and often being left with nothing on which to retire. Indeed, there was a great irony in the teaching profession: for most of American history, many teachers clearly fit the PMC paradigm, enforcing notions of temperance and middle-class morality, and some helped discipline new generations of working people and stanching social unrest just as Horace Mann had hoped. And yet, it was largely during the times when teachers acted as working-class people did—organizing in unions, participating in demonstrations, and withholding their labor (or at least threatening to)—that they were able to win sustainable salaries, job security, and more control over their workday.[37] Though the NEA certainly appreciated Carter's racial liberalism, the promise of elevating the status of education was its major reason for backing him.

Democrats held enormous majorities in both houses of Congress going into the election of 1976, and so even though Carter beat Ford by a slim margin, he came into office with his party in the driver's seat. Though Democrats had unified control of government for the first time since the Johnson presidency, Carter's commitment to broad social democratic principles was limited, and the vision of the new generation of Democrats elected after Watergate was similarly limited. Organized labor believed Carter would work with Congress to pass a sweeping law to even the odds against the growing attempts by corporations to prevent workers from organizing. Many working people hoped Carter and Congress could strengthen the position of American jobs in an increasingly global economy in which capital much more systematically sought cheaper labor elsewhere.[38] Public employee union leaders like Albert Shanker, president of the AFT, sought a federal law ensuring collective bargaining rights, including the right to strike, for all state and local workers.[39] Social democrats such as Humphrey, California representative Augustus Hawkins, and civil rights activist Coretta Scott King tried to work with the new administration to finally guarantee every American the right to a job.[40]

Though the New Deal had prioritized families and the family wage, the fight for Humphrey-Hawkins and labor reform occurred during a moment in which feminists, welfare activists, and others had worked to disconnect economic security from the breadwinner model. Though they were not fully successful—and provoked a backlash of "breadwinner conservatism" in the 1970s and beyond—feminists had very much changed the parameters of how many Americans thought about jobs. Women workers were entering the workforce in large numbers in the decade, in part a consequence of the decline of manufacturing and pressure on male workers' wages, but also because of equal opportunity enforcement stemming from the Civil Rights Act of 1965 and the Equal Opportunity Commission led by women's rights activists. So too were Black workers breaking into jobs from which patterns of discrimination in the law and union-created seniority provisions had excluded them. Both groups were at the forefront of new organizing drives to unionize for greater economic security in the decade.[41] Had a robust version of Humphrey-Hawkins and a labor reform bill been passed in the late 1970s, the United States may have been able to move forward with a broader and more inclusive version of social democracy.[42] Anyone hoping Carter would commit to this path during his administration, however, would be sorely disappointed.

The effort for a jobs guarantee was already in the works when Carter was on the campaign trail. By 1976, persistent unemployment on a level Americans hadn't seen since before World War II put the notion of a full employment policy—much more robust than the public jobs offered by CETA—at the center of the nation's political agenda. The coalition that came together pushed for a bill with both a stronger version of economic planning and a robust government jobs guarantee. It included Humphrey, and importantly, African American social democrats (like King and Hawkins) who had seen unemployment ravage Black communities. In addition to labor leaders, the effort also included intellectuals like the economist Wassily Leontief, who by the 1970s was calling to resurrect the National Resources Planning Board, and economist Leon Keyserling, a veteran of the New Deal and key adviser on the Freedom Budget.[43]

Humphrey and Hawkins were, of course, the loudest congressional voices of the bill they sponsored. Hawkins, who had backed Upton Sinclair's socialist bid for governor back in 1934, served in the California state assembly from 1935 to 1963, when he won election to the US House. The Democrat, representing a district that included the Watts neighborhood in Los Angeles, was heavily influenced by A. Philip Randolph. He had authored Title VII of the Civil Rights Act and was a cofounder of the Congressional Black Caucus (CBC). Connecting civil rights and jobs, in 1974 he proposed a federal jobs guarantee, in which anyone who could not get a job in the private sector would be entitled to a job at the prevailing wage rate, enforceable by lawsuit. Hawkins and the CBC saw a jobs program as paramount, particularly as the already substantial gap between white and Black unemployment had begun increasing in late 1973.[44]

Humphrey had been a decades-long supporter of civil rights, too, pushing for a greater commitment in the Democratic Party plank in 1948, and was crucial in breaking a filibuster of the Civil Rights Act in the Senate. Elected vice president in 1964, he garnered the overwhelming support of labor in the ill-fated campaign of 1968, after which he was elected to the Senate again in 1970. In 1975, the Minnesota senator had worked with Leontief and Senator Jacob Javits (R-NY) to develop a bill called the Balanced Growth and Economic Planning Act, which proposed a microeconomic planning process to reduce unemployment and strengthen

American industry. Humphrey then threw his support toward a revised version of Hawkins's bill. In 1976, he flirted with another presidential run. Instead, he made full employment his political priority in the nation's bicentennial year.[45]

That March, Hawkins and Humphrey once again introduced a version of the bill, now called the Full Employment and Balanced Growth Act, to Congress. This version provided an enforceable jobs guarantee (at the larger rate of either the minimum wage or local prevailing wage), with a 3 percent unemployment goal within four years. Proposed as an amendment to the Employment Act of 1946, the bill also obligated the president to put together a full employment budget.[46] The Federal Reserve and the Council of Economic Advisors would develop and implement the planning policies to ensure full employment, and the Department of Labor would establish an "Office of Full Employment" to ensure the unemployed had access to federally funded reservoirs of public service jobs.

As soon as Humphrey and Hawkins introduced the bill, Coretta Scott King and Murray Finley, the co-chairs of the Full Employment Action Council (FEAC), began working to mobilize the "wide support" that already existed.[47] FEAC was the legislative arm of the National Committee for Full Employment (NCFE). Formed in 1974 with more than one hundred representatives of unions and other political organizations, NCFE's board of directors included the president of the UAW (Leonard Woodcock, who had succeeded Reuther after his death in 1970); I. W. Abel, president of the United Steelworkers; and Roy Wilkins, the executive director of the NAACP, in addition to leaders from the National Organization for Women, Americans for Democratic Action, and Common Cause.[48]

Finley was the president of the Amalgamated Clothing and Textile Workers Union (ACTWU). Scott King, of course, was Martin's widow, and she argued that Humphrey-Hawkins represented his legacy. King, murdered in Memphis in 1968, had become a highly persuasive advocate for both racial justice and for all workers for economic security by the end of his life: he had endorsed Randolph and Rustin's Freedom Budget, and in February 1968 he announced the demand of an annual $30 billion investment in a jobs guarantee, a minimum income, and housing as part of the Poor People's Campaign. Indeed, when King traveled to Memphis, he was working with other leaders from the Southern Christian Leadership Council (SCLC) to mobilize a sustained occupation of Washington, DC, to force Congress to recommit to social democratic change.[49]

In 1976, congressional Democratic leadership supported full employment policy and sought to make it a major campaign issue.[50] Congressional hearings highlighted the proposal's widespread support, and Senate hearings that May are especially illuminating. Humphrey expertly placed the effort to plan an economy in which everyone would have a job within the legacy of other social democratic

advances, arguing for the promise of America's founding in contrast to economists' critiques about "market forces":

> There's not a word in the Constitution about market forces, and . . .
> there's not one word, may I say, in the Emancipation Proclamation
> about the market forces. But there are a lot of words about justice, fair
> play, compassion, decency. . . . The whole purpose of the Declaration
> of Independence doesn't talk about market forces and that's what this
> year is all about—life, liberty, and the pursuit of happiness. You don't
> pursue much happiness if you're ground down in the dirt by so-called
> market forces. It says governments are instituted to secure these rights.
> How do you pursue happiness in filth and degradation and slums and
> unemployment and misery and sickness?[51]

Likewise, Hawkins argued, "The moral tragedy of current policies is that they
deliberately create and countenance high levels of unemployment. . . . I think that
we listen too darn much to some economists at least who are talking about inflation and the other problems who perhaps haven't read the bill but who neglect to
mention the physical, social, and psychological impact of the waste which is now
being created by mistaken policies."[52]

The bill had its share of critics, including some Keynesian economists who
worried about inflation.[53] Senator William Proxmire (D-WI), chair of the Senate
hearings, also worried about inflation, for instance, while conservative economist Alan Greenspan testified that funding "nonproductive" jobs would hold
back the nation's economy. The Chamber of Commerce rekindled the argument
made to stifle Senator James Murray's Full Employment Act in 1945, arguing that
the planning envisioned by Humphrey-Hawkins would stall "free enterprise."[54]

Though the bill would have been unlikely to get Ford's signature in 1976 (Ford
faced his own challenge from Reagan, who mobilized the growing conservative
populist forces on the campaign trail), some Democrats—particularly from
urban areas and with labor ties—hoped to pass it in order to highlight a sharp
contrast between their party and the GOP.[55] Other congressional Democrats,
particularly those elected in 1974, however, prevented the bill from a floor vote
in either chamber. Many of these new Democrats felt politically vulnerable since
they came into office following a unique election marked by the nation's reaction
to Watergate.[56] Further, the wave of new Democrats in 1974 did not seek a vote
on Humphrey-Hawkins because they likely saw themselves as more accountable
to the growing numbers of professional-class voters—not at the precarious end
of the labor market—who elected them. And, more recently elected Congress-
people believed government action should be more limited. As a young Delaware
senator named Joe Biden criticized Hubert Humphrey, "He is not cognizant of

the limited, finite ability government has to deal with people's problems. And I wonder whether Humphrey has the intestinal fortitude to look at some programs and say, 'No.'"[57]

Still, Democratic leaders used the employment issue in the election of 1976, and with good reason, since polls in 1975 had almost 80 percent of the country supportive of "a federal program to give productive jobs to the unemployed."[58] The party platform in 1976 committed "to the right of all adult Americans willing, able and seeking work to have opportunities for useful jobs at living wages." These efforts included the direct creation of public-sector jobs after the exhaustion of efforts to create jobs in the private sector.[59]

Carter was lukewarm to a jobs guarantee, however. Though he pitched incentives to create private-sector jobs on the campaign trail, he did acknowledge that public service jobs might have been necessary, agreeing grudgingly that "government should be the employer of last resort."[60] He stated that he "favor[ed] federally created jobs similar to the CCC and WPA during the depression years, particularly for young Americans who have an extremely high unemployment rate—in excess of 40 per cent for black young people."[61] Though African Americans represented a "decisive" vote in a very close election, his support for Hawkins's proposal quickly diminished, in spite of the fact that both the CBC and prominent Black leaders like the Urban League's Vernon Jordan had prioritized full employment.[62] Carter's commitment to the right to a job had always been under political duress, and his economic advisers—including CEA chair Charles Schultze—prioritized curtailing inflation over job creation.[63]

The new president's initial budget proposal in 1977 sought dramatic increases in funding for public service jobs through CETA, but Carter continued to be cool to the notion of a jobs guarantee.[64] Further, by 1977 the United States had experienced a rise of "business consciousness" from the Chamber, Business Roundtable, and other organizations that had grown increasingly confident in their ability to stymie social democratic reform.[65] Business opposition ratcheted up a massive lobbying effort to defeat the bill following Carter's election.[66] But FEAC continued to push, holding a Full Employment Action week in 1977, for example, that brought out 1.5 million people across three hundred cities.[67] Though unemployment fell over the course of 1977, it remained at about 6.5 percent at the beginning of the next year. Carter's 1978 State of the Union address, however, made clear his distaste for anything approaching a jobs guarantee: "We really need to realize," he argued, "that there is a limit to the role and the function of government. . . . Government cannot eliminate poverty or provide a bountiful economy or reduce inflation or save our cities or cure illiteracy or provide energy." Though Carter offered the possibility of some public service jobs to reduce racial and age disparities, he argued for business incentives and tax cuts as the solution, making clear he would only support a Humphrey-Hawkins bill that did not guarantee a job or include economic planning.[68]

Ultimately, the bill was reintroduced, but in 1978 was amended by conservatives so that it provided very little beyond an unenforceable goal of reducing unemployment to 4 percent by 1983, and, later, at an unspecified time, to "full employment," which was not defined. The bill also set goals for eliminating disparate unemployment rates based on race, gender, disability status, veteran status, and age. Finally, the law amended the Federal Reserve Act to instruct the Fed to take unspecified action in support of the goals of the Humphrey-Hawkins Act, but it also included a section on "overcoming inflation," that also obligated the Fed to do the opposite.[69]

The administration's congressional support for full employment is illuminating, as it implicitly blamed workers for unemployment and emphasized the importance of making workers more employable rather than ensure jobs existed as the 1976 version of Humphrey-Hawkins would have done. Labor Secretary Ray Marshall's Senate testimony in May 1978, for instance, explained how the Humphrey-Hawkins Act of 1978 would allow the Labor Department to facilitate "such measures as training, improved coordination with private firms, public service employment, youth programs, improved labor market information, antidiscrimination enforcement, and limitations on the entry of undocumented workers. The general policies must be aimed at improving the employability of a variety of specific groups that have high unemployment rates." Marshall went on to say that welfare reform and CETA reauthorization would be necessary to create the training and transitional public service jobs necessary to reduce the unemployment rate.[70]

Business interests, however, opposed even the watered-down version of the law for what it vaguely promised. Jack Carlson, the Chamber of Commerce's chief economist, made explicit Marshall's implication that the unemployed were in that situation because of their own inadequacies. Carlson argued that, rather than use government tools to create jobs, "our schools, training system, the transition from school to career job, and many other things must improve over long periods of time. One thing we can do to reduce unemployment is to make people employable."[71] Business Roundtable representative Lewis Foy also opposed Humphrey-Hawkins's "overpromises" to be achieved by "national planning," instead offering the Roundtable's support for potential job-training programs in a reauthorized CETA.[72]

By May, the Chamber and BR were working to kill another major social democratic reform, also with the assistance of a lukewarm Carter administration: labor reform legislation. Initially, labor hoped for a repeal of Section 14(b) of the Taft-Hartley Act, which allowed states (like Carter's Georgia, which did so in 1947) to pass laws allowing workers to benefit from a collectively bargained contract without paying for union representation costs. Instead, the AFL-CIO settled for a bill to make it harder for employers to intimidate workers in representation elections and to delay bargaining. The bill would have expanded the size of the National Labor Relations Board, increased penalties for companies that fired workers who organized, made union elections fairer, and mandated bargaining when employers didn't do so in good faith. By the late 1970s, this reform was badly needed: unrepresented manufacturing workers in the South and in service industries (increasingly composed of women and African American workers as discriminatory barriers had been broken down) across the country tried to organize unions in large numbers, but employers' tactics prevented a greater portion than in years past from winning union representation elections.[73]

Antiunion interests, like the Chamber, the Business Roundtable, and the National Right to Work Committee, mobilized an unprecedented effort to kill the bill. Republican senators led by Orrin Hatch (UT) and Richard Lugar (IN) filibustered in May and June 1978. Its proponents amended it to make it more palatable to senators on the fence, but even the watered-down version fell two votes short of breaking a filibuster. The Carter administration, which had publicly supported the reform, focused much more on negotiating the votes to get the Senate to ratify a treaty to return control of the Panama Canal to Panama than it did on getting votes for labor reform.[74]

In October, Carter signed the mostly toothless version of Humphrey-Hawkins into law. Coretta Scott King celebrated the bill, hoping its goals could be employed to make a difference. "This is indeed a great historical occasion, perhaps as significant as the signing of the Civil Rights Act of 1964 and the Voting Rights Act of 1965," she argued. "Perhaps in the future, history will record that it may be even more significant, Mr. President, because I think it deals with an issue on a basic human right that's the most basic of all human rights, the right to a job. And that is a central priority now of our economic policy with the signing of this act into law today."[75]

King's thinking, unfortunately, was largely wishful, and the right to a job would not really be a priority for either Democrats or Republicans for decades. Taken together, the first half of the Carter administration crushed any possibility of a renewed promise of American social democracy. Millions of private-sector workers, many of whom were nonwhite workers and women in precarious jobs, lost their best chance to gain real union rights. The universal expansion of public-sector labor rights was never seriously considered. And the promise of the right to a job foundered on the shoals of a set of unenforceable goals. Carter's presidency represented the future of the Democratic Party: one that enabled capital while allowing possibilities for workers to wither.

In fact, perhaps the most consequential aspects of Carter's economic policy were, first, a major tax reduction for capital gains (without any mechanism for ensuring these cuts would resurrect investment in American manufacturing) while raising the tax burden on the middle class and, second, appointing Paul Volcker to chair the Federal Reserve. In that office, Volcker severely restricted the money supply to show the federal government's seriousness in wringing inflation out of the economy.[76] Already high unemployment increased. American industries like steel hemorrhaged blue-collar jobs that had been the backbone of economic security for so many workers, and even when Carter worked to save jobs, as in the auto industry when he brokered a deal to bail out Chrysler, it came at the high cost of concessions.[77] Indeed, by 1979, Carter had unequivocally turned away from the possibility of robust social democracy in order to fight inflation and advance the agenda of neoliberal economics.

In one other way, Carter's administration represented the harbinger of Democrats future: in the second half of his single term in office, he finally signed into law a bill to meet the NEA's calls for a stand-alone Department of Education, symbolically cleaving education from its connection to the promise of a more robust set of enabling freedoms. The Department of Education Organization Act highlighted the increasing shift toward human capital as the major avenue for working people to acquire what Carter had called, in his State of the Union address in 1978, the "chance to earn a decent living."

Reorganizing Government, Reorganizing Priorities

Perhaps the most significant domestic achievement for Carter was the controversial creation of the Department of Education in 1979. Carter's promise of a stand-alone department in 1976 had been an awkward fit in his campaign given his other pledges to limit government. "Generally, I am opposed to the proliferation of federal agencies," Carter had admitted. "But a Department of Education would consolidate the grant programs, job training, early childhood training, literacy training, and many other functions currently scattered through the government. The result would be a strong voice for education at the federal level."[78]

The federal Office of Education, after it was created in the 1860s, was quickly demoted to a bureau in the Department of the Interior, and in 1929, it was once again elevated to "office" status. In 1937, the increased role of the federal government in providing social services led a presidential commission to propose a Department of Social Welfare; instead, the Federal Security Agency was created in 1939. It took until 1953, however, when President Eisenhower's Reorganization Plan No. 1 created the Department of Health, Education, and Welfare (HEW) for the federal government to have a comprehensive cabinet department devoted to social welfare. As Eisenhower pointed out, "Such action is demanded by the importance and magnitude of these functions, which affect the well-being of millions of our citizens."[79]

Eisenhower's remark illustrates the fact that American policymakers after World War II continued to view health, education, and other social welfare programs as part of one interrelated effort. When the Johnson administration was putting together ESEA, some had argued to elevate Education to its own department. Education Commissioner Keppel, however, opposed it and not just because conservatives feared greater federal control over education. Indeed, Keppel argued, "There was so much convergence between the Great Society's education, health, and antipoverty programs that it made sense to house them under one umbrella department."[80]

Even so, during the 1960s, liberal senator Abraham Ribicoff (D-CT) introduced legislation for a separate cabinet department, and in 1972, McGovern supported a cabinet department during his presidential run. Though Carter had promised to elevate education in 1976, he did not make it an immediate priority—likely because he knew the effort would face stiff opposition. As early as the campaign in 1976, Albert Shanker, for instance, pushed back against the notion of a separate department. Elected president of AFT in 1974, Shanker was clearly a social democrat. By the mid-1970s, he was not only advocating for teachers' labor rights, but he was pitching a wide-ranging program of lifelong learning called "educare" and in 1975, Shanker supported a bill by Senator Walter Mondale (D-MN) and Representative John Brademas (D-IN) that would have funded an extensive program of childcare, prenatal care, and early childhood education.[81]

The Carter campaign in 1976 set up an education policy task force, featuring both Shanker and NEA president John Ryor, in addition to Keppel, former HEW secretary Wilbur Cohen, and other notables. At the very first meeting, Ryor advocated for the department proposal while Shanker opposed it. The AFT president worried that a separate department "might upset effective coalitions and produce less for all by creating new competition among former allies." Cohen agreed with Shanker, pointing out the proposal would "delay any substantive progress because the turf fights involved would use up everyone's energies; the issue would prevent new money for education."[82]

After the election of 1976, the AFT sprang into action against the possibility of a separate department. While admitting it had "surface appeal," Shanker argued that "rather than encouraging the traditional go-it-alone tendencies of many educators by setting education's administration off by itself, we should launch a coordinated health, welfare, and education approach to the major problems our nation faces—poverty, equal educational opportunity, welfare, youth unemployment, and health security."[83]

The NEA and its members pushed Carter hard the other way. In September 1977, the union established the Citizens Committee for a Cabinet Department of Education (CCCDE), a coalition of education, labor, civil rights, and business leaders. The proposal garnered wide support, including from the president of the National Congress of Parents and Teachers (NCPT) and the National School Boards Association. As NCPT president Grace Baisinger pointed out, "We must insure that this great priority of parents—the education of their children—is a national concern. The best assurance . . . that this will be met is a Department of Education with cabinet status."[84] The Citizens Committee also included Coretta Scott King (at that point, also advocating for a federal jobs guarantee); Vernon Jordan, director of the National Urban League; AFSCME president Jerry Wurf; UAW president Douglas Fraser; former US commissioner of education Keppel (who now supported the cabinet proposal); and Republican Terrel Bell (who would later be tasked by Reagan with dismantling the department).

The NEA asked members to write to Carter, and in the fall of 1977, the letters poured into the White House, calling on the president to fulfill his campaign promise. In September, Connecticut teacher Marilynn Parnell charged, "You have now been in office for almost a year and still we hear nothing solid or specific about the establishment of a separate Department of Education." Massachusetts high school teacher Gerry McDonough wrote to Carter in October, "I do not believe that education has been receiving its fair shake, nor will it ever receive the attention it demands, while it is under HEW."[85]

Carter called for a Department of Education in his January 1978 State of the Union, which he also recommended as a priority in a message to Congress on education on February 28. In the summer, Representative Jack Brooks (D-TX) introduced a bill to create the department in the House.[86] Over the course of 1978, forces lined up in support and opposition to the proposal, sometimes connecting the bill's necessity to economic opportunity. HEW secretary Joseph Califano, for instance, sent a letter to the Senate Committee on Governmental Affairs, officially agreeing with President Carter's "judgment that education is a ranking domestic priority which requires visible, high level leadership of its own. That need is heightened by a perceptible decline in the quality of public schools, an inadequate level of basic functional skills for young people seeking employment."[87] NEA president Ryor full-throatedly supported the effort in

Senate hearings, arguing, "Surely the education of our citizenry with its dramatic and profound impact on the productive capacity and future economic and social well-being of this Nation demands as much Presidential time and attention as the development of programs designed to physically transport our citizens and our goods."[88]

The most important opponents of the proposed department were the AFT, the AFL-CIO, and their allies in Congress, who all opposed the effort on the grounds that public education should be connected to other aspects of the social democratic promise. The AFL-CIO Public Employees Department (with which the AFT affiliated) opposed the cabinet position as did the full AFL-CIO, which passed a resolution at its convention in December 1977.[89] The same month, Shanker, highlighting the AFT's push to connect childcare and public education, envisioned connecting education and job training to a wider social democratic vision: "If welfare is to become more work-related, unskilled adults will need skills to obtain and hold jobs—a huge educational undertaking for our schools. Day care must be readily available for their young dependent children. The AFT's proposal that day care be combined with early education under the auspices of the public schools would gain new force."[90] Indeed, a broader social democratic vision capable of moving the United States beyond the limited, breadwinner-focused version of economic security that grew after World War II would clearly have required universal childcare.

New York Democratic representative (and founding member of the CBC), Shirley Chisolm referenced organized labor's "vigorous support for equal opportunity and social justice" in pushing for civil rights legislation over the years. She concluded that "labor groups have carefully constructed coalitions around major national issues such as poverty, equal access to educational opportunities, as well as welfare and health assistance. Now, to thoughtlessly destroy these coalitions . . . in order to achieve the dubious goal of formation of a separate department appears a little foolhardy."[91]

In 1978, the bill easily made it through the Senate, but it took until 1979 to get a floor vote in the lower chamber as the bill's opponents leveraged the body's packed schedule to delay a vote until the next session. Carter again called for a cabinet-level department, and after a bruising battle, the bill finally passed. A new version in the House escaped the chamber's Government Operations Committee by a single vote on May 2, and the floor vote could not have been closer (210–206) that July. The conference committee worked into the fall to reconcile with the Senate, eliminating House amendments opposing busing and racial quotas. Unlike with labor reform in the Senate, Carter put significant energy into lobbying wavering House Democrats to pass the conference bill, turning enough votes to ensure it passed. In the end, seventy-seven Democrats opposed the bill, and thirty Republicans voted for it.[92]

The Gathering Storm

In several ways, President Jimmy Carter supported public education. He stayed true to campaign promises to advocate for much more federal funding in the budget: in his first term, he increased funding 60 percent above Ford's last budget.[93] And, the Department of Education Organization Act did what the NEA and its allies hoped it would do, elevating the political significance of public education in the United States. In an NEA press release issued after Carter signed the bill into law, newly elected president Willard McGuire compared the law to the 1862 Morrill Land-Grant Act in terms of its impact on shifting public support for education.[94]

But to what end? In *The Coming of Post-Industrial Society*, Daniel Bell had charted a course to navigate the emergent tensions of the 1970s, and he pointed out that equality of opportunity in education would not suffice. Even if educational opportunity could be equalized, and Bell was skeptical of that possibility, the United States would still fall short of constructing a "fair" meritocratic competition. Citing social science work on inequality, Bell argued there was simply too much luck involved in determining how one's opportunities translated into social and economic outcomes. He concluded his masterwork by arguing for what he called a "just meritocracy" in which everyone's social and economic needs would be taken care of, on top of which Americans would have opportunity for greater reward, though not at the expense of diminishing the basic needs of their fellow citizens.[95]

Establishing a stand-alone Department of Education could have represented one important strand of a significant expansion of American social democracy along the lines of a "just meritocracy"—had it accompanied other enabling freedoms that included a jobs guarantee, healthcare, and labor reform. But by only elevating education, the Carter administration contributed to the rise of the myth that education could, as if by magic, ensure access to economic security for those willing to get the right skills.

Other Democrats, however, continued to fight for broader social democratic possibilities even after the defeats of labor reform and a meaningful jobs guarantee. In 1980, Massachusetts senator Ted Kennedy entered the Democratic primary in a bid to unseat Carter. Though a long shot, Kennedy garnered support from influential political entities on the left. While the NEA enthusiastically endorsed Carter, for instance, the AFT endorsed his opponent. In part, Kennedy responded to Carter's epic unpopularity, much of which, like his fruitless attempt to rescue American hostages in Iran, stemmed from the perceived failures of his administration. But Kennedy's campaign was also premised on the effort to ensure all Americans had access to good healthcare and as a critique of Carter's unwillingness to enforce the goals of Humphrey-Hawkins.[96] Others on the left continued to advance different social democratic possibilities too. Lane Kirkland, president of the AFL-CIO, for instance, advocated a massive industrial program to revitalize American manufacturing in 1980.[97]

Kennedy won twelve states and around 38 percent of the votes cast in the Democratic primaries, both a major sign of weakness for Carter and a reminder that there was still a thirst in the US for extending broad enabling social and economic freedoms. In 1980, however, California governor Ronald Reagan capitalized on Carter's politics of diminished expectations with promises to restore American prosperity by decreasing regulations and lowering taxes. Reagan, indeed, had a very different vision for America, and unlike Carter's lukewarm, professional-class drift, engaged in an all-out war against social democracy. Even so, Reagan did not arrest the growth of the education myth; the notion that economic opportunity acquired through access to education could compensate for the loss of other social supports continued to grow more powerful during the California Republican's administration too.

"AT RISK"

The Acceleration of the Education Myth

On January 20, 1981, Ronald Reagan was inaugurated as the fortieth president in American history. The previous November, the Gipper resoundingly defeated Carter in an unequivocal rejection of the former Georgia governor, which was the first time since 1932 an incumbent president had lost a reelection campaign. Reagan won by almost ten points in the popular vote in addition to winning a resounding 489 electoral votes. A large explanation for this rejection was Carter's abject failure on the economy, and support for Kennedy's primary challenge suggested that, for most Democrats at least, Carter's problem had not been an excess of social democracy. Union households, for example, had gone for Carter 62–38 in 1976; after the Democrat's failure to deal with the nation's economic challenges, that margin was sliced to 48–45 in 1980, and Carter may have lost that demographic entirely were it not for third-party candidate John Anderson siphoning votes from Reagan.[1] Indeed, Carter had failed to pass any significant social democratic reforms, instead opting for regressive tax policies and allowing the Federal Reserve to send the American economy into recession. Then he had lectured Americans against too much material want in his famous "Crisis of Confidence" speech in 1979. Reagan's campaign, however, promised a presidency to make the economy great again.[2]

Reagan began his political career in California, as a governor (1967–75) who took on higher education and the growing professional class. In 1976, he ran as a conservative populist against the incumbent Gerald Ford. Indeed, Reagan attempted to mobilize resentments similar to those Nixon targeted in 1968 and

1972 and that were, at least in part, built on opposition to educated elites.[3] Further, Reagan's campaign consciously sought to take on the public sector, framing social goods like public education as taking from productive taxpayers. Here Reagan tapped into the heightened prominence of Gary Becker and Milton Friedman's conservative version of the education myth, which touted the importance of education but sought to privatize investment as much as possible.[4]

Reagan and other Republicans employed the landslide in 1980 to argue that Americans *had* rejected social democracy and thus to further reduce the state's role in ensuring economic security. In fact, his inaugural speech sounded like a mirror image of the vision FDR laid out in 1944. As had been the case in the 1930s, Reagan pointed out that "these United States are confronted with an economic affliction of great proportions." In the 1970s, Americans suffered "from the longest and one of the worst sustained inflations in our national history. . . . Idle industries have cast workers into unemployment, human misery, and personal indignity. Those who do work are denied a fair return for their labor." If working people could relate to this state of events as their grandparents had in the 1930s, however, Reagan flipped the promise of the New Deal on its head: those who worked, he argued, suffered from a "tax system which penalized successful achievement and keeps us from maintaining full productivity."

Carter's policies had brought on the worst of both worlds: he had raised the relative tax burden for many working-class people while failing to substantively improve their lives with any new government interventions—except for elevating the tenuous narrative that government could help individuals develop their own human capital through education. Reagan, however, proposed a drastically new course. "In this present crisis," he asserted, "government is not the solution to the problem; government is the problem." Separating "the people" from a government beholden to special interests, Reagan argued that "this administration's objective will be a healthy, vigorous, growing economy that provides equal opportunities for all Americans with no barriers born of bigotry or discrimination." Reagan's color-blind language intended to leverage that mythology to convince Americans, wrongly, that government interventions had hurt them. He concluded, therefore, it was "time to check and reverse the growth of government, which shows signs of having grown beyond the consent of the governed."[5]

President Reagan, fully at war with social democracy, spent eight years putting this vision into action. Bargaining with a Democratic Congress, the president won huge tax cuts that disproportionately helped the already wealthy. Reagan sought economic deregulations, particularly those begun in finance and banking, creating an economy structured around leveraged buyouts and corporate takeovers that further undermined blue-collar jobs. And, he threw down the gauntlet against unions, firing striking air traffic controllers in 1981 and populating the

National Labor Relations Board with appointees hostile to workers.[6] Following the Reagan recession of 1982–83, the economy turned around just in time for his reelection campaign in 1984, and he was easily reelected over social democrat Walter Mondale. By the end of his second term, the economy overall had improved since the stagflation of the 1970s, but poverty also rose dramatically as the Gipper's budgets cut social programs.

One of the areas of government Reagan could not ultimately roll back, however, was public education. Breaking with a decades-old consensus around increasing federal support for education, Reagan did win federal cuts. But his larger goal to significantly curtail federal influence in education by abolishing the federal Department of Education failed. The growing importance of the education myth had become too politically entrenched by then. In fact, Reagan's own secretary of education, Terrel Bell, convened a task force that crafted the momentous report, *A Nation at Risk*, which blamed the diminishing economic security of Americans on the failure of the education system to keep them internationally competitive. Despite Reagan's views on the federal role of education, the education myth continued to grow, particularly as a political response to an increasingly unequal economy. Further, Reagan himself helped to facilitate this myth by pushing fantasies that increased federal investment in job training would help workers whose livelihoods were under duress from the combination of antiunion practices and capital flight.

The Reagan administration also sought to renew the role of education in deepening American patriotism, particularly during the former actor's second term. Appointed by Reagan in 1985, Education Secretary William Bennett, a staunch cultural conservative, sought to restore his version of American values and the tradition of Western civilization to prominence in the nation's education system. This effort sought to cast Democrats, particularly beginning in the late 1980s and 1990s, as unconcerned with the values of the American polity. Seeking to combat Reaganism, a growing group of neo-liberal Democrats shifted course, seeking to move the party in a winning direction by touting entrepreneurialism and the alchemical power of public investment in education.

A Nation at Risk

After Reagan's inauguration in 1981, he worked with a Democratic Congress to pass an enormous tax cut, at the time the largest in American history.[7] Reagan believed in supply-side economics, which postulated that the United States government could offset the revenue lost from tax cuts with larger revenues generated by the economic growth the cuts would stimulate. This supposition was not borne out in reality as large tax cuts, in fact, led to greater federal deficits, not greater taxation income. Reagan also cut funding to social programs, particularly those he believed should not be funded by the federal government. The latter prominently included the Educational Consolidation and Improvement Act of 1981, which slashed the budget for education, particularly for desegregation programs, and replaced categorical funding with block grants.[8] Over the course of his two terms, further cuts reduced the proportion of the federal budget spent on public education from about 2.5 percent of total spending in fiscal year 1979 to just 1.7 percent in FY 1989. These cuts hit the poorest school districts the hardest.[9] As a cultural conservative, Reagan also sought, unsuccessfully, to bring prayer back into schools and to provide tax credits for private school tuition. Building on his efforts as governor of California to connect tuition-free higher education with welfare and government handouts, Reagan's first budget also slashed student aid for higher education, limited Pell grants, and made student loans less accessible.[10]

The Reagan administration's most dramatic goal, however, was abolishing the cabinet-level Department of Education Congress had just created in 1979. This effort failed to gain traction in part because of Reagan's own education secretary. A moderate Republican from Utah, Terrel Bell played a role in building the mainstream political consensus around the importance of federal funding for education that had emerged by the 1980s. Having served as US Education Commissioner in 1970–71 and 1974–76, Bell supported the elevation of the cabinet-level Department of Education, and the NEA approved of his appointment as the department's second secretary in 1981.[11] Bell was tasked by Reagan, however, with eliminating the very department he was appointed to administer. His four years in the administration were tumultuous, as Bell constantly fought with the "right-wing radicals" who wanted, in his view, to cut education spending to the bone.[12]

In part an effort by Bell to prevent the department's demotion, the new secretary created the National Commission on Excellence in Education in 1981. (Reagan, in fact, had declined to appoint the presidential commission for which his secretary of education had asked.) Bell appointed David Gardner, a former colleague from Utah, as chair, and the remainder of the eighteen-member commission included teachers, parents, corporate leaders, school board members, university professors and presidents, and school administrators (including from private schools). Bell tasked the commission with examining teaching and learning, the connection between "social and educational" changes and student achievement during the past twenty-five years, and in particular, the state of education at the high school and college levels. By focusing on secondary and postsecondary education, the commission could connect students' skills with their future economic livelihoods, and this charge was made more evident when Bell tasked the commission with "comparing American schools and colleges with those of other advanced nations."[13]

Indeed, the economic turmoil for working people over the course of the 1970s and early 1980s found its way prominently into the report's findings, which historionically blamed the decline of the American education system for the fact that other industrial nations—especially Japan—had caught up to the United States in manufacturing performance. Indeed, *A Nation at Risk* (*ANAR*), began by breathlessly invoking threats to the economic structure of the United States:

> Our Nation is at risk. Our once unchallenged preeminence in commerce, industry, science, and technological innovation is being overtaken by competitors throughout the world. . . . The educational foundations of our society are presently being eroded by a rising tide of mediocrity that threatens our very future as a Nation and as a people. What was unimaginable a generation ago has begun to occur—others are matching and surpassing our educational attainments.[14]

Setting the tone for an explicit international competition, the commission pointed out that the world was now "one global village." Though characterizing the world as a village might mean nations collaborated with each other, *ANAR* instead pointed to the economic competition in which the United States was purportedly falling behind. The Japanese made "automobiles more efficiently than Americans and have government subsidies for development and export." The South Koreans had built "the world's most efficient steel mill" and American machine tools were "being displaced by German products."[15] It was true that other manufacturing nations were catching up to the United States in productivity and gaining market share in many industries in which the profitability of American industry had been unmatched. Focusing on the education system, however, was far from a natural leap. One way to make the United States more competitive, for instance, as the report implied with its references to Japanese subsidies, could have been to develop a national industrial policy. As business consultant Ira Magaziner and public policy expert Robert Reich argued, in fact, around the same time, an overarching industrial policy may very well have made American manufacturing more internationally competitive.[16]

Instead, *ANAR* connected competition between industrial nations to education, asserting that "knowledge, learning, information, and skilled intelligence are the new raw materials of international commerce and are today spreading throughout the world as vigorously as miracle drugs, synthetic fertilizers, and blue jeans did earlier." Though the report dutifully argued Americans should revivify the "intellectual, moral and spiritual strengths of our people which

knit together the very fabric of our society," this entreaty was clearly secondary to the economic importance *ANAR* larded onto public education. The
report highlighted some of the supposed deficiencies of an education system
in which the aggregate of American students failed to score higher on standardized tests than students in other nations did, especially in math and science. Unsurprisingly, however, none of *ANAR's* "indicators of risk" quantified
Americans' supposed lost moral, intellectual, or spiritual strength relative to
other nations.

Scholars have since shown that fears about declining test scores at the time
were seriously exaggerated.[17] The most representative longitudinal test in the
United States—the National Assessment of Educational Progress (NAEP)—for
instance, showed that from 1973 to 1982, math scores for Americans remained
virtually unchanged with a slight increase overall for thirteen-year-olds and a
slight decrease for seventeen-year-olds. African Americans and Hispanics saw
increased scores, in fact, in virtually every age range tested, and racial achievement gaps decreased.[18] In fact, Americans might have actually celebrated such
scores given the economic turmoil of the decade that challenged school budgets
and the ability of students to do well. Nevertheless, the decreased competitiveness on standardized tests relative to other nations, *ANAR* argued, was a serious
issue because of the supposed demand for new jobs in computers, robotics, and
other technologies.

ANAR pointed to testimony from students, parents, and teachers expressing
frustration that "more and more young people emerge from high school neither
ready for college nor for work." The report could have concluded with an argument for ensuring everyone had access to good jobs. Instead, it strengthened
fears that the education system was not doing enough to make workers ready for
the jobs that would supposedly become available, asserting that "this predica-
ment becomes more acute as the knowledge base continues its rapid expansion,
the number of traditional jobs shrinks, and new jobs demand greater sophistica-
tion and preparation."[19]

As the answer to these problems, the commission argued the nation must prepare "through the education and skill of its people to respond to the challenges
of a rapidly changing world."[20] Such a society would be committed to life-long
learning, ensuring students got the skills they needed and workers were invested
in retraining, a clear attempt to navigate the decade-long downward pressure on
livelihoods for nonprofessional workers. The report called for a greater focus on
math, reading, science, and technology; higher expectations and more rigorous
standards; enhanced instructional time in the schools; and recruiting and retain-
ing better teachers by setting higher standards and providing performance-based
pay. Importantly, in a stark departure from Reagan's vision of dismantling the

federal presence in education, the commission also called for greater fiscal support to make these changes: "The Federal Government has the *primary responsibility* to identify the national interest in education. It should also help fund and support efforts to protect and promote that interest."[21]

In sum, though Reagan sought to reduce federal support for education, his administration through *ANAR* both sustained and heightened the growing bipartisan consensus that education could solve the nation's economic problems. Though the report recommended buttressing the nation's human capital stock, the premise had shifted from that of the NDEA back in the 1950s, which was based on the notion that total human capital advanced the collective goals of the United States during the Cold War. The myth asserted by *ANAR* certainly followed the premise that the collective education level of the nation was important, but primarily because it would facilitate individual opportunities to access sustainable jobs. As the Reagan administration cut into the social welfare state, such a narrative became all the more important. Indeed, the conclusions of *ANAR* fit perfectly with Reaganism because it blamed government and American workers for their own "deficiencies," even if those deficiencies supposedly represented the product of poor schools.

Though it was the most prominent, *ANAR* was not the only arena for this argument. Other education reports, such as the Twentieth Century Fund's *Making the Grade* (which came out the same week as *ANAR*) and the Committee on Economic Development's *Action for Excellence*, made similar arguments about the necessity of improving education.[22] Surprisingly, Albert Shanker of the AFT seconded *ANAR*'s call to improve public education. The union president, who had sought to temper criticisms of public education in the 1970s, agreed in 1983 that the *ANAR* report was right, and the nation's schools needed serious reform. Shanker further argued that teacher unions should work with business, particularly since he believed the necessity of a more educated workforce made improving schools imperative. Doing so would also prevent businesses from supporting dramatic moves like vouchers, Shanker believed, and with union support, greater consensus around the importance of education outlined in *ANAR* would prevent more federal budget cuts from the Reagan administration.

In fact, Shanker even argued teachers should "rise to the challenge of corporate willingness to spend billions more on education provided that there are improvements." And, presaging George H.W. Bush's national conversation about education in Charlottesville in 1989, Shanker, in 1983, called for a "national summit" of business and education leaders to determine how to improve public education.[23] According to historian Richard Kahlenberg, Shanker's intervention in support of *ANAR* was "pivotal" in elevating public consensus for the document's argument, and it influenced other union leaders like the NEA's Bob Chase, who would, a decade later, push the nation's other union to embrace education reform and collaboration with business too.[24]

But in the early 1980s, the NEA stood out in its opposition to the findings of *ANAR*, seeing the recommendations instead, in the words of one historian, "as a continuation and intensification of the Republican attacks on public schools and public teachers."[25] Representing a clear alternative to the calls to link the downward pressure on workers with the supposed deficiencies of the American education system, the NEA at the time responded to the proliferation of these dire education reports by rejecting the notion that public education should serve the interests of job training. In July 1983, the NEA's national representative assembly formed a Blue-Ribbon Task Force on Educational Excellence, which issued a report in the wake of *ANAR* entitled, "Open Letter to America on Schools, Students, and Tomorrow" (1984). While the union welcomed calls to improve public education, the teachers laid out an agenda that refuted the assumptions of *A Nation at Risk*. The letter pointed to the necessity of building a robust public education system that taught students to be good citizens and held high standards without resorting to calls to reduce student outcomes to job readiness. While the NEA report pointed out there would certainly be new technologies in the future, they should be thought of as new opportunities for learning, not threats to the livelihoods of working people. In fact, the report pointed out that in 2001, not only would Americans be able to "return to school to learn new work skills. They will also find myriad opportunities in schools to enrich their lives outside of work."

The "Open Letter to America" called for students to become "active participants in the learning process" and for schools to coordinate a systematic response to students facing trauma from poverty or drug abuse. "Children whose families are going through crisis cannot devote their full attention to instruction," the letter pointed out, calling on schools to be at the center of guaranteeing social services: "Local governments [should] coordinate badly needed health and welfare services for our students through the school." Further, eschewing merit pay, the report instead called for "the proportionate across-the-board salary increases all teachers need and deserve" to be treated as professionals.[26]

The Political Economy of Reaganism

While furthering the myth that improving education could help Americans thrive in a leaner economy, the Reagan administration also helped to make that economy significantly leaner. Perhaps most important, Reagan accelerated efforts on the right—from both corporations and conservative politicians—to weaken unions. In 1981, members of the Professional Air Traffic Controllers Organization (PATCO), a union that had endorsed Reagan, walked off the job over salaries that had been eroded by inflation and to improve working conditions. Consistent with a similar critique he made of striking Los Angeles teachers in 1970 as governor of California, President Reagan fired and replaced them.[27] Reagan's actions in 1981 motivated private-sector employers, such as Greyhound Bus Lines and Eastern Airlines, to use striker replacement as a tactic to reduce worker power too.[28]

The "Reagan recession" of 1981–82 caused unemployment to spike into double digits, as the president accepted an economic downturn to fight inflation by keeping interest rates high. How much the effort actually reduced inflation is debatable; prices stabilized in part because of shifts in global oil prices. Nevertheless, inflation declined, and the economy grew in the 1980s. Much of this growth, however, was not due to increases in productivity but in financial services and the proliferation of credit. Reagan's economy was characterized by deregulating banking and the emergence of new forms of financial transactions in which investors leveraged debt to take charge of productive assets, extract value—often by laying off workers and/or reducing labor costs—and then sell them for a profit.[29] Tax cuts combined with cuts to social services significantly increased the wealth gap between the very rich and the very poor.[30]

States like Wisconsin, which had a disproportionate amount of stable, blue-collar jobs, fared the worst, as Reaganism exacerbated trends already underway in the 1970s. Wisconsin's economy comprised about 36 percent manufacturing in 1963, a number that declined to 33 percent by 1977, and fell even further to 28 percent by 1986. These jobs were replaced by service-sector jobs that paid significantly less and were much less likely to have a union.[31]

In fact, a strike at Briggs and Stratton illustrates the impact of Reaganomics and its war on social democracy following a decade in which Democrats at the national level failed to advance meaningful industrial policies capable of supporting blue-collar jobs. In 1983, Briggs and Stratton, a highly profitable small-engine manufacturer based in Milwaukee, leveraged the wave of concession bargaining occurring in manufacturing outfits across the United States in the early 1980s and trumped-up fears about Japanese competition to demand workers accept a wage freeze, a two-tier wage system, and to subcontract work to nonunion contractors. Briggs and Stratton provoked a strike and began moving jobs to a non-union factory in Georgia. In the ensuing years, workers continued to make even deeper concessions, but the company further shifted production to the south and to Mexico anyway. After years of exploiting loose credit policies to acquire other companies and buy back stock rather than invest in new research and development, the company enriched its executives and shareholders. Its two factories in

Milwaukee's North Side, which provided jobs to a number of African American workers, were shuttered, and the company finally declared bankruptcy in 2020.[32]

One social service Reagan was willing to invest in during this time, however, was job training, furthering fictions that American workers could do better for themselves just by getting the right human capital. Reagan's vision of government sought to limit access to higher education to stanch the growth of the professional class: first as governor of California where he sought to diminish public investment in the state's generous system of higher education and as president by limiting federal investment in Pell grants and student loans. Indeed, Reagan clearly sought to stoke the resentments Bell foresaw in 1976 and that the Carter administration made worse.

But Reagan was willing to invest in nonacademic job training. The much-diminished Humphrey-Hawkins Act had set federal goals for unemployment and provided the government, at least in theory, with some limited tools to meet those goals. Reagan, however, believed the government should play even less of a role in creating jobs than Carter had. When he came into office, CETA had already been reauthorized until 1982. The program funded almost 750,000 public service jobs in 1978 and despite cuts pushed by the Carter administration, still provided about 400,000 when Reagan was inaugurated. The new president hoped to quietly eliminate CETA's funding for public service jobs when the law expired. The high unemployment rate of the Reagan recession (rising from 7 percent in January 1981 to over 10 percent by the end of 1982), however, forced Reagan to do something to show he was helping Americans acquire jobs.[33]

For Reagan, and for the business community that supported him, fictions that federal support for job training would significantly reduce unemployment replaced even the vestigial promise of a jobs policy that existed at the end of the Carter administration. As economist Gordon Lafer has shown, job-training policy before Reagan constituted merely a "minor backwater of federal employment policy." After working with Congress to pass the Job Training Partnership Act (JTPA), in 1982, however, "the administration of President Ronald Reagan explicitly replaced job *creation* with job *training* as the focus of federal employment policy."[34]

JTPA passed Congress with wide majorities in both houses in 1982. The bill promised short-term job training to more than one million workers at the low-wage end of the job market. Empowering local business councils to decide how to spend training funds, it would ultimately lead to about $3 billion in spending each year from 1984 through 1998.[35] The premise of the JTPA was fundamentally flawed, however, and in reality, did very little to improve the livelihoods of working people. This stagnation occurred not because workers lacked skills, but

because during the 1980s employers were able to pay substandard wages (sometimes assisted by stoking fears of shifting jobs overseas), unions were weaker, and
racial discrimination continued unchecked.[36]

Though Reagan's economic agenda departed in some dramatic ways from
postwar liberalism, the fundamental assumptions around job training were not
all that different from those embedded in the Great Society. Indeed, as had been
one of the central assumptions of the War on Poverty, poverty and unemployment to Reagan were explained by the individual deficiencies of workers. The
president's argument, however, removed the Great Society's limited recognition
that structures existed that might make it difficult for those with fewer resources
to access good jobs and, as a consequence, that the poorest Americans should
have a safety net. Instead, focusing on job training allowed politicians to convey
the "unlikely hope," in Lafer's words, "that poverty can be ended without conflict."
Reagan's JTPA, indeed, helped to shoehorn nonacademic job training into the
education myth too.[37]

Conservative Protectors of the Nation

Reagan's political economic vision was, rhetorically at least, tied to reinstill-
ing pride in American nationalism. The administration had no interest in any
national industrial strategy of the kind called for by Magaziner and Reich that
might have facilitated broad prosperity for Americans in a more competitive
global economy. Reagan, however, argued that the GOP would restore American
power and national pride in a changing world. Particularly after the humiliating
limits on the nation's previously unfettered international standing in the 1970s—
including the fall of Saigon and the global energy shocks caused by petroleum
exporting nations in the Middle East—Carter's volitional cession of American
power further opened space for Reagan's argument. In particular, Carter's failure
to bring home fifty-two American hostages following the Iranian Revolution in
1979 loomed large, as did even his signature success as president. Indeed, the
Panama Canal treaty in 1978, for which Senate ratification likely came with the
high price of losing labor reform, was met with disapproval from Reagan, who
had made the negotiation into a major campaign issue in his challenge to Ford
in the 1976 primary.[38] After it was ratified, Reagan portrayed the treaty as one of
many examples of the decline of American exceptionalism, only this time perpetrated willingly by Democrats. On the campaign trail in 1980, he often employed
some version of the line "We bought it, we paid for it, it's ours, and we should
tell [Omar] Torrijos [the leader of Panama] and company that we are going to
keep it."[39]

It is no surprise, then, that, even while cutting budgets, Reagan's vision for restoring American nationalism included the public education system. He found an enthusiastic advocate for this effort in conservative Catholic William Bennett, whom Reagan appointed to head the Department of Education following Bell's resignation in 1985. Bennett, after earning a Ph.D. in philosophy from the University of Texas and a J.D. from Harvard Law, was hired as a professor and assistant to John Silber, the conservative president of Boston University. In 1981, Reagan appointed him chair of the National Endowment for the Humanities (NEH) before elevating him to secretary of education four years later.[40] A Democrat at the time of his appointment, Bennett, like Reagan, was driven by the fear that liberal permissiveness threatened the American values that had made the nation exceptional. He believed revitalizing those values, which stemmed from America's emergence from the Western Christian and enlightenment tradition, would strengthen American nationalism.

A key part of this argument centered on the fiction that the United States was defined by the ideal of colorblindness. In fact, Bennett's most highly publicized effort at the helm of the NEH was to refuse to comply with a directive from the Equal Employment Opportunity Commission (EEOC) to set goals for more women and minority hires. In a letter to EEOC chairperson Clarence Thomas, Bennett argued, "It was the glory of America to proclaim to the world: all men are created equal. . . . Blindness to color, race, and national origin is the hallmark of civilized justice as embodied in the principles of this Republic."[41]

Here Bennett's argument fit within a broader strategy by some conservative elites to arrest the development of multiracial democracy in the 1970s. The growing culture wars around issues of affirmative action and racial inclusivity, for instance, emerged at just the time when many middle- and working-class Americans were expecting a more democratic politics and economy that could truly make progress toward eliminating racial inequality. Bennett's argument for safeguarding the legacy of American "culture" by deepening the nation's commitment to the humanities in higher education appears not to be directly linked to the service of stifling the economic demands of working Americans. Still, Bennett's time heading the NEH corresponded with the continued growth of corporate "business consciousness" and the empowerment of free-market think tanks and conservative politicians like Reagan who helped the already wealthy at the expense of working people. Using culture as a wedge to divide Americans by race and class, as Bennett did, certainly helped the political economic goals of the right.[42]

Bennett's intellectual project, then, beginning with the NEH and ramping up as secretary of education, was to restore nationalism by pushing Americans to connect their identity to the supposedly timeless values of the Western tradition.

Indeed, Bennett sought to revitalize study of the classics and as chair of NEH, castigated left liberal professors for politicizing the humanities.[43] Bennett appeared to truly believe Americans' commitment to their nation would be improved with a common cultural appreciation, even if such a call was tone-deaf, or even outrightly hostile, to the inclusion of minorities. He reportedly argued that "the greatest advances in the humanities have already been made" between ancient Greek history and the Renaissance and saw little place for work that wasn't done by white men. Stemming from this premise, the NEH during Bennett's years at the helm significantly reduced grants to fields in Black studies and women's studies.[44]

As chair of NEH, Bennett also oversaw a series of meetings with higher education faculty (which included Silber and conservative education professor Checker Finn) on undergraduate instruction in the Humanities. This work led to a published assessment by Bennett entitled, "To Reclaim a Legacy: A Report on the Humanities in Higher Education." As the title suggests, Bennett argued that "the humanities, and particularly the study of Western civilization, have lost their central place in the undergraduate curriculum." He lamented both the plummeting decline of humanities majors and that most undergraduates received a degree without studying ancient Greece and Rome. For these developments, Bennet blamed "a failure of nerve and faith on the part of many college faculties and administrators." In the 1970s, many colleges and universities had shifted more programs toward professional fields as students viewed them as increasingly necessary to find a sustainable job. Bennett clearly sought to defend Western civilization from the perils of the professional class, while not understanding that students were choosing professional degrees because of the growing difficulty of finding good jobs without them. Nevertheless, Bennett suggested that "study of the humanities and Western civilization must take its place at the heart of the college curriculum."[45] Bennett's report received a good deal of attention as one of the most prominent in a series of similar arguments by conservatives in the 1980s, such as Allan Bloom's *The Closing of the American Mind*, which also criticized universities for cultural relativism and shifting away from the classics that, when refracted through the great American thinkers, had supposedly formed the genesis of national greatness.[46]

Bennett, therefore, was a perfect appointment for Reagan, who often mobilized historical examples of American exceptionalism to tout individual initiative and conservative values while justifying diminishing government services for the poor. In this way, the war on the livelihoods of most working people continued apace. In higher education, Bennett followed the lead of Reagan, who had ignited his political career by arguing that university faculty and students represented a threat to American values during his 1966 run for governor of California.[47] Upon leading the Department of Education, Bennett became, in the words of one historian, "an unofficial minister of morals, calling for more personal responsibility, higher standards, and improved test scores."[48]

As Bennett framed it very early in his tenure as secretary, he sought to advance "three C's" in American education: Content, Character, and Choice, which he described in a series of speeches during his first year in office. Though he never directly criticized the premise of *A Nation at Risk*, Bennett argued that American education needed more than just enhanced instruction in math and reading. In fact, the education secretary overtly argued that skills were not enough for American workers to get good jobs. On the contrary, he believed the education system should discipline future workers, many of whom saw a much leaner opportunity for economic security in the Reagan years. Just as Mann highlighted how public education made workers more docile as early as the 1840s, Bennett argued that "evidence shows that when recent high school graduates fail in their jobs, it's usually not for lack of skills. They usually get fired because of poor work attitudes and habits, tardiness, and undependability." Bennett thus concluded that to ready new generations for the job market, schools should teach students "a sense of honor, independence, degrees of thoughtfulness, fidelity to task and to people, kindness, honesty, respect for the law, diligence, fairness, standards of right and wrong, and self-discipline."[49]

Further, the humanities were crucial in understanding why Americans should take pride in their nation. In another speech from 1985, he chastised schools for teaching a superficial version of American history: "Too often our high school graduates know too little or nothing of the Magna Carta or even the Bible, the Greek polis, the Federalist papers, or of the Lincoln-Douglas debates." He went on to excoriate "cultural relativism": "If all traditions are equally valid, then there is clearly not much point in transmitting a *particular* cultural heritage, a *distinctive* set of social and political values." Bennett believed, by contrast, there were timeless American values that were diminished when the history of those Americans who were never able to fully access their rights as citizens were included.[50]

Bennett, also like Mann in the 1840s, understood education as advancing a particular vision of the nation, and one that could discipline unruly workers and political critics alike. Unlike Mann, though, Bennett did not seek to compel Americans to attend public schools. Over the course of his four years as secretary, Bennett sought to bestow on Americans the means to choose private schools. By advocating for various forms of vouchers, Bennett sought to further "common values."[51] Bennett, however, never seemed to grasp the irony of attempting to restore a common American culture by undermining the institution perhaps most responsible for encouraging that culture in the nineteenth and twentieth centuries. By the late 1980s the most successful arguments for the conservative human capital mythology around vouchers connected education to economic opportunity. The education secretary, interestingly, did not make an economic argument for school choice, however. The best argument for vouchers, for Bennett, was to allow parents to "choose . . . schools where their own values will be extended instead of lost."[52]

Given Bennett's place in the administration and his push for a conservative version of American history, it is unsurprising that he left the Democratic Party in 1986, viewing the GOP instead as the party that would protect American values.[53] Bennett believed in and advanced a version of civic nationalism that was consistent with the conservative economic position of Reagan Republicans. For Bennett, nostalgic fictions about America as a color-blind, classless society in which opportunity could be had by all fit neatly into Reagan's economic argument. Importantly, conservative Republicans like Bennett made this forceful case for culturally strengthening the nation at a time when Democrats had begun to cede the idea that the American tradition meant social democratic interventions to improve people's lives and instead began to fully embrace the global economic race to attain human capital.

The Democrats: Neo-Liberals Rising

Over the course of the 1980s, the Democratic Party was thoroughly remade. In spite of Carter's dramatic defeat in 1980 after shifting away from the social democratic center of the postwar era, a growing number of Democrats took the lesson from Reagan's victory that Americans were supposedly moving right, particularly on economic questions. The ascendant education myth thus represented the linchpin of their new vision for giving working people a crack at economic security in a more competitive world.

This wave of Democrats formed the foundation of what journalist Randall Rothenberg, in 1984, called "neo-liberals."[54] Not reducible to the growing "neoliberal" wave of politics, economics, and intellectual theory that has become essential in understanding the seismic shifts in American and global society since the 1970s, the neo-liberals who emerged in the Democratic Party in the late 1970s and early 1980s were part of that trajectory.[55] Rothenberg counted among them Democrats who were some of the most important leaders in Congress, statehouses, and on the perennial shortlist of presidential candidates in the 1980s: Colorado senator Gary Hart, Massachusetts senator Paul Tsongas, New Jersey senator Bill Bradley, Missouri representative Dick Gephardt, Tennessee representative Al Gore, California governor Jerry Brown, North Carolina governor James Hunt, and Governor Michael Dukakis of Massachusetts. Among the intellectuals Rothenberg listed were Charles Peters, founder of the *Washington Monthly*, and Robert Reich, then a lecturer at Harvard. These neo-liberals believed in stronger investment in defense and opposed "interest group politics" and bureaucracy in the name of economic growth. In short, they were "prepared to leave the mechanism of the New Deal behind."[56]

A central aspect of their growth agenda was entrepreneurial creativity. As Peters argued in an influential piece in the *Washington Monthly*, "Economic growth . . . is essential to almost everything else we want to achieve. Our hero is the risk-taking entrepreneur who creates better jobs and better products."[57] Hart, Brown, Bradley, Gephardt, and others were sometimes called "Atari Democrats" because of their support for a burgeoning "information" economy built on entrepreneurial activity, new technology, and knowledge.[58] To turn the page on Rooseveltian social democracy would require new "human capital," and government should invest in education, but only if the investment was subject to market forces. As Peters argued, "We aren't against government, period, as . . . many conservatives appear to be. But we are against a fat, sloppy and smug bureaucracy. We want a government that can fire people who can't or won't do the job. And that includes teachers. Far too many public school teachers are simply incompetent." Writing in the wake of *ANAR*, Peters concluded, "Public schools have to be made better, much better, if we are to compete economically with other technologically advanced countries, if we are to have more Route 128s [in suburban Massachusetts] and Silicon Valleys." To ensure supposed equality of opportunity for people of color, a growing obsession of the Democrats who wanted to shift the party to the right, schools were crucial: "The urban public schools have in fact become the principal instrument of class oppression in America, keeping the lower orders in their place while the upper class sends its children to private schools."[59]

Rothenberg argued that neo-liberals were set apart from other Democrats because they recognized the "postindustrial economy is 'human-capital intensive,' meaning that the rapid pace of industrial change demands not workers skilled at single repetitive tasks, but workers with the knowledge, education, and ability to adapt to a variety of tasks as the needs of industry shift." Neo-liberals thus sought out new methods for using government investment to satisfy the needs of employers for human capital. For example, Brown worked to spur development in Silicon Valley, Dukakis along the Route 128 corridor outside Boston, and Hunt the North Carolina research triangle, while "traditional liberals" had focused their efforts on older urban areas.[60]

Neo-liberals sought to make education more responsive to market forces by experimenting with ideas like using private-industry employees as teachers and merit pay in the public schools. In contrast to what they viewed as the low expectations of JTPA, they also sought retraining programs that would give adult workers skin in the game and thus more tangible rewards by adding new skills. Neo-liberal economist Pat Choate, for example, developed a plan for "Individual Training Accounts"—modeled on Individual Retirement Accounts—jointly financed by contributions from employees and employers, which would only pay off for workers when they received training that bore fruit in higher wages.[61] Whereas conservatives in the GOP wanted to keep education costs down in order to finance tax reductions, neo-liberals wanted to spend money, but only if it would lead to economic growth by providing workers the skills new businesses desired.

The most important of these Democrats was Gary Hart. Hart's high-profile campaign for the presidential nomination in 1984 and in 1988 (before revelations of an extramarital affair forced him out of the latter race) put his views squarely in the national political mainstream. Further, of everyone in the group, Hart was best able to articulate a vision for a future built on entrepreneurialism, a renewed emphasis on market forces, and investment in human capital.

In his 1983 book *A New Democracy*, for instance, Hart painted a picture of a country whose citizens were wracked by economic insecurity, but he argued the problem was bigger than taming inflation and limiting government: "The United States has increasingly become part of an international economy. We are no longer self-sufficient, nor the undisputed leader. New actors on the world stage influence American economic conditions to a degree that is unprecedented, and to many of us, disquieting." The key to succeeding in such a world was recognizing the path forward would come "not through simple solutions nor through sheer power but primarily through creative use of our ingenuity and inventiveness—and by working together."[62] Here was an optimistic vision of American renewal to rival Reagan's. If Americans just got on the right side of the learning curve, they could all be winners in the new global capitalism.

Hart, anticipating the argument George H.W. Bush and Bill Clinton would make in support of the North American Free Trade Agreement (NAFTA), welcomed a competition in which he believed Americans would thrive when trade barriers were removed. Paralleling the conclusions of *ANAR*, Hart believed Americans would excel in this competition as long as education was deployed properly: "Fundamentally . . . we need a new employment strategy that invests in our human assets to obtain the highest and most productive return for the economy, the nation, and the workers themselves."[63]

Also, as with *ANAR*, Hart paid lip service to the importance of education in developing good citizens, but when it came to federal investment, he clearly prioritized the technical and scientific. For example, in *A New Democracy*, he cited his work authoring the American Defense Education Act in 1982, a clear attempt to leverage the notoriety of the 1958 National Defense Education Act.

The bill was designed to "provide incentives and support to schools that, first, set targets for improving the instruction they offer in mathematics, the sciences, communications skills, foreign languages, and technology, and second, meet the goals they have established."[64] Here, Hart had the strong backing of the NEA, which invoked similar arguments to *ANAR* about the importance of technology.[65] An NEA policy paper predating the publication of *ANAR* from February 1983 argued, "We face the dawn of a new century, a period accompanied by the most profound changes that our nation and the world have yet to see. We are part of one of the deepest, yet perhaps most subtle, revolutions in the history of the human race—brought on by the continuing wave of technological innovation." In words that could have been lifted directly from *ANAR*, the paper argued NDEA was necessary to "prepare U.S. citizens to ride the crest of this wave of technology into the future. [Doing so] remains our best hope for maintaining our stature as a nation and as a world leader."[66]

Hart further cited his support for Senator Paul Tsongas's High Technology Morrill Act to pair federal investment with contributions from state governments and businesses to increase the numbers of science and engineering degrees from American universities. Tsongas's bill, which assumed an international competition with other nations that prioritized "the relationship between education and economic growth" consciously invoked the Morrill Act as "a useful model for fusing the interests of government, industry, and education into a national policy for economic growth."[67] Hart also endorsed Choate's ITA proposal.[68] Though the Colorado senator inveighed against the "simple solutions" of Reaganism—specifically he slammed supply-side economics as a "quick fix"—his own brand of entrepreneur-driven capitalism was similarly built on easy choices: simply invest smartly in the education of America's working people, and nothing would need to be done to upset the nation's social, political, or economic structure.

The 1984 presidential primary provided Hart the platform to push the Democratic Party toward an embrace of neo-liberal ideas. Former Minnesota senator Walter Mondale, who had been Carter's vice president (and was selected as a running mate in 1976 in part because of his high regard by labor unions and the traditional New Deal coalition), was the front-runner. Civil rights activist and social democrat Jesse Jackson also entered the race. Hart, with strong showings in New Hampshire and Iowa, ascended to join Mondale and Jackson as one of the three major candidates. Mondale ended up easily winning enough delegates for nomination, but his cumulative popular vote margin over Hart's was small (about 38 percent to 36 percent).

Though the social democrats Mondale and Jackson combined to win a large majority of Democratic voters, Hart's campaign made a major impact on the party. Indeed, the Colorado senator set up a dynamic in which he framed his ideas in *A New Democracy* as a fresh contrast to the Mondale campaign. (Mondale had sought to undermine this framing by asking, famously, "Where's the beef?") In a debate in Chicago, featuring a physical copy of the book from which Hart read and Mondale criticized, the former slammed the latter for playing the politics of "old agendas and old arrangements." Jackson, by contrast, prioritized the "25,000 in this sub-zero weather homeless tonight and 600,000 malnourished" in Chicago, arguing for an "industrial policy that makes sense" to solve the problems of poverty and unemployment.

Hart, in response to a question about how his presidency would help African Americans, highlighted his shift from the postwar social democratic promise of the Democratic Party, arguing for an entrepreneurial fix to racial inequality. "I have put forward proposals, as I have for this entire economy, that seek to open up economic opportunity in the future, particularly for those young Blacks getting into our economy," Hart argued. "If I have the chance ... to say that the issue in the 1980s is not whether Rosa Parks rides in the front or back of the bus but whether her son can own and operate the bus company, then I think I will get my share, or more, of the Black votes." Under questioning from a *Jet Magazine* reporter about high unemployment rates for African Americans, Hart answered with a pitch for urban enterprise zones and human capital investment, characterizing himself as a "strong proponent of a whole range of new education and training initiatives, including individual training accounts for all workers, including Blacks, and the ADEA, that would increase educational investment across the board, including urban schools."[69]

In the end, Reagan handily won the general election in 1984 with almost 59 percent of the popular vote and a massive electoral college majority. Mondale only won his home state and Washington, DC. Opposite Reagan's enormous advantage of being an incumbent in an economy entering a period of growth, Mondale faced an insurmountable challenge. While Democrats lost sixteen seats in the House, however, they still maintained a huge majority of seventy-one seats and picked up two Senate seats. These circumstances left it unclear whether voters were truly rejecting a broad version of social democracy, but for some party insiders, that was the clear lesson they took from Mondale's massive defeat.

The formation of the Democratic Leadership Council (DLC) in 1985 represented the most important development in this shift following Reagan's reelection. Al From, a former congressional staffer, founded the DLC to push the center of the Democratic Party toward a new electoral coalition focused on "ideas, not constituency groups." Never a grassroots organization, the DLC was comprised of party insiders and elected officials and was backed almost exclusively by wealthy donors solicited by its elected official members. Its initial base of elected officials from the South and the West (Al Gore from Tennessee and Arizona governor Bruce Babbitt, for instance, were important early figures), the DLC hoped to recapture voters who had supported Reagan in 1980 and 1984. Like the more loosely organized neo-liberals, the DLC would focus its energy on pushing the party toward "sustained economic growth, equal and expanding opportunity and the aggressive defense of freedom with the promotion of democratic values abroad."[70]

If that agenda sounds like a more palatable version of Reagan conservatism, that's because it was. (Social democrats like Jackson and Iowa senator Tom Harkin, for example, would employ that exact critique as a pejorative.)[71] The key idea that distinguished the DLC agenda from Reagan conservatism, in fact, was education: that by investing in human capital, all Americans could have the chance to prosper in the global economy. As From remembered it, the "party's first imperative was to revive the American economic opportunity by fostering broad-based economic growth led by a robust private sector generating high-skill, high-wage jobs. . . . Government's proper role is to foster private sector growth and to equip every American with the opportunities and skills that he or she needs to succeed in the private economy, not to pick 'winners' and 'losers,' and not just to redistribute wealth."[72] Beginning in 1985, then, the DLC began to recruit "New Democrats"—often from Sunbelt states where voters had been abandoning the party—and pushing for an economic growth agenda built around free trade and investment in human capital.[73]

From 1985 to 1988, the DLC did not push too hard, trying to avoid contention that might cost Democrats elections and instead worked to alter the rules in the party primaries to favor southern candidates like Gore. In fact, we have the DLC largely to thank for the southern-heavy composition of "Super Tuesday" that persists to this day.[74]

Though Jackson's strong showing in the South in the 1988 primary highlighted the continuing purchase of social democratic ideas in the party, the central ideas of the DLC, nevertheless, were on the rise. Though Massachusetts governor Dukakis was not connected to the DLC, he won the nomination in 1988 largely on the strength of the growing suburban knowledge workers in the Democratic Party. Indeed, though Dukakis was derided on the right as a "Massachusetts liberal," his support for public-private investment in technology, human capital, and welfare reform symbolized not the old politics of New Deal labor-liberalism but the continued shift of the Democratic Party toward the interests of postindustrial knowledge workers and the growing myth that economic opportunity stemmed from one's ability to acquire the right kind of human capital in a meritocratic competition.[75]

Nevertheless, Dukakis's dramatic defeat by Reagan's vice president George H.W. Bush—an enormous lead for the Massachusetts governor dissipated over just a few months as the Bush campaign portrayed Dukakis as soft on crime—led the DLC to take a much more adversarial stance toward the Democratic Party. William Galston and Elaine Kamarck (who had worked for Gore and for Babbitt, respectively), argued that, in spite of the fact that Democrats had gained seats in Congress in 1988, Dukakis's defeat showed the party was outside the American mainstream. Unsubtly titled *The Politics of Evasion*, their statement argued for cultivating middle-income voters by moving right: "The next nominee . . . must squarely reflect the moral sentiments of average Americans; and he must offer a progressive economic message, based on the values of upward mobility and individual effort, that can unite the interests of those already in the middle class with those struggling to get there."[76]

In short, the lesson DLC Democrats took from the 1988 election was to more vigorously push toward targeted government intervention that would facilitate the competition of working people in the global economy. It presumed that those (disproportionately white) workers who had made it into the "middle class" deserved to do so, and that somehow those struggling to get there could do so with more "effort." The obvious contradiction was that it would be impossible for everyone to move up in such a competition. By the end of the 1980s, however, DLC Democrats were not the only group to hunt political points by employing the education myth. Seeking to develop an identity that would distinguish him from the callousness of Reagan conservatism, former vice president Bush sought to harness the power of the ascendant myth for Republicans.

"WHAT YOU EARN DEPENDS ON WHAT YOU LEARN"

Education Presidents, Education Governors, and Human Capital Rising

While Reagan's presidency shrunk the promise of American social democracy, it did not arrest the growth of the notion that investing in education could serve the alchemical purpose of ensuring all Americans had the equal opportunity to compete in an uncertain world. As the Democratic Party shifted right, employing education as the means to arm working Americans with the skills to compensate for the government interventions that would no longer be there, some Republicans like George H.W. Bush sought to show their education bona fides too. Supporting public education allowed Bush to separate himself from the hard-hearted approach of Reagan while cultivating a conservative version of the education myth. Indeed, Bush was responding to the fact that public education had grown as a political concern for Americans, particularly in the years after *A Nation at Risk* and myriad other reports asserted the system was in decline. The 1988 campaign, in fact, was the first in American history to have a primary debate (there was one for each party in fact) solely on education. Dukakis could tout his experience with education reform as governor of Massachusetts, and Bush sought to counter it by prioritizing human capital on the campaign trail.

At a New Hampshire high school in January 1988, Bush proclaimed, "I want to be the Education President. I want to lead a renaissance of quality in our schools."[1] Elsewhere, splicing together Lyndon Johnson's assumptions about education and the clarion call of *ANAR*, Bush asserted, "I believe as I look into the future—our ability to compete around the world, our ability to solve the problems of poverty that are unsolved in this country . . . whatever it is, education has got to be the priority. Better schools mean better jobs."[2]

Bush had run as an establishment Republican against Reagan in 1980, famously referring to the Gipper's supply-side fantasies as "voodoo economics." After winning the primary, Reagan added Bush to the ticket that year for ideological balance. More conservative Republicans continued to be skeptical of Bush in 1988, and he had had to move to the right on abortion and evangelical Christianity in order to win the nomination.[3] Still, on a number of issues, he remained more moderate than Reagan, and with heavily racist undertones, he attacked Dukakis for permitting a "revolving door" policy on crime. Bush easily defeated the Massachusetts Democrat by 7 percentage points in the popular vote and a large majority in the electoral college (426–111). Initiating the push for national standards, Bush as president helped to further advance the idea that human capital through education represented the means for American workers to find opportunity and, if they succeeded, security, in a globalizing world. Given the increasing characterization of education as a commodity, it is not a surprise that more conservative political figures than Bush also, for the first time, successfully won market-based education reforms like vouchers. In Wisconsin, Governor Tommy Thompson developed the latter policy in concert with civil rights activists in 1989. This reform leaned on the education myth to do the work of building consent for school choice: its proponents argued that the connection between education and economic opportunity was too important—particularly for communities who had been locked out of good jobs—to deny parents a choice.

Democrats, however, were best equipped to employ the education myth for political gain. The DLC became much more politically assertive after 1988, and its most important figure, Arkansas governor Bill Clinton, was the nation's single loudest purveyor of the education myth. Clinton's coronation as chair of the DLC in 1990 represented the culmination of a major shift in the Democratic Party. In a more globally integrated America, Clinton and other new Democrats believed American working people could no longer hope good blue-collar jobs would come back, and it was folly to even try to protect them. Instead, they should embrace change, and one of government's most important roles would be to ensure everyone had a fair shake, without any guarantees, in the world economy.

Indeed, during his career as governor of Arkansas and on the campaign trail in 1992, Clinton consciously turned his back on political support for those Americans who sought blue-collar livelihoods.[4] To even attempt to credibly advance such a move, however, Democrats like Clinton had to argue they could ensure public education functioned better. Schools, they believed, had to respond to market forces by meeting the needs of employers for more skilled workers in a meritocratic economy increasingly centered on "knowledge." As had earlier efforts at federal education policy such as ESEA, the agenda of Clinton and the DLC used education and other social policies to overcome supposed "deficiencies" that existed in those left behind by American capitalism. Clinton's campaign rhetoric, marked by the often-repeated phrase "What you earn depends on what you learn," highlighted the fact that by 1992, investing in public education and advancing the notion of meritocracy represented the central economic argument of the Democratic Party. Indeed, the social democratic alternatives FDR proposed in the Second Bill of Rights or those for which Randolph, Rustin, King, Humphrey, Hawkins, and Scott King had advocated in the 1960s and 1970s were increasingly absent from the party's political center.

From Charlottesville to America 2000

True to his campaign promise, President Bush made public education a rhetorical priority during his first year in office. In the years after *ANAR*, calls to make the American education system more competitive to enhance human capital for economic purposes had continued at a rapid pace. For example, the Committee for Economic Development, an organization comprised of business executives and educators, in 1985, pointed to "increasing evidence that education has a direct impact on employment, productivity, and growth, and on the nation's ability to compete in the world economy." The committee contrasted low graduation rates and the "lack of preparation for work" among those who did graduate against the higher graduation rates and science and math test scores of the Japanese.[5]

Workforce 2000 (1987), a futurist report based on the research of experts published by the conservative Hudson Institute, argued that the nation's new jobs would require more education. Funded by Reagan's Department of Labor, the study essentially advocated more focus on job preparation—both in and out of schools—which would purportedly make American workers more competitive. *Workforce 2000* predicted that the economy of the 1990s would be marked by relatively steady growth, a more diverse workforce, and a larger share of service jobs (a trend Daniel Bell had pointed to in *The Coming of Post-Industrial Society*). It would be pointless to try save manufacturing work, the report argued, and instead Americans should focus on training workers for jobs that required "much higher skills."[6]

The report called on the United States to continue its shift away from worrying about its share of world trade. Instead, *Workforce 2000* asserted American policymakers should work to improve overall economic growth, particularly in the Global South, while making the new service industries (in healthcare, education, retail, and government) in the United States more productive. To do these things, American policymakers needed to better tap the nation's human potential, making the workforce more inclusive by "reconcil[ing] the conflicting needs of women, work, and families" and "integrat[ing] Black and Hispanic workers fully into the economy." *Workforce 2000* rightly advocated for policies improving working conditions and benefits for women workers. As for integrating minorities excluded from the job market, however, the report continued the well-worn path of the Great Society, Reagan's job-training fantasies, and Hart's call for entrepreneurialism to argue that minorities needed "both cultural changes and education and training investments." Schools were vital, because "as the economy grows more complex and more dependent on human capital, the standards set by the American education system must be raised" by introducing more market competition.[7]

Economist Gary Becker also pointed out that in 1989, the diminished wages of young Americans by the end of the Reagan years had "stimulated renewed academic interest in the analysis of human capital." Giving the University of Chicago's Ryerson lecture in 1989, Becker asserted, without accounting for the downward pressure on wages from capital flight, lack of a jobs plan, or the concerted war against unions, that

> trends in the earnings of young persons in the United States provide good reason for concern about the preparation they are receiving. The trend has been disastrous for the 15 percent of all students and much larger percentage of inner-city blacks who fail to complete high school. Their real wage rates have fallen by more than 30 percent since the early 1970s. Whether because of school problems, family instability, or other forces, young people without a college education are not being adequately prepared for work in modern economies.[8]

Governors, particularly those leading southern states, also sought to make public education more responsive to the supposed needs of employers, assuming it would attract more business to their region. The National Governors Association (NGA), for instance, became a prominent proponent of the notion that improving education outcomes would, in the words of Tennessee governor Lamar Alexander, allow Americans to "meet stiff competition from workers in the rest of the world." That year, in fact, the NGA put into place an "action plan" creating seven task forces representing, in the words of one observer, "probably the most concentrated effort ever mobilized [in the NGA's history] for the improvement of education."[9] The next year, the NGA published a report entitled *Time for Results: The Governors 1991 Report on Education*, which pushed for higher standards for teachers and students, new technologies, and more efficient use of resources in schools.[10] In an appearance on *Meet the Press* to discuss American teaching practices, Alexander argued that state governments sought reforms because "this goes to the bottom line of every American family—will your paycheck be less in the '90s because we can't compete with Koreans who are ready to outdo us? I think the public is going to demand of us that we do it and the governors, I believe, are ready to push."[11]

Though the southern governors who supported this argument included Republicans like Alexander, prominent proponents also included DLC education reformers like Arkansas's Bill Clinton, South Carolina's Richard Riley, and North Carolina's Jim Hunt. (Clinton and Riley, for instance, had each chaired one of the NGA's task forces in 1987.) Clinton was the most prominent of a group of southern governors who consciously sought to employ what historian Brent Cebul has called "supply-side liberalism"—good fiscal stewardship and state-led postindustrial economic development—to move in the 1980s beyond the assumptions of the New Deal.[12] Education and human capital played a prominent role in that overarching vision.

President Bush believed the states were vital in improving America's schools and had pledged on the campaign trail to prioritize working with governors. Once in office, his administration organized a national education summit, held in September 1989 in Charlottesville, Virginia. For Bush, the purpose of the summit, just the third time in American a history a president had organized a meeting with the nation's governors, was twofold: cultivating an image as a prominent supporter of education and developing strategies for helping states improve education.

Democrats went into the summit seeking investment: Clinton, by then chair of the Democratic Governors Association, called for dramatically enhanced federal funding for education and saw reform as vital for the future of poor and minority students.[13] The NEA also argued for more federal education funding. Citing education cuts since Reagan took office, President Keith Geiger pointed out, "There is no issue more important to our nation's future than education. . . . Money will not cure every problem that ails education, but it is short-sighted to believe that the cure won't require any more money."[14]

At the summit, there was ample time built in for informal conversations, many of them shielded from the gaze of the media. The meeting featured six working groups, each of which was co-chaired by one Democratic and one Republican governor. The working groups included the topics of teaching and learning, governance, school choice, postsecondary education, and perhaps most important, "A Competitive Workforce and Life-Long Learning."[15] Employing assumptions pushed extensively since *ANAR*, the latter working group took as given that "as a nation we face the twin challenges of educating our youngsters in the latest technologies while encouraging our older workers to acquire new skills. We cannot afford a poorly trained workforce if we are to maintain our position of world leadership." The group called for businesses to partner with schools to ensure students had the right education for the supposed growing number of jobs requiring advanced learning, lauded the JTPA for providing valuable job training, and called on states to invest more of their funds in similar programs. It also proposed greater assessment of college graduates and for "strengthening the teaching of math, science, engineering, and increasing the number of graduates in these fields."[16]

The summit's conclusions, a joint statement by the president and the governors, framed future recommendations by calling for a set of national goals:

> As a Nation we must have an educated workforce, second to none, in order to succeed in an increasingly competitive world economy. Education has always been important, but never this important because the stakes have changed: Our competitors for opportunity are also working to educate their people. As they continue to improve, they make the future a moving target. We believe that the time has come, for the first time in U.S. History, to establish clear, national performance goals, goals that will make us internationally competitive.[17]

The next January, Bush, after working with the governors, announced six national education goals in his 1990 State of the Union address. In a speech that reflected on the winding down of the Cold War, the president asserted:

> In the tough competitive markets around the world, America faces great challenges and great opportunities. And we know that we can succeed in the global economic arena of the nineties, but to meet that challenge, we must make some fundamental changes—some crucial investment in ourselves.
>
> Yes, we are going to invest in America. This administration is determined to encourage the creation of capital, capital of all kinds: physical capital—everything from our farms and factories to our workshops and production lines, all that is needed to produce and deliver quality goods and quality services; intellectual capital—the source of ideas that spark tomorrow's products; and of course our human capital—the talented work force that we'll need to compete in the global market.
>
> Let me tell you, if we ignore human capital, if we lose the spirit of American ingenuity, the spirit that is the hallmark of the American worker, that would be bad.

Then after thanking Clinton and a handful of other governors, Bush called on the nation, by 2000, to ensure every student went to school "ready to learn"; every student was assessed at least once every four years; the high school graduation rate increased to 90 percent; the United States had the best students in the world in math and science; the nation's schools would be drug free; and most fantastically, that "every American adult [would] be a skilled, literate worker and citizen."[18] The next summer, the president and the NGA established a National Education Goals Panel, comprised of officials from the executive branch, six governors, and four congressional leaders, which would measure both the federal and state governments' progress.[19]

While Bush and the nation's governors did the most to advance the human capital imperative in the late 1980s and early 1990s, business interests did their part to further the notion that investing in education was necessary for workers to succeed in a competitive global economy. *Fortune* magazine, for instance, began hosting an annual summit on education beginning in 1988. The 1990 summit illustrates how businesses pushed for investment in individual human capital. Jim Hayes, publisher of the magazine, lauded Clinton for his work in advocating for public education before pointing out that "business executives are indeed taking a leadership position in the long-term revolution to save public education." Lamenting the decline of standards for students, Hayes argued that "corporate America is determined to find ways to help schools turn out a new generation of workers who can read, write, compute, and yes, think, if for no other reason than for pure survival."[20]

The evening's featured speaker, however, went even further. President of Brown University, Vartan Gregorian, placed the moment in the broader sweep of American history. Citing the support for education in the nineteenth century, Gregorian pointed out that "America placed its fate in the future by developing public schools for all. It did so in the belief that a better-educated citizenry would inevitably provide a stronger democratic society and a more prosperous one." Following the well-worn path of declension charted by *ANAR*, Gregorian fretted that the system now faced four challenges: "functional illiteracy, growth and explosion of knowledge and complexity of learning, a mismatch between skill and talent, and the decline of our public-school system." Because of the rapid shift of technology, "the age of industry . . . is yielding to the age of information. Technical knowledge becomes obsolete so quickly that one can no longer bank on the skills of a single specialty. What we need learn, therefore, is how to learn, ever over and over again."

Citing the leaders of Xerox and Apple Computers, in addition to the *Work-force 2000* report, Gregorian worried about the slow growth of the economy and pointed out that women, minorities, and immigrants were increasingly entering the American workforce, making it much more diverse than before. Specifically referring to the "new knowledge economy," Gregorian argued, "investing in science and engineering and having a well-educated technical and skilled work force is becoming a high national priority of our Nation." He then lauded the corporate leaders—Coca Cola, R.J. Nabisco, IBM, and GE, for example—taking it on themselves to invest their own money and "prestige" into pushing the American education system onto the right course. He concluded by calling for a "new form of alliance" between businesses and the nation's schools and universities to ensure students had the skills they needed to compete in this new global economy. Of course, Gregorian's argument said little about the necessity of higher minimum wages, more power for workers in the workplace, or social supports for those who could not make it in this more competitive world. But an argument that education was responsible for the problems inherent in the American economy was palatable to corporations and politicians alike because it meant little had to fundamentally change.[21]

By the end of 1990, Bush worried about his reelection prospects without a major political achievement in public education. He swapped out his education secretary Lauro Cavazos (a holdover from the Reagan administration who replaced Bennett in 1988) with Lamar Alexander. Alexander was an articulate public advocate for education reform, and in April 1991 he and Bush unveiled a plan called America 2000, which called for tests that governors could voluntarily adopt to measure progress toward the nation's education goals. It also proposed the New American Schools Development Corporation, to be led by business leaders to "generate innovation in education"; merit pay schemes for teachers; and report cards for states and school districts. Most controversially, the plan also called for private school vouchers. Congressional Republicans opposed the increased federal presence in education, while Democrats opposed both the voucher scheme and the proposal's limited fiscal investment. The bill that left the Democratic Congress conference committee rejected most of Bush's initial proposals, including vouchers, the business innovation corporation, and testing. The conference bill was filibustered in the Senate and died before reaching the president's desk.[22] While Bush failed to pass any major education reforms, by turning so much public attention to the schools, his four years in office did a good deal to strengthen the education myth, particularly since he was the most prominent Republican up to that point in American history to push it.

Vouchers for Human Capital

The movement to make schools "accountable" galvanized space for disruptive education reform efforts. Some of these reforms built on calls from far right, free-market conservatives to have schools compete in the same way private busi-nesses competed for sales or even in the way nations supposedly competed with each other in a zero-sum game for economic opportunities. Some of these plans continued Bennett's argument for choice, that families should choose schools that taught their preferred values, while others argued choice would ensure those who lacked opportunity could maximize it by shopping around for better educa-tion. The latter represented a rational response for parents who had been told for two decades that the acquisition of human capital would, as if by magic, make their children successful in a supposed economic meritocracy. By the end of the 1980s, this competition appeared to be even more critical as the possibility of other aspects of social democracy—such as public-sector jobs, union representa-tion, and under Reagan, in particular, social services—had been stripped away. In other words, though the impetus for choice-based models largely came from education reformers, more choice in public education—particularly when deep inequities existed, as in the case of race—made sense as a rational response to neoliberalism.

The Charlottesville summit had featured a working group on Choice and Restructuring that took as its premise that "the more parents accept responsibil-ity for the educational progress of their children, the more likely it is the children will succeed." The group concluded that choice "stimulates efforts to improve our schools by inspiring constructive competition among schools and encourag-ing parents to get involved in school improvement efforts." The working group lauded Minnesota, which had passed two laws in 1987 and 1988 under Democrat-Farmer-Labor governor Rudy Perpich giving families in the state the opportu-nity to choose schools across districts. While it did not get into the discussion of charters (at that time, a conversation just beginning) or vouchers (as Bennett had been pushing) the working group argued that states should expand choice by creating more public magnet schools.[23]

Charter schools would ultimately become the primary avenue for reformers to push school choice in America, but conservative advocates in the late 1980s and 1990s mainly advocated for the more obviously market-based voucher model. Given the years of calls for developing human capital as the only solution to ensure Americans had a shot at long-term economic security, it made sense that calls for vouchers would be strongly linked to the education myth.

The first argument for vouchers in the United States dates to 1955, when neo-classical economist Milton Friedman (a colleague and mentor of Gary Becker at the University of Chicago who also espoused a conservative version of the educa-tion myth) made the case that Americans should be free to spend the dollars allo-cated for their children's public education at any institution of their choosing. In an essay entitled "The Role of Government in Education," Friedman outlined the principle that government intervention should be as limited as possible. In fact, he believed there were only three basic functions for government: (1) enforcing contracts and ensuring free markets, (2) mitigating "neighborhood effects" in which an individual's actions imposed costs on other people for which they could not be individually compensated, and (3) "paternalistic concern for children and other irresponsible individuals." Friedman believed that since society required a citizenry with a minimum level of common values and literacy (though he had a much less grand vision for society than Horace Mann), and since there were so many differences between the means of parents, schools should be supported by the state. He argued, however, that government should not have the authority to determine the kind of education for which tax dollars paid. In Friedman's ideal system, government

> would give each child, through his parents, a specified sum to be used solely in paying for his general education; the parents would be free to spend this sum at a school of their own choice, provided it met certain minimum standards laid down by the appropriate governmental unit. Such schools would be conducted under a variety of auspices: by private enterprises operated for profit, non-profit institutions established by private endowment, religious bodies, and some even by governmental units.

But Friedman also argued government should not directly subsidize education—here he largely referred to professional education—that primarily enhanced one's human capital. Because these investments paid off directly to individuals, Friedman believed the state should stop subsidizing such programs and instead offer additional financing for such "capital" just as businesses could borrow to attain physical capital. He argued such investments should be paid off over time as workers earned higher wages.[24]

In the years since Friedman's essay, voucher schemes—called "tuition grants" to private schools—were employed by southern segregationists to circumvent court-ordered desegregation. They were also supported by some liberals as a creative method for desegregating schools. By 1980, Friedman had won the Nobel Prize for Economics for his work on inflation and gained a prominent platform to push for vouchers in the ten-part series that aired on PBS that year called *Free to Choose* (an entire episode was devoted to arguing for school vouchers). Constituencies frustrated by teacher strikes in the early 1980s, inspired by Friedman, also advocated for vouchers as an alternative to the public school system.[25]

In addition to Friedman, William Bennett, of course, had also pushed for vouchers in the Reagan administration, in service of preserving American values. But it wasn't until notions about the importance of accessing human capital had become political commonsense that conservative voucher advocates were able to gain traction with other political constituencies. The best example of this is the influential book published in 1990 by John Chubb and Terry Moe, two fellows at the centrist Brookings Institution. Chubb and Moe spent the 1980s studying public schools. Building from the premise that the nation's schools were failing, the duo diverged from the recommendations of *ANAR*, arguing that the "existing institutions cannot solve the problem, because they *are* the problem." The authors pointed to the growing realization, particularly among the business community, that the education system, as the institution "responsible for shaping America's 'human capital,' understandably attracted close scrutiny. . . . From an economic standpoint, America clearly needed better—and more rigorous education. But beyond that, it needed education of a different kind." A "dynamic economy well suited to modern conditions," Chubb and Moe agreed with the education system's critics, "requires workers who are not only technically knowledgeable and well trained, but who also have the capacity for creative, independent thought and action—since technology and the requirements of productivity are constantly changing and cannot be learned once and for all."[26] To complete the reforms necessary to achieve educational excellence, reformers needed to circumvent the teacher unions and other education professionals with a vested interest in maintaining the status quo.

Chubb and Moe's analysis of the nation's schools argued that private schools were "organized more effectively than public schools are and . . . this is a reflection of their far greater autonomy from external (bureaucratic) control." This premise led the authors to conclude that public schools needed to be liberated to meet the supposed needs of businesses and consumers, and the way to do that was through choice. Parents should be able, the authors argued, to send their kids to any school that met their needs. Chubb and Moe assumed parents had both the knowledge and motivation to help their kids acquire the appropriate human capital, and a competition on these grounds would force public schools to improve once they began losing students.[27]

A major problem with this logic, of course, was the assumption that schools that "do a better job of satisfying consumers will be more likely to prosper and proliferate."[28] For how would parents, even if they approved of a school's pedagogical goals or believed their children were prospering, know whether their kids' long-term human capital needs were actually being served by schools until years after they entered the job market? Further, even if this logic worked, what would happen to those students whose parents had no interest in helping them select the right schools? And what if, even after students acquired the right "human capital," they still lived in a community in which there were few jobs and they lacked either the will or the resources to relocate?

Despite these obvious problems, Chubb and Moe proposed the education system be realigned through a system of indirect vouchers, as their scheme would ensure that states remove most regulations, including tenure protections and reducing standards for teachers to the bare minimum. "Any group or organization that applies to the state and meets these minimal criteria," they concluded, "must then be chartered as a public school and granted the right to accept students and receive public money. Existing private schools will be among those eligible to participate."[29] Though this system was not technically a voucher system, by opening up public dollars to virtually any school, it was a voucher scheme in all but name.

Indeed, though all-out voucher schemes have not been nearly as prevalent in American school districts as charters have, vouchers attained their first permanent toehold in American politics in 1989 in Wisconsin, just as Chubb and Moe finished the empirical research that supported *Politics, Markets, and America's Schools*. The Wisconsin story is illustrative since it brought together a surprising coalition of conservative Republicans under Governor Tommy Thompson and Democratic-leaning civil rights activists.

Milwaukee followed the pattern of many American cities in the twentieth century: thousands of African Americans after World War II moved there seeking good jobs and to escape the unapologetic white supremacy of the South. In the 1960s, civil rights activists sought to desegregate schools and housing and faced brutal resistance from whites in the city, prompting the moniker the "Selma of the North."[30] Though these efforts led to some important changes, Milwaukee continued on its path as one of the most racially unequal cities in America, a distinction it still holds today. In part, this inequality was exacerbated by the fact that the city lost the most manufacturing jobs of any in the country between 1960 and 1985.[31] As had been the case elsewhere, this decline disproportionately impacted African Americans.

In the 1970s and 1980s, Black Power activist Howard Fuller led a fight for community control over schools and resisted integration schemes that put the burden on African Americans to leave neighborhood schools to go elsewhere.[32] Fuller worked with Polly Williams, an activist elected to the state legislature, in 1987–88, to establish an independent, all-Black district within Milwaukee. The plan was premised on the idea that integration efforts had failed, and so Blacks needed control over their own schools. Opposed by the NAACP and the Milwaukee Teachers Education Association (MTEA), the bill made it through the state assembly but ultimately failed in the senate.[33]

A Democrat, Williams believed liberalism had failed to provide her constituents in Milwaukee access to good jobs, housing, and schools, which motivated her to work with Republicans when she thought doing so would expand these opportunities. "If you're drowning and a hand is extended to you," she argued at a conservative PAC's American Opportunities Workshop hosted by Newt Gingrich in 1990, "you don't ask if the hand is attached to a Democrat or a Republican. From the African American position—at the bottom, looking up—there's not much difference between the Democrats and the Republicans anyway. Whoever is sincere about working with us, our door is open." Williams's support for vouchers made her a favorite of conservatives, and she counted Bennett, Alexander, and President Bush among her supporters. Williams, in fact, served as the featured speaker at conferences sponsored by Bush's Department of Education, the conservative Bradley Foundation, the Heritage Foundation, and the conservative newspaper the *Washington Times*.[34]

Catholics in Milwaukee had sought vouchers in the city since the 1950s, and many Republicans across the country took an interest in vouchers in the late 1980s.[35] One of those Republicans was the state's governor Tommy Thompson, who had won election in 1986 in part by feeding off the resentments of white Wisconsinites toward public employees, Native Americans, and African American welfare recipients.[36] After taking office, Thompson garnered national attention for seeking to discipline the poor. Working with a Democratic legislature, Thompson succeeded in passing two programs—Workfare and Learnfare— which tied welfare payments to job training and the school attendance of the kids of AFDC recipients, respectively.[37]

In his 1988 budget address, influenced by Bennett's call for using religious schools to build conservative values, Thompson proposed a voucher program for secular and religious schools in Milwaukee County. Prominent supporters of vouchers in Milwaukee also included the Bradley Foundation. Chartered in 1942 as a philanthropic organization funded by the Allen-Bradley Company, the foundation's assets exploded in value when Allen-Bradley was sold in 1985, and it became a prominent political actor bankrolling conservative politics and think tanks across the country. Bradley, in fact, was a major funder of Chubb and Moe's study.[38]

For African Americans in the city, the call for vouchers came at a time in which activists were looking for new ideas for schools that had not been successful in overcoming the poverty and trauma Black students experienced. In this context, though Williams opposed programs like Learnfare, she was open to working with Thompson on vouchers. After the legislature deleted Thompson's voucher plan from the budget, he introduced a new version in 1989. Though this proposal did not pass either, the idea was picking up steam. In March, Milwaukee Area Technical College hosted a conference on education, which included Chubb, Moe, and Fuller. The crowd, according to historian James Nelsen, "clearly favored the voucher advocates."[39] Williams developed her own voucher plan, in part to counter a school district plan that would only allow vouchers for the families of "at-risk" kids. Williams's proposal was centered on Milwaukee and only included nonsectarian private schools. The Parental Options Choice Bill, as it was eventually called, was introduced in the assembly in October 1989, and after making it through both houses of the legislature, Thompson signed it into law on April 27, 1990. Though liberal white Democrats, the NAACP, and teacher union lobbyists opposed it, Williams and Fuller both supported it, and enough Democrats joined the legislature's Republicans to pass the nation's first voucher program outside the South. The law would pay for 1 percent of Milwaukee students to go to private, nonsectarian schools. Several years later the program would be expanded to include religious schools, too. Other states have since experimented with vouchers, including Ohio, which in 1995 also passed a law funding private school vouchers in Cleveland.[40]

Williams's perspective on vouchers, connected to the promise of economic security, is notable. The Democrat supported the proposal because the effort to integrate schools in Milwaukee, she argued, had failed miserably to serve Black children. "Our children are filling up white schools that were half empty," she remarked in 1990. "The only value black students had was (state) money. . . . They want to keep the white neighborhood schools stable and keep their people employed. . . . Our kids are put in 'cages'—put on buses. Their kids are safe and secure in their own environments with their mommies and daddies."[41] As her comments make clear, despite the promise of *Brown v. Board of Education* as well as the efforts of social democrats like the Kings, Randolph, Rustin, Hawkins, and Chisolm, the United States had failed in powerful ways to ensure many African Americans access to economic security. After decades of failures by Democrats—and the growing disregard of social democracy by Republicans like Reagan and Thompson—it made sense to seek greater choice, particularly if access to human capital represented the only shot at a good job. In many important ways, the voucher movement signified the fracturing of the American tradition of common culture through public schools, an irony indeed given the argument Bennett and others had made for providing families more choice.

The GI Bill in a Funhouse Mirror

Perhaps no political effort in the Bush years best illustrates how far the United States had shifted from the promise of a broader social democratic vision than the president's proposal in June 1992 for a "GI Bill for Children." At that point, Bush was mounting a reelection defense against Bill Clinton, and the bill was essentially a voucher plan, providing parents up to a thousand dollars to spend on a school (public or private) of their choice. In the words of one scholar, the plan was "clearly designed to help Bush repair his damaged relationship with the right wing of the Republican Party," in part caused by his support for greater federal involvement in public education evidenced by America 2000.[42] And, it is no surprise Bush pushed for the so-called GI Bill for Children after several years in which Republicans sought market-based approaches to education. In fact, Bush's announcement of the bill lauded both Thompson and Williams by name.[43] Beyond firming up his right flank, however, Bush's comments in support of the bill elsewhere illustrate the continued growth of the myth that education should serve as the primary means for facilitating the possibility of economic security in America. "For too long," he asserted, "we've shielded our schools from competition . . . it is time we began thinking of a system of public education in which many providers offer a marketplace of opportunity, opportunities that give all of our children choices and access to the best education in the world."[44]

Referring to the plan as the GI Bill was highly misleading, however. It is indisputable that the 1944 GI Bill systematically discriminated against Black service members, a legacy that was never rectified by the time Fuller and Williams pushed for vouchers in Milwaukee. But the GI Bill of 1944 also included a much broader set of social supports for employment and housing, even if those supports were limited to veterans and thus mostly accrued to men. Bush's GI Bill for Children, however, only offered a pittance of opportunity through education. It certainly did not include the right to be free from poverty or the right to healthcare and other important services that are essential if students are to do well in school. Not only that, but for the Education President, the bill likely would have destabilized public schools by siphoning students toward private schools. As NEA president Keith Geiger pointed out: "The real G.I. Bill helped millions of poor and middle-class Americans have access to education. Bush's parody on the G.I. Bill will not only block that access, but is a dangerous threat to our public education system."[45]

Bush and other conservatives criticized unions like the NEA for hamstringing education reforms. Ironically, however, while teacher unions opposed vouchers (rightly, as threats to public education), they nonetheless invoked the education myth to fight, too, as it had gained a stranglehold on political possibilities in the United States. In 1992, for instance, Geiger supported a national fund for education technology, arguing that "the federal government must expand educational opportunity so that business and industry can take full advantage of our nation's diversity, improve productively, and compete as a nation." Why? Because "to revitalize the American economy, the United States must do more to make sure all citizens are fully prepared for the high-skill, high-productivity, high-wage jobs. . . . At present, the skills needs in the emerging workplace of tomorrow don't match the educational opportunities available to students today."[46]

Moving into the 1990s, it seemed more and more evident that while politicians might still disagree on how students would access new opportunities to attain human capital, the notion that doing so was the best—perhaps the only—way to given individual Americans a shot at economic security was all but beyond reproach. For Democrats, this put the education myth at the center of the party's political strategy for the next generation.

Reinventing Democrats: The Rise of the DLC

In the wake of Dukakis's defeat in 1988, the DLC went beyond simply recruiting and serving as a platform for candidates. In 1989, the DLC organized a think tank, the Progressive Policy Institute (PPI), modeled on the conservative Heritage Foundation, to push the party further toward ideas that, while more systematically distributed, were not all that different than those of Hart, Dukakis, and the neo-liberals.[47] The DLC also began publishing a magazine called *The Mainstream Democrat* later that year, which soon became *The New Democrat*.

The *New Democrat* in the early 1990s served as a hub for the DLC agenda, in which market-based, human capital intensive education reform played a critical role. In the September 1991 issue, for example, an unattributed piece skewered President Bush's America 2000 education plan as woefully insufficient, calling it nothing more than "a little pork barrel" that would not solve the "nation's education crisis."[48] Liberal Democrats, however, did not escape criticism. As the next issue of the *New Democrat* argued, a budget proposal for more federal investment in education was, by itself, only likely to facilitate more bureaucracy: "At a time when Democrats and Republicans are agreeing with parents that some sort of school choice is needed to improve the system, the Democratic plan seems to be just another old style liberal reaction to a problem: don't fix what's broken, just throw more money at it."[49]

In September 1991, Seymour Martin Lipset argued that redoubling efforts to enable African Americans to be more competitive in the schools was necessary to eliminate the disproportionate poverty of Blacks. Indeed, like much of the material that came out of *The New Democrat*, Lipset had no reservations that the nation's education system was a meritocracy. It just needed to be made fairer: "To return to the image of the shackled runner, Americans are willing to do more than remove the chains. They will go along with special training programs and financial assistance for previously shackled runners, enabling them to catch up with those who have forged ahead because of unfair advantages. But most Americans draw the line of predetermining the results of the competition." The author concluded that more national service would help to level the playing field: "Those with inadequate education and skills could be trained for positions which are in demand, while helping to rebuild publicly supported infrastructure or delivering social services."[50]

For New Democrats, even a tougher stance on crime needed to be paired with support for the right education. Democrats—especially Clinton—supported "tough-on-crime" laws that massively increased incarceration in the United States in the 1990s. In a *New Democrat* piece criticizing Bush for being soft on crime, David Kurapka argued Democrats should lock up more Americans, "because the record shows that locking up criminals does reduce crime, particularly with repeat offenders." But education was the key to preventing crime in the first place: "We need to improve the economic opportunity in the inner city, with ideas like national service, which provides an education in exchange for community work, and youth apprenticeship, which provides training for those not attending college."[51] As was the case with the assumptions policymakers in the Johnson administration had made regarding the kinds of "deficits" poor people needed to fix before they could get good jobs, this piece also bought into fantasies that getting those in the inner city the right skills and proper attitude would reduce crimes that stemmed from poverty and chronic lack of economic opportunity. Unfortunately, given the long postwar history of American jobs moving away from inner cities, enhanced education was at best a partial solution to a massive structural problem that persists to this day.[52]

Perhaps the most representative issue of the *New Democrat* in the early 1990s was devoted to David Osborne (a PPI senior fellow) and Ted Gaebler's *Reinventing Government*, an influential book that served as the DLC manual for how to reshape government. As the *New Democrat's* editor's note summed it up:

> Those of us at the Progressive Policy Institute and the Democratic Leadership Council have been intrigued by David Osborne's work since we met him three years ago. Since then, we have shamelessly parroted his ideas and routinely refer to the kind of twenty-first century government we are searching for as "Osbornian." We believe that the foundation for a new politics—one that focuses on solutions and ultimately restores people's faith in democratic government—can only be based on government which is in keeping with the world of the twenty-first century.[53]

Osborne and Gaebler's book argued that "our governments are in deep trouble today" and required dramatic change. Government, the two argued, had been "last reinvented . . . during the progressive era and New Deal. . . . Today, the world of government is once again in great flux. The emergence of a postindustrial, knowledge-based, global economy has undermined old realities throughout the world, creating wonderful opportunities and frightening problems." The book relayed "snapshots of existing entrepreneurial governments" in the hope that officeholders elsewhere would follow suit, and the authors referenced Total Quality Management (TQM), based on W. Edwards Deming's business philosophy that centered customers in the production process and favored a decentralized approach to management. Though Osborne and Gaebler were not the first to do so, they would use Deming's methodology as the core of their vision, particularly as it related to public education.[54]

Indeed, Osborne and Gaebler prominently featured education in their analysis of dysfunctional government and argued that schools should be forced into meritocratic competition. Citing a few anecdotal examples of school districts (made up disproportionately of poor families) where students failed to do well on standardized tests, the authors asserted the nation's "public schools are the worst in the developed world." Osborne and Gaebler positively referenced examples of school choice—in East Harlem and in Minnesota—and performance incentives for teachers and principals in South Carolina. "When it comes to the effects of competition," the authors asserted, "education is no different than any other service industry."[55]

Osborne and Gaebler believed that investing in public education was not enough: to fully endow education with the right market signals, the system needed to be opened up to choice. In fact, the authors enthusiastically quoted Governor Thompson, fresh off his deal to bring vouchers to Milwaukee: "Competition breeds accountability," Thompson asserted. "Schools providing a higher quality education would flourish, the same way as a business that improves its quality for its consumers. Schools failing to meet the needs of their students would not be able to compete, and in effect would go out of business."[56] The impact of TQM in Thompson's breathless zeal for treating education like a business is obvious.

The *New Democrat* special issue on *Reinventing Government* touted Florida Democratic governor (and DLC member) Lawton Chiles, Chicago mayor Richard Daley, and Philadelphia mayor Ed Rendell for bucking union resistance to institute market-based reforms.[57] As DLC founder Al From summed it up, "Democrats should demand radical change: in education with charter schools and more choice, not private school vouchers; in vocational education with European-style apprenticeship programs to provide an upward mobility track for non-college bound youths; and in college aid with national service so young people earn scholarships by serving their country."[58]

By 1992, the DLC had established a clear vision for the Democratic Party: a turn away from the social democratic promise of the New Deal, market-based reforms to public institutions, and crucially, investment in human capital as the way to arm individual working Americans for a global economic Battle Royal. Though the organization's ideas featured a number of high-profile champions, undoubtedly the most important moment in the DLC's history occurred in March 1990 when rising superstar governor Bill Clinton replaced Georgia senator Sam Nunn as chairperson.

Clinton, a Rhodes Scholar from Arkansas, unsuccessfully ran for Congress in 1974 at the age of just twenty-eight during the election that catapulted New Politics Democrats to a huge majority following Watergate. Four years later, Clinton was elected governor of his home state, becoming the youngest state executive in the country. During his first term, he focused largely on roads and transportation. Booted out of office following the 1980 election (he was blamed for a revolt of Cuban refugees in a federal facility in Fort Chaffee, Arkansas, and saddled with an unpopular tax hike on vehicle registrations), Clinton won the office back in 1982. From 1983 on, Clinton pushed entrepreneurialism and postindustrial development, establishing entities like the Arkansas Science and Technology Development Authority and the Arkansas Development Finance Authority.[59] Significantly, as part of this effort, he consciously chose to make education reform his political focus as governor, seeing it as a winning strategy, particularly in the wake of *ANAR*. His wife Hillary chaired the state's Education Standards Committee during his second term, and Bill built on the committee's recommendations to successfully increase education funding, adopt new accountability measures for schools, begin high school entrance exams, and initiate controversial teacher testing opposed by the Arkansas Education Association. Clinton was credited with modest increases in student graduation rates, and he gained a national reputation as a brilliant education reformer (media often made a point of emphasizing that he was a Rhodes Scholar).[60] This work catapulted him into a leadership position on education in the National Governors' Association, most prominently at the Charlottesville summit in 1989.[61]

Clinton had been a member of the DLC from its onset, and From recruited him for chair both because of the Arkansas governor's prolific fundraising and because he believed the rising star had an excellent chance of bringing the DLC's agenda onto the national stage should he win the presidency in 1992. Clinton spent 1990 and 1991 proselytizing for the DLC and working to build up state chapters across the country. These chapters would then provide delegates to the May 1991 Cleveland Convention, a "seminal event in the history of the New Democrats" in the words of one insider, in which the DLC "unveiled its most detailed—and hence most controversial—policy manifesto; showcased its organizational breadth across the country, and arguably, launched the presidential candidacy of its chairman."[62]

More than a thousand delegates attended the gathering. Standing atop the work of the neo-liberals, the convention began with the premise that global competition with other industrial nations was leaving the United States behind. Too many people in the United States lacked healthcare, American prisons locked up too many people, and there was no path for working people without college degrees to get good jobs. As Clinton, who chaired the convention, framed it, Democrats had to offer "opportunity for all." Economic growth was paramount, which for the Arkansas governor meant expanding free trade and new technologies, and education and job training were vital in facilitating the meritocracy that would grow the pie without upsetting the nation's economic structure. As DLC chair, Clinton found another platform for pushing the education myth in the late 1980s, work begun as governor of Arkansas, and then through the NGA.[63]

Though Osborne and Gaebler's book hadn't yet been published, the delegates at Cleveland referenced their ideas, specifically calling to streamline government. Clinton used the very term *reinventing government* in his framing mantra of "opportunity, responsibility, choice, a government that works, and a belief in community." One of the convention's most important resolutions explicitly used the term too: "*We believe in reinventing government.* We want to eliminate unneeded layers of bureaucracy, and give citizens more choice in public services, from child care and care for the elderly to public schools."[64]

Human capital thus played a major role in the DLC's vision for prosperity in a global society, and the New American Choice Resolutions explicitly blamed workers' lack of education for diminished standards of living and downward pressure on wages:

> Whereas, economic growth and individual prosperity in American now depend on the ability of U.S. workers and businesses to outperform foreign competitors in both U.S. and world markets;
>
> Whereas, in the new global economy, as investment capital and advanced technologies flow freely among many nations, the critical factors in outperforming foreign competition are the skills, training, and talents of a nation's workers, and the ability of a nation's businesses and government to organize and marshal these skills and talents. . . .
>
> Whereas, policies that have neglected making investments to train, develop, organize, and marshal Americans' skills and talents, or that have tried to shield America's businesses and workers from the challenge of the global economy, have produced the slowest gains in

working Americans' incomes and productivity since the Great Depression and declining average wages;

.... Now therefore, be it *RESOLVED* by the 1991 Democratic Leadership Council Convention, that our government should take the necessary steps to increase the prosperity of all Americans by enabling them to meet the challenge of global competition.[65]

The last "whereas" specifically went after labor and social democratic policies designed to uphold the place of workers in a world in which their employers had gone to war against them.[66] In fact, with the right investments in human capital in place, the delegates welcomed free trade, urging Congress to "fast track" a deal with Mexico.[67] Meanwhile, union activists protested the DLC's position on NAFTA outside the convention.[68]

The delegates in Cleveland proudly drew on the work of Robert Reich.[69] Reich, who met Clinton as a fellow Rhodes Scholar, graduated from Yale Law School, which he attended with both Bill and his future wife Hillary. After serving in Carter's Federal Trade Commission, Reich took a position at Harvard's Kennedy School of Government. In the early 1980s, Reich, with Ira Magaziner, had argued that the declining competitiveness of American industries required a national industrial policy to make the US manufacturing sector more competitive. At that time, Reich had already begun to advocate for "programs of retraining, relocation, and targeted investment [so that] hardships caused by industrial restructuring can be remedied in ways that do not hinder economic progress." Still, in 1982, Magaziner and Reich also argued for the US government to promote specific industries—as the Japanese did—rather than simply cede manufacturing jobs to other nations or allow the wages of blue-collar workers to spiral ever downward under pressure from employers shifting work to cheaper locations. In fact, Magaziner and Reich had sharply criticized both Reaganomics and American corporations, asserting they had "overemphasized the importance of cheap labor in production at the expense of productivity improvements and long-term market penetration."[70]

It was Reich's argument for public investment in human capital, however, that gained wide purchase in neo-liberal circles by the end of the 1980s. Reich had been an important adviser to Dukakis, for instance, and had also advised the Clintons on education reform in Arkansas.[71] Osborne and Gaebler, in fact, thanked Reich for "significant intellectual debts" in the acknowledgments of *Reinventing Government*.[72]

By the early 1990s, in fact, Reich had shifted decidedly away from arguments for industrial policy and toward a full-throated embrace of investment in human capital. In *The Work of Nations* (1991), a clear reference to Adam

Smith's classic argument against mercantilism in 1776, Reich pushed for a more liberal version of Schultz's human capital than that of Becker and Friedman's conservative version. Reich believed there was still a place for a robust state, but it should focus on equipping workers to compete in an economy increasingly built on knowledge.

Arguments about the shift in the United States toward a "knowledge society" originated in 1960, when management expert Peter Drucker coined the term *knowledge work*. By 1993, Drucker was arguing that the United States had already shifted to a full-blown "postcapitalist" knowledge economy increasingly divided into knowledge workers and service workers. The former alone directed "wealth-creating activities," however: "The leading social groups of the knowledge society will be 'knowledge workers'—knowledge executives who know how to allocate knowledge to productive use, just as the capitalists knew how to allocate capital to productive use." Though Drucker massively underestimated the wealth and power that "knowledge executives" such as Jeff Bezos, Mark Zuckerberg, and others would amass in the years since the 1990s, he argued that nations were turning the page on manufacturing, and as Bell had argued in *The Coming of Post-Industrial Society*, he believed ensuring the "dignity" of service workers would be a monumental challenge.[73]

Reich's argument in *The Work of Nations* represented the growing intellectual shift among both Democrats and Republicans away from arguments for sustaining the livelihoods of manufacturing workers. In *Minding America's Business*, he and Magaziner had sought to provide a governmental framework for American manufacturing firms to become more competitive internationally in order to increase workers' wages and continue to provide permanent, sustaining jobs moving forward. The necessity for such a policy was existential, they argued, for on that question, "the future prosperity of the United States will be won or lost."[74]

By the early 1990s, however, even those like Magaziner who had argued for a national industrial policy were moving toward education and job training as the solution to make Americans broadly prosperous. A good example of this trend is the report by the National Center on Education and the Economy, called *America's Choice: High Skills or Low Wages* (1990). Chaired by Magaziner and co-chaired by Carter's former labor secretary Ray Marshall and Reagan's labor secretary Bill Brock, the report brought together liberals and conservatives, and also included former Democratic governor James Hunt; former chair of the EEOC Eleanor Holmes Norton; Karen Nussbaum, director of feminist labor organization 9to5; and Howard Samuel, president of the AFL-CIO's Industrial Union Department (IUD).

The report began by citing the fact that, recently, the "incomes of our top 30 percent of earners increased while those of the other 70 percent spiraled downward."

The difference mapped onto the approximate number of Americans who had college degrees. Instead of offering political supports for the bottom 70 percent, however, such as facilitating good jobs, a higher minimum wage, or stronger unions rights, the report argued that "the key to maintaining, to say nothing of improving, our standard of living is productivity growth—more products and services from every member of the workforce." To do so employers needed to reorganize work, and workers needed more skills to facilitate this shift.[75]

Oddly, the report admitted there was no immediate skills shortage since employers mostly prioritized workers with a "good work ethic and appropriate social behavior." *America's Choice* argued, nonetheless, that raising education standards and requiring companies to invest more in job training (it suggested 1 percent of their annual budget) would force organizations to employ labor models closer to those of the supposedly more productive nations of Taiwan, Korea, and Singapore. "The reason we have no skills shortage today," the report concluded, "is that we are using a turn-of-the-century work organization. If we want to compete more effectively in a global economy, we will have to move to a high productivity work organization."[76]

By the early 1990s, resigned to the belief that not only was the economy global, but most major corporations were effectively global, too (or would be soon), Reich had gone even further than that. Only by ensuring American workers were contributing the knowledge work to these corporations, Reich believed, would the United States be successful as a nation. Here, Reich built on globalist trends in both politics and in the public intellectual sphere. In 1987, for instance, the Hudson Institute's *Workforce 2000* study asserted that "as the world economy has become more integrated, the United States, like all other nations, has pro-gressively lost control of its economic destiny. The growing importance of trade means that no nation can expect sustained growth unless the world economy grows."[77] And, adding to his argument about the postcapitalist knowledge society, Peter Drucker believed the nation-state was losing its ability to help its citizens: "Certain it is that in politics we have already shifted from the four hundred years of the sovereign nation-state to a pluralism in which the nation-state will be one rather than the only unit of political integration."[78]

Building on a decade of work in the neo-liberal and DLC milieu, Reich con-cluded that American workers could only guarantee themselves a livelihood if they were able to become "symbolic analysts" whose primary tasks were to "solve, identify, and broker problems by manipulating symbols." These workers included engineers, financial and management consultants, research scientists, public relations executives, journalists, and others. Most symbolic analysts, according to Reich, were college graduates, and he supposed the key in getting all Ameri-cans to succeed in the growing knowledge economy was simply to bring more

of them into it. To do that, he believed the symbolic analysts who had pros-
pered had an obligation to invest in the training and education of manufacturing
and service-sector workers. Thus, the nation needed major public investment in
education—at the primary, secondary, and tertiary levels.[79] The massive investment in public education represented a clear distinction from conservative
versions of the human capital argument, but it shared the basic premise that the
economy was a meritocracy in which broader social democratic policies were
both undesirable and unnecessary.

Reich's argument drove the DLC agenda on education. Building on almost a
decade of jeremiads, beginning with A Nation at Risk in 1983, about the failed
state of American education, the DLC delegates in Cleveland in 1991 resolved
that "this nation guarantee upward mobility and equal opportunity through a
sweeping reorganization of public schools and an assured way for all citizens
to have an ability to obtain a college education." The convention endorsed the
National Education Goals for the year 2000 that came out of the Charlottesville
conference. It also pushed for more accountability through rewards and punish-
ments, public school choice plans, charter schools, alternative certification for
teachers, and "greater incentives to get and keep good teachers." The delegates
also endorsed a "new, civilian GI Bill that would promise a college education in
return for voluntary national service."[80]

The Rise of Clinton

The growing influence of the DLC and its vision for that which would not disrupt
existing social and economic structures nourished Clinton in his ascendance to
the nomination of the Democratic Party. In fact, the array of candidates in the
1992 primary highlighted the shift of the Democratic Party toward the DLC
agenda: aside from the more social democratic populist Tom Harkin (Iowa),
Clinton's major competition came from the neo-liberals Paul Tsongas and Jerry
Brown.[81] Indeed, as it was for Tsongas and Brown, investment in postindustrial
knowledge industry and education served as critical components of Clinton's
pitch to the American people in the election of 1992. The backing of the DLC,
in addition to Clinton's political skills, however, gave the Arkansas Democrat an
advantage the others lacked, and he locked up the nomination.

Education was central in Clinton's general election campaign, particularly
since reform had been one of his signal claims to achievement as governor of
Arkansas. Bush also integrally involved education in his reelection argument, as
he had tried to claim the title of Education President. In fact, as Becker noted in
the third edition of Human Capital (1993), in 1992 "both President Clinton and

President Bush emphasized the importance of improving the quality of the labor force. A dozen years ago, this terminology would have been inconceivable in a presidential campaign."[82]

Even so, Clinton, employing the slogan "Putting People First," more prominently featured the human capital argument. Indeed, Clinton made his friend Robert Reich's argument a centerpiece of the vision: "In the emerging global economy, everything is mobile: capital, factories, even entire industries. The only resource that's really rooted in a nation—and the ultimate source of all its wealth—is its people. The only way America can compete and win in the twenty-first century is to have the best-educated, best-trained workforce in the world, linked together by transportation and communication networks second to none."[83]

The Clinton campaign advocated for more government investments, but only did so in line with Osborne and Gaebler's notion of "reinventing government" through more market incentives and public-private partnerships. The absence of any broader social democratic alternatives was notable. A proposed $20 billion Rebuild America Fund, for example, would be "leveraged with state, local, private sector, and pension fund contributions. User fees such as road tolls and solid-waste disposal charges will help us guarantee those investments." Education, specifically, investment in human capital, was absolutely fundamental: "Putting people first demands a revolution in lifetime learning, a concerted effort to invest in the collective talents of our people. Education today is more than the key to climbing the ladder of opportunity. In today's global economy, it is an imperative for our nation. Our economic life is on the line."[84]

Clinton's campaign, therefore, paralleled Reagan's in 1980 in one very concrete way: in the context of economic downturn, the Arkansas Democrat offered the dreamy promise of economic prosperity for all without any tough choices. In Reagan's case it had been to limit government; in Clinton's, it was to make the right investments so workers, as if by magic, would all get the right skills to excel. Indeed, the latter campaign's explanation for rising income inequality is telling: "In an era when what you earn depends on what you learn, education too often stops at the schoolhouse door. While our global competitors invest in their working people, seven of every ten dollars American companies spend on employee training goes to those at the top of the corporate ladder. High-level executives float on golden parachutes to a cushy life while hardworking Americans are grounded without the skills they need."[85]

The campaign argued that no fundamental realignment in the American economy was necessary. Instead, the new Democratic regime would simply "give students the chance to train for jobs or pay for college, and provide workers with the training and retraining they need to compete in tomorrow's economy."

Neither diminishing workers' rights, the growing power of employers, nor the shift of jobs from the United States to lower-wage workers elsewhere was a part of the discussion. Instead, once the government closed the human capital gap by forcing multinational corporations to spend more on training, the enhanced skills would somehow lead them to treat their workers better.[86] In Clinton's acceptance speech at the Democratic National Convention, in fact, he pointed out that human capital was his priority: "The most important family policy, urban policy, labor policy, minority policy, and foreign policy America can have is an expanding, entrepreneurial economy of high-wage, high skill jobs."[87]

Clinton handily won the electoral college race by 370–168. The popular vote was much closer, however, as the Arkansas governor won 43 percent of the popular vote and Bush won about 37.5 percent. However, 18 percent went to third-party protest candidate Ross Perot, which highlighted the fact that many Americans were not happy with either major party (exit polls showed Perot's votes came at about the equal expense of both Bush and Clinton). Importantly, much of Perot's support came from his rejection of free trade and support for an American industrial policy.[88] Compelling evidence, in fact, indicates that Clinton won largely because Americans blamed Bush for the recession.[89] Nonetheless, as had been the case with Reagan in 1980, the defeat of an unpopular president gave the incoming chief executive a seeming mandate. In Clinton's case, that would mean more myth making.

PUTTING SOME PEOPLE FIRST

The Total Ascendance of the Education Myth

In 1993, Bill Clinton was inaugurated as president, with a Democratic Congress and the hope he could enact much of the DLC agenda. In his inaugural address that January, he called on Americans to "face hard truths." "Profound and powerful" forces of globalization and technology were "remaking our world." In this context, the only path for "renewal" would come from the understanding, building on Reich's *Work of Nations*, that the world was one in which "we must compete for every opportunity." His speech called for no big social democratic alternatives, but instead investment and "sacrifice" to win the future.[1] Its ideas ascendant in the administration, the DLC vision permanently altered the political narrative around how Americans understood economic opportunity, tipping the scales definitively toward the education myth. Clinton's first term, in fact, brought a major free trade deal that signified once and for all to nonprofessional-class workers that the Democratic Party would have little for them aside from promises of training for better jobs. Federal education policy, including Goals 2000, the Improving America's Schools Act, and the School-to-Work Opportunities Act, built on the assumptions of the Bush administration and furthered the notion that schools should serve primarily to build human capital.

But these policies brought a stinging rebuke in the 1994 midterms, at least in part because organized labor did little to help Democrats that had just negotiated NAFTA. Clinton, however, moved even further right, agreeing to a draconian welfare reform in the reelection year of 1996. The combination of these policies meant that those left behind were disproportionately African American and

Latino, particularly as the manufacturing working class had grown increasingly more diverse in 1970s and 1980s.

Reelected with a strong economy behind him, however, Clinton used his second term to continue to push for connecting public education to human capital, and national teacher union leaders supported this "reinvention" of American public education too. Taken together, by the end of the 1990s, intellectuals like Reich, political figures like Clinton, the DLC, and top union leaders—indeed, the nation's political center—had shifted decisively toward a new set of assumptions that structured mainstream politics for the next two decades: public investment in education and retraining workers to meet the needs of increasingly empowered employers would bring opportunity for prosperity and security, but only when workers could appropriately commodify themselves. In this context, there no longer existed, at least in the political mainstream, even the faintest social democratic alternatives to assist the victims of continuously growing economic inequality. Populist conservatives like Pat Buchanan, building on the strategy Nixon and Reagan had employed in the 1970s and 1980s, respectively, continued to channel the anxieties of some Americans excluded, either economically or culturally, from this "meritocracy."

The DLC President

One of Clinton's immediate priorities, rightly, was expanding access to healthcare, as this was a growing worry among Americans as costs, premiums, and deductibles were all on the rise while real wages grew slowly.[2] However, after sinking a great deal of political capital into healthcare reform that would not have radically restructured workers' reliance on employers for care, Clinton watched his proposal, developed in large part by Hillary, die without even garnering a vote in Congress. The president also developed divisive solutions to social policies such as whether homosexuals would be allowed to serve openly in the military. In addition, deficit hawks in the administration almost immediately stymied serious consideration of the investments in education and training Reich envisioned in *The Work of Nations*.[3]

The failure of healthcare reform and other parts of the Clinton agenda led many immediate postmortems to see the first two years of Clinton's first term—before his embrace of a softer version of the GOP's agenda in the 1994 Contract with America—as a major failure. Reich, for example, whom Clinton appointed secretary of labor, felt let down by Clinton's lack of attention to his human capital agenda, as the title of his memoir of his time in the administration—*Locked in the Cabinet*—makes clear. The first half of Clinton's first term, however, elevated the education myth in two important venues: first, the successful negotiation of the North American Free Trade Agreement (NAFTA), and second, federal education and training policy that, while lacking the massive investment Reich wanted, nonetheless strengthened the expectation that schools should be accountable to the needs of employers.

Indeed, Clinton's biggest achievement, which further weakened the promise of secure blue-collar jobs, was NAFTA. George H.W. Bush's administration initially negotiated the deal, which created a free trade bloc between the United States, Canada, and Mexico. Like Bush, Clinton argued the treaty would boost the American economy.[4] But many Americans were unconvinced, and congressional ratification was highly controversial. Ross Perot articulately criticized NAFTA, for instance. In a televised debate with Vice President Al Gore on CNN in 1993, the populist political candidate pointed out that NAFTA would motivate American corporations to seek out cheaper labor in Mexico.[5] Labor unions hoped Clinton would negotiate strong worker protections—thus limiting the job losses of American workers—into the agreement before it was ratified. The administration negotiated a side agreement on labor rights, but it lacked enforcement provisions, and the AFL-CIO led a massive opposition drive. Labor was, therefore, incensed that the agreement passed with more Republican votes than Democratic votes (132 House Republicans backed it, while only 102 Democrats did). Clinton pledged to defend any Republicans who voted for it in the 1994 midterms.[6]

For many blue-collar workers, however, NAFTA was merely the latest and most spectacular example of seeing their interests sold out in favor of the professional-class notions of meritocracy driving American politics. For example, in Wisconsin, NAFTA came on the heels of a prominent fight for the jobs shipped elsewhere by American Motors Company (AMC). In the 1960s, AMC was the largest employer in Wisconsin, and the benefits of the autoworkers' union contract accrued to white workers as well as the African American and Latino workers who had moved to the city during and after World War II. In 1988, the plant in Kenosha (by then owned by Chrysler) closed, costing workers 5,500 jobs and in the process, altering the entire political culture of the city. The workers organized to save their jobs, and Jesse Jackson even made the effort a cause célèbre during the presidential primary campaign that year. The growing professional class in the city, however, which included the new mayor and the teachers who sought to ensure working-class students bought into public education, saw the workers as getting what they deserved for failing to seek an education and relying on the prospect of a blue-collar livelihood and a union. The workers viewed the situation differently: believing in their work as a contribution to the nation, they saw the country letting them down when their political leaders failed to do anything to save the labor equity these workers had put into the company and thus the promise of a decent retirement.[7]

Indeed, the battle over NAFTA showed that for many working people, Clinton's agenda had little to make workers' lives better. Though Clinton did see his ambitious plans to fund postindustrial, technological development stymied by deficit hawks and conservative Republicans, his tone-deafness on NAFTA nonetheless stemmed from an overly optimistic attitude about the economy and the myth of economic advancement through education that he and Reich worked for years to elevate.[8] An interaction with Lane Kirkland, president of the AFL-CIO, early in Reich's tenure as secretary of labor in 1993, was illuminating. Reich was clearly aware that the labor movement faced trouble in 1993, in part because of structural changes in the economy: "Workers in big industries dominated by three or four companies," he pointed out, "were easier to organize than workers in the small and medium-size service businesses (retail, restaurant, hotel, hospital, office), which have been creating most of the jobs for twenty years. And blue-collar male factory workers were easier to mobilize than pink-collar Hispanics, Asians, and blacks—mostly women—in rapidly expanding but low-paying clerical, custodial, cashier, child-care, data entry, and telemarketing jobs."[9]

Still, the labor secretary seemed unconcerned about the growing leverage of employers under a dysfunctional labor law. By the end of the Kirkland years, the labor movement had made its fair share of mistakes. In fact, its lack of investment in organizing was a major reason why John Sweeney of the Service Employees International Union (SEIU) led an insurgent campaign for AFL-CIO president in 1995. But the AFL-CIO had invested significant money and energy into Clinton in 1992, and the organization hoped that with a Democratic Congress, the president would prioritize a bill to ban striker replacements, a tactic used increasingly by corporations to break unions' most important leverage in labor stoppages.[10]

Instead, labor's most important agenda item did not even make it onto the long list of the new administration's priorities for the first term. While Reich did float a compromise to the National Association of Manufacturers (NAM)—that they not oppose striker replacement in exchange for labor getting out of the way of NAFTA—it was a nonstarter, and the effort died in a Senate filibuster after businesses lobbied hard against it. Reich tried unsuccessfully to sell NAFTA by arguing to its union opponents that "workers who lose their old jobs because of free trade can be retrained for new jobs that pay as well or better."[11]

Education became a major part of the Clinton human capital agenda with the passage of Goals 2000: The Educate America Act of 1994. Here Clinton worked closely with fellow southern Democratic governor Richard Riley (South Carolina, 1979–87) whom Clinton appointed secretary of education in 1993. Like Clinton, Riley was an education reformer: during his tenure as chair of the Southern Regional Education Board (SREB)'s Commission for Educational Quality, for example, the SREB published a report titled *Goals for Education: Challenge 2000*, which issued twelve national goals that looked similar to what Bush and the governors eventually proposed in 1990.[12]

In the Education Department, Riley drafted Clinton's signature education policies: Goals 2000 and the Improving America's Schools Act of 1994 (a reauthorization of ESEA). Though this legislation faced opposition from conservatives for increasing federal involvement, it hardly revolutionized education in the United States. It did, however, significantly strengthen the argument, gaining wider purchase among both Republicans and Democrats, that aligning the skills of the nation's young people with the needs of American employers represented the main avenue for facilitating individual economic opportunity.

Goals 2000 built on the six education goals emanating from the Charlottesville summit in 1989. The bill proposed eight national goals for the year 2000, as well as a National Education Standards and Improvement Council (NESIC), which would be responsible for "certifying" state standards-based education reform plans, required to receive grant funding from the Department of Education.[13] Another portion of the bill established a National Skills Standards Board to connect worker training outcomes to the needs of employers.

Indeed, proponents of the bill, including both Riley and Reich, argued for more accountability and a tighter connection between education and labor to meet the needs of American employers and, presumably, create more economic opportunity for workers. At House subcommittee hearings in April 1993, Riley breathlessly asserted that "I am deeply concerned about the quality of elementary and secondary education in America. We must improve our education system if we are to prosper as a democratic country and build a high-skill, high-wage economy." Repeating an argument that could have come from *ANAR* or any number of similar reports since, Riley elaborated, "The other countries against which we compete for jobs expect all of their students to take challenging course work in a variety of academic areas. . . . As we approach the 21st century our prosperity and dreams hinge upon education as never before. The global economy is characterized by an information-rich world dependent upon technology and filed with high-skill, high-wage jobs." Further, previewing the landmark 2001 reauthorization of ESEA, Riley argued, "We cannot afford to leave any student behind."[14]

Though Riley gave lip service to the "social imperative" of education in "an ever-changing democracy," his examples of high-quality education to which the nation's schools should aspire were mostly about teaching Black and Latino kids mathematics (Riley referenced Jaime Escalante, for instance, made famous by the 1988 film *Stand and Deliver*). Indeed, education was vital for the future economic opportunity of Americans, as Riley employed Clinton's language on the 1992 campaign trail: "In a world in which what you earn depends on what you learn, today's young people will be destined for lower pay unless we can help many more of them take and master more challenging subject matter."[15] Riley's argument was human capital with no alternative: without a robust education built on math and science, economic insecurity was simply destiny.

The next week, Reich testified to the same committee. He pointed out that as the United States recovered from the recession that began during Bush's presidency, fewer Americans than expected had ended up getting their jobs back. Companies continuing to cut payroll (a trend begun in the 1980s), advances in technology, and increased international trade all added up to "enormous structural changes." The committee members would not be surprised to learn that little could be done except for people to seek new work: "This means people have to change jobs, more than ever before. Americans have to get new skills, more than ever before. They have to know how to get the skills, where to get the skills, what skills they need, and where the jobs are."[16]

But there was a second problem: "Most American workers have seen their real inflation-adjusted earnings for their cohorts, for their age group, continue to decline, on average, since 1977. . . . Even Americans who have jobs are seeing that it is getting harder and harder to get a job that pays well, that pays as well as the jobs we had before." Who was falling behind? Those without college degrees. As Reich pointed out, college graduates were the only workers seeing inflation-adjusted raises. Thus, for the secretary of labor, the "moral of the story is that much of the decline in nonsupervisory wages, I believe, can be attributed to educational deficiencies, simply not being ready for the new world of work." Though he eschewed "simple or easy solutions," Reich argued that the Goals 2000 legislation would help solve the problem of "educational deficiency" as well as the "mismatch" between those who had the skills and the jobs that were out there. While Reich certainly wanted more Americans to be able to access higher education, the nationally recognized skills standards Goals 2000 promised would also help those without college degrees make sure they could attain the "credential that will get them a good job."[17]

Under questioning from the committee chair, Reich, however, pointed to a stark reality in the future of the nation's economy: "Employers around America are spending approximately $30 billion a year training their employees. . . . It turns out, on closer inspection, that approximately two-thirds of this sum, about $20 billion, is spent on employees who already have college degrees. The 75 percent of Americans without 4-year college degrees, who are in the most need and are most in danger of losing their way economically, are getting a relatively small portion of that $30 billion package."[18] After the 1980s, when budgets had squeezed education and employers had increased downward pressure on their workers—all while Democrats lost three presidential elections—one could understand why a moderate argument about job training for American workers was palatable. But, as Reich argued for funding for Goals 2000, corporations continued to seek lower labor costs from the bottom echelons of their workforces—either through cheaper labor elsewhere, automation, or eliminating union protections that had defended workers from that competition. In such a climate, new retraining standards were unlikely to move the needle.

The assumptions embedded in Goals 2000 were important because they also formed the basis for the reauthorization of ESEA during the Clinton presidency: the Improving America's Schools Act of 1994. The law changed American education by shifting the formula for Title I appropriations toward schools with greater needs while increasing expectations for the accountability of these schools toward their students' performance. To receive federal funds, states now had to develop content standards in core academic areas and develop plans to improve schools. Schools received more flexibility in using Title I funds but faced the possibility of being taken over by either a school district or the state if their test scores did not improve. An important bridge to No Child Left Behind (2001), disadvantaged students now faced no-excuses expectations, no matter what kind of impediments there might be to learning.[19]

Finally, the Clinton administration's School-to-Work Opportunities Act, also passed into law in 1994, furthered the connection between education and jobs by providing seed money for states to link high school learning with the workplace. As the legislation made clear, the goal was to "improve career prospects and academic achievement in high school, and thereby boost enrollment in postsecondary education and increase the likelihood of high-skill, high-wage employment."[20]

In fact, Clinton's education and training policy and NAFTA represented his two major achievements in the first half of his first term. Though Reich may have been disappointed there had not been more investment in human capital—certainly nothing like a civilian GI Bill came close to materializing—the administration's first two years powerfully advanced the myth he, Clinton, the neoliberals, and the DLC had been pushing for more than a decade.

Right Moves

Clinton's first-term accomplishments were purchased with a high price, however. Because of his push for NAFTA, labor turned against Clinton, which helped facilitate the Republican takeover of Congress in 1994.[21] Further, his education agenda was criticized by the GOP's conservative wing for extending the reach of the federal government, and it also played a role in some Republicans' critique of Clinton. (In fact, the GOP-led Congress of 1995–96 repealed key elements of the Goals 2000 Act, including NESIC.)[22] In 1994, the GOP picked up ten governors, eight seats in the Senate, and fifty-four seats in the House, giving them control of both chambers for the first time since the 1940s. New House Speaker Newt Gingrich and a much more conservative caucus pushed for draconian versions of DLC policy items like "tough-on-crime" laws and limiting the social safety net to force the poor to work harder. The GOP vision was all sticks and no carrots.

In this milieu, Clinton pivoted right, too, seeking "triangulation" by softening some of the most stringent aspects of the Republican agenda.[23] Perhaps the signal statement of that strategy was Clinton's famous 1996 State of the Union speech, in which he declared big government dead but differentiated himself from the hard-core antigovernment nostrums of the Gingrich Republicans:

> The era of big government is over. But we cannot go back to the time when our citizens were left to fend for themselves. Instead, we must go forward as one America, one nation working together to meet the challenges we face together . . . Our goal must be to enable all our people to make the most of their own lives—with stronger families, more educational opportunity, economic security, safer streets, a cleaner environment in a safer world.[24]

That vision, in fact, drove Clinton's efforts at shaping the most significant limit to American social democracy during his two terms in office: the Personal Responsibility and Work Opportunity Reconciliation Act (PRWORA) of 1996.

Clinton and the DLC had long been fascinated with using government "sticks" to enforce personal responsibility to reduce poverty, and that personal responsibility took the form of "family values," where government could use punishment to reinscribe two-parent, heteronormative gender roles.[25] A *New Democrat* article from September 1991, for instance, about the problem of "deadbeat dads," pointed out that in Arkansas, where Clinton was governor, the state had been working with credit agencies to "wreck their credit."[26] It took Republicans, however, as had been the case with NAFTA, to give Clinton the space to enact an agenda built on "personal responsibility" for the poor.

Calls to reduce "welfare" as an entitlement had long been a goal of conservative proponents of human capital. Feminist welfare rights activists in the 1960s and 70s challenged a system of economic security built around male breadwinners, and though they never fully established the right of all Americans to sustainable social support, their lobbying had resulted in dramatically expanded access to welfare benefits. In the decades since, conservatives sought to limit welfare since many recipients, particularly Black women, were seen as not having "earned" benefits. Ironically, by the 1980s, some welfare opponents, rather than continuing to criticize the construction of poor families, were instead pointing to changing gender norms to advocate for combining limits to benefits to the promise of job training. The Hudson Institute's *Workforce 2000* (1987), for example, linked calls for higher education standards and the shift of the national economy toward the service industry with a recognition that women, in the future, would make up a larger portion of the labor force. The report leaned into the trend, and in fact, sought to force more women to work in order to limit welfare benefits: "Now that a majority of non-welfare women with young children work, it no longer seems cruel to require welfare mothers to do so. The current system should be replaced with one that mandates work for all able-bodied mothers (except for those caring for infants) while providing training, day care, and job counseling."[27] In Wisconsin, Governor Thompson had made welfare reform a major priority, too, signing into law a program to replace AFDC before Clinton completed federal reform in April 1996. The Wisconsin Works program required low-income parents either to get a job or to complete an "employability plan" that included work training for those not yet deemed "job ready" to continue to receive funding. Clinton's welfare reform also allowed Thompson to go even further, capping lifetime benefits.[28]

The GOP takeover of Congress made welfare reform into a pressing agenda item for Clinton. Though historians have argued Clinton used his veto power to prevent even more punitive versions of reform, the bill he signed on August 22, 1996, was plenty draconian, forcing states to create work requirements for public assistance, replacing benefits with block grants, limiting lifetime benefits to a maximum of five years (and allowing states to set even shorter limits), and strengthening child support enforcement.[29] As had been the case with NAFTA, proponents of welfare reform touted education and job training as the missing pieces that would combine with the "motivation" of no longer having welfare cash payments to allow poor Americans, disproportionately African American and Latino, to succeed in a knowledge-based economy. Welfare reform, however, did little more than continue to punish poor Americans for the structural lack of jobs in neighborhoods bereft of economic investment. To the extent that inner-city welfare recipients engaged in behavior that shut them out of the job market, as the sociologist William Julius Wilson explained in 1996, such responses were logical adaptations to a social fabric in which work had "disappeared."[30]

The overarching result of Clinton's first term was to exacerbate the upsurge of inequality in the United States. In fact, in the twenty years after 1996, the number of Americans living in extreme poverty skyrocketed. Further, the version of PROWRA Clinton signed actually diminished the possibility of using job-training programs to help workers at the lower end of the job market get the skills for a living wage job; instead, training programs, according to economist Gordon Lafer, began "to focus almost exclusively on an ideological agenda aimed at reinforcing the value of hard work at low wages." Predictably, though millions of working people lost financial support in the years after PROWRA, most of these workers were unable to find stable jobs that could support their families.[31] The education myth represented the glue that made the further diminution of social democracy palatable for many Democratic policymakers.

Teacher Unions and the Education Myth

National teacher unions that had supported Clinton embraced the education myth too, likely for strategic reasons. Both the NEA and AFT had endorsed Clinton by large margins in 1992, and that support did not wane four years later.[32] By the 1990s, a growing chorus on the right argued teacher unions were preventing the education reform necessary to advance the human capital of future generations of Americans. For example, as Republican presidential nominee Bob Dole asserted in his acceptance speech at the party's national convention on August 15, 1996: "If education were a war, you would be losing it. If it were a business, you would be driving it into bankruptcy. . . . And to the teacher unions I say, when I am president, I will disregard your political power, for the sake of parents, the children, the schools, and the nation."[33] In this context, the choice to support Clinton's more palatable vision of education reform made tactical sense.

Albert Shanker, despite the trepidation of much of the AFT membership, was an early supporter and advocate of more rigorous standards in education. Shanker called Bush's proposal for America 2000, which included specific language about the "knowledge and skills necessary to compete in a global economy," "bold and comprehensive. More so than any President or Secretary has come up with."[34] As part of Bush's Education Policy Advisory Committee, Shanker suggested the administration focus on "letting kids know that they are going to have to perform in school to get into college or get a job."[35]

In 1992, Shanker was even more enthusiastic about Clinton and standards-based reform, offering early support for the Arkansas Democrat while most union leaders backed Tom Harkin, and the two remained very close until Shanker's death in 1997. During the Clinton administration, Shanker was a prominent supporter of tougher standards for both schools and students, and all that implied about education's role in facilitating economic opportunity. In 1993, for example, Shanker argued in his column *Where We Stand* that Congress should support Goals 2000 because it would help the poorest Americans to become more "employable," pointing out that "they could qualify for jobs that are now moving to other countries because our young people don't have the skills to do them."[36]

NEA national leadership helped advance the education myth too. In a 1996 speech at an Education International roundtable, for instance, NEA president Bob Chase attempted to defend public education from Republicans' voucher schemes and to advocate for greater racial equity in America's schools. Chase, a Connecticut teacher who had risen to NEA vice president, was elected president in 1996. In the speech Chase conceded public education needed to be reformed to accommodate its important function of facilitating human capital acquisition in a global economy.

Indeed, it is notable how closely Chase's account of the changing landscape in the United States resembles that of Clinton and Reich: "The constant realignment going on in the world—and the nation—demands a labor force that is well educated, increasingly versatile and continually learning to reshape itself to the needs of the economy. And that brings added urgency to the need for all schools to do a better job." Chase went on to assert that educators should "view their students as clients and partners—capable of performing to higher standards, given enough time and adequate resources." The speech invoked management techniques like Total Quality Management and asked if schools could be modeled along business practices, but Chase neglected to mention any structural barriers an increasingly diverse student population faced in American cities. Nor did Chase assert that teachers bore much responsibility in the classroom beyond building the capacities of students to "possess higher-level thinking skills and to utilize the tools of the Information Era."[37]

By 1997, Chase went on to outline a widely circulated vision for a "new unionism" to reform public education, built on ensuring kids would acquire the right skills for the twenty-first century. In the late 1980s, the NEA Research Division's series of publications called *Eye on the Economy* had begun touting the connection between education and economic growth. The "new unionism" embraced by Chase as a "cornerstone" of his presidency, then, gave voice to trends already emergent in the NEA.[38] Further, given Dole's dark characterization of teacher unions, the NEA's doubling down on supporting Clinton in 1996 made perfect sense. But embracing the agenda of Clinton and the DLC meant embracing human capital as the primary function of the nation's schools.

Clinton's State of the Union address in February 1997, the first after his successful reelection campaign, was a victory lap that envisioned an even greater role for connecting education and human capital to economic opportunity. After a first term in which "we have won back the basic strength of our economy" Clinton warned the nation not to become complacent: "The new promise of the global economy, the Information Age, unimagined new work, life-enhancing technology—all these are ours to seize. . . . if we do not act, the moment will pass—and we will lose the best possibilities of our future."[39]

Clinton's "number one priority for the next four years" was ensuring "all Americans have the best education in the world." Continuing to push the accountability argument of his first-term agenda, Clinton pitched a major education investment—around $50 billion—in his Call to Action for American Education. The plan was built on ten principles. As had been the case for virtually every other proposed human capital investment from Gary Hart onward, Clinton nodded to "character" education, asserting in the sixth principle that "we must teach our students to be good citizens." But virtually every other principle called to create higher standards in the service of skills acquisition in an internationally competitive economy.

Principle #1, in fact, asserted the need for "a national crusade for education standards . . . representing what all our students must know to succeed in the knowledge economy of the 21st century." Anticipating No Child Left Behind, Clinton called for every state to "test every 4th grader in reading and every 8th grader in math to ensure this standard is met." Another principle pushed for greater community college access: Clinton had not given up on the DLC idea of a GI Bill for America's Workers comprised of new training programs for those who could no longer access union manufacturing jobs. Most controversially, Clinton pushed hard for more school choice to "foster competition and innovation that can make public schools better." Just six years after Minnesota had authorized the nation's first charters, Clinton envisioned three thousand new charter schools by the end of his second term.[40]

But what about those workers who could not benefit from investment in public education, school choice, or worker retraining? What about the Americans who would be dropped from welfare rolls under PRWORA? Clinton's plan amounted to imploring corporations, out of the goodness of their hearts, it seems, to give them a job: "I challenge every religious congregation, every community non-profit, every business to hire someone off welfare. And I'd like to say especially to every employer in our country who ever criticized the old welfare system, you can't blame that old system anymore, we have torn it down. Now do your part. Give someone on welfare the chance to go to work."[41]

The day after Clinton's address, Chase enthusiastically endorsed it in a signature speech at the National Press Club. Indeed, he left no doubt that the NEA had moved in the same direction as the AFT in embracing education reform and tougher standards.[42] Similar to the many other reinventions the DLC wing of the Democratic Party had imagined, Chase's speech—"The New NEA—Reinventing Teacher Unions for a New Era"—argued the union had to change: "The imperative now facing public education could not be more stark. Simply put, in the decade ahead, we must revitalize our public schools from within, or they will be dismantled without." Chase believed the union had sometimes "protect[ed] the narrow interests of our members, and not to advance the interests of students and schools." And what were the interests of students and schools? These became apparent in the series of pledges with which Chase concluded his speech:

> To parents and the public, NEA pledges to work with you to ensure that every classroom in America has a quality teacher. This means we accept our responsibility to assist in removing teachers—that small minority of teachers—who are unqualified, incompetent, or burned out.
>
> To the business community, NEA pledges to work with you to raise and enforce standards for student achievement, to ensure that high school graduates are—at a minimum—literate, competent in the basic skills, equipped for the workplace.
>
> To President Clinton and the Congress, we at NEA pledge our enthusiastic support for the extraordinary agenda—a truly 21st century agenda for children and education—set forth in last night's State of the Union address.[43]

A 1999 NEA publication entitled *Investing in Public Education: The Importance of Schools in the New Global Economy* showed just how far the national union had come toward embracing the education myth. The work began by explaining, in language that could have come from Hart's *A New Democracy*, Reich's *The Work of Nations*, or Clinton's 1997 State of the Union: "The agricultural and manufacturing industries that made America great in the middle and late twentieth century are becoming less important economically. In this new and emerging economy, access and control of electronic information and technology will greatly determine both individual and national economic accomplishments."[44]

In making the case for enhanced public education funding, the publication, citing Gary Becker, referenced the importance of human capital in an increasingly global and service-oriented economy. In fact, the changing needs of employers led the study to conclude with the same inequality as destiny argument Richard Riley made in support of Goals 2000 in 1993: "If a person living in the United States does not possess the knowledge and skills to master technology, their wages will drop continuously until they equal the wages of similarly 'unskilled' workers who live in less economically developed countries."[45]

Given the political realities of the 1990s and the trajectory of the Democratic Party, one can understand why making such an argument would be attractive. But, given that trade policy—a political choice—further motivated American manufacturers to seek cheaper labor elsewhere, and given the shrinking social safety net, this argument effectively gave up on doing anything for those who couldn't get the right education.

Clintonism and Its Discontents

As Bill Clinton reflected in 2013, his goal as head of the DLC had been to elevate a vision that, by somehow doing all things for all people, would not upset the global capitalist order. "The DLC believed that the Democratic Party's fundamental mission," Clinton remembered, "was to expand opportunity, not government. . . . And we called for an end to the era of false choices. We were pro-growth and pro-environment; pro-labor and pro-business; pro-work and pro-family; pro-middle class and pro-antipoverty efforts that work."[46]

Clinton's view, however, was based on the mythology that embracing meritocracy and investment in human capital could paper over any negative repercussions caused by dismantling the government safety net and making American jobs more susceptible to capital flight. The promise that a greater pie would compensate those who lost in the global competition was fanciful. All the way back in 1984, neo-liberal Randall Rothenberg had argued the labor movement represented the main source of resistance to a market-driven, human capital approach to economic prosperity:

> A clash seems inevitable, for virtually every single issue promoted by the neo-liberals seems to run counter to the interests of organized labor as they are currently expressed. . . . And of course, no single issue currently divides the Democrats as the problem of free trade versus the protectionism that organized labor so dearly wants. But there is more. . . . Labor's vitality has been dependent on large, national industries; collective bargaining has thrived on the ability of centralized unions to negotiate with centralized industries . . . an economy that requires constant adaptation to improve productivity and match the needs of the global market cannot admit of a labor movement whose very existence is predicated on a rigid system of rules.

As Rothenberg also pointed out, the neo-liberals would face resistance from "special interests"—among them, African Americans, who were also largely being excluded from the spoils of the postindustrial society.[47]

Rothenberg could not have been more prescient. Indeed, unions and their "rigid system of rules," as well as other "special interests" such as the civil rights movement, had been important advocates for social democracy. Carter's lukewarm embrace of unions and the failure of labor reform hinted at this conflict, and the clashes between Reich, Clinton, and the AFL-CIO over NAFTA would prove it. As the power of "special interests" like labor diminished, there would be fewer vocal advocates protecting those who could not become "symbolic analysts" in the global economy.

In *Putting People First*, Clinton and Gore had promised to ban striker replacements and to repeal Section 14(b) of Taft-Hartley, which allowed states to make union security clauses illegal. But Clinton's time in office highlighted how right was Rothenberg's account of the choice Democrats would face in the United States. Clinton, Gore, Reich, and the DLC prioritized market-driven, human capital policies because they promised economic prosperity without altering the growing power that employers were amassing at the expense of working people. They put little political capital into social democratic protections like enhancing the ability of workers to collectively bargain, and as with welfare reform, actively undermined other protections. Under Democrats in the 1990s, any possibility of broad social democratic alternatives to neoliberal capitalism shriveled into nothing more than desiccated remains.

In the 1990s, the economic inequality emergent during the Reagan years continued to rise dramatically as almost all of the profits of economic growth were racked up by multimillionaires and billionaires or, to a lesser extent, the symbolic analysts Reich had hoped would include a much broader group of people. Indeed, as the former secretary of labor noted in his 1998 memoir, the economy was quite strong in the decade, corporate profits and the stock market had exploded, and both unemployment and inflation were low. And yet, he pointed out, "half of all workers are still earning less than they did in 1989. And despite modest gains among the working poor, the 1990s have witnessed greater polarization of income than at any other time since the Second World War. We are fast becoming two cultures—one of affluence and contentment, the other of insecurity and cynicism."[48]

Some economists have argued that increased inequality since the 1980s derived in large part from "lethargic" education growth in the late twentieth century, since new technologies demanded more college-educated workers, while the education system failed to supply them.[49] It is hard to imagine, however, that an expansion of education of any kind could have come close to compensating for the disastrous national policy choices made during the Carter, Reagan, and Clinton years. But even the political efforts to expand access to higher education in the 1990s further exacerbated inequality. In fact, a key piece of Clinton's second-term agenda was a college tuition tax credit signed into law in 1997. While asserting that this credit would help all Americans, Clinton knew it would disproportionately help wealthy families. Clinton's own pro–Wall Street treasury secretary Robert Rubin, in fact, opposed them for this reason. Not only did these credits expand inequality, but they also helped inflate college tuition costs for everyone else while the Pell Grant program continued to lose relative value.[50]

In summary, even if more education *were* the answer, the increase in the college wage premium—the extra income the average college graduate could expect—would not have been enough. Simply put, not everyone could be upwardly mobile, and for those in the vast group of Americans in the bottom two-thirds of the economic distribution, the policies of the DLC championed by Clinton facilitated the flight of blue-collar jobs and made it ever more difficult to access the social safety net. And they replaced these jobs and social supports with false promises. Further, the 1994 Crime Bill, touted by Clinton and other Democrats like Delaware senator Joe Biden, which stiffened penalties on a series of infractions, provided funding for new prison construction and institutionalized inequitable penalties for crack cocaine. Even though crime rates had been declining, the bill would play a major role in expanding the percentage of Americans incarcerated.[51] Thus the combination of NAFTA and the failure of striker replacement reform made blue-collar jobs more precarious, the PRWORA removed the floor from beneath the poor, and criminal justice policy locked increasing numbers of impoverished Americans in prison for long sentences. By overemphasizing the connection between education and economic opportunity through the rhetoric around Goals 2000 and other education policies, the Clinton administration made it even more difficult for working Americans to understand what had gone wrong. Instead, for many of these Americans, resentment and disaffection with the political system grew.

Indeed, as Reich also pointed out in his memoir, the midterm election of 1994 represented a revolt of white men in the downwardly mobile middle class who feared their long-term economic outlook. "The largest defections from the Democratic Party," Reich highlighted, "were men without college degrees—nearly three out of four working men—whose wages have been dropping for a decade and a half. They tilted to Republicans sixty-three to thirty-seven percent."[52] Telling these voters to simply get a college degree or to retrain for jobs that were no longer secure was a recipe for political disaster. The United States certainly was shifting toward a society in which many jobs required more knowledge than had been the case in the past, something both Bell and Drucker had foreseen decades before. Further, more and more jobs in knowledge and service, especially in the growing fields of health and education, were filled by women workers.[53] The threat to male blue-collar jobs in the 1990s contributed to the continued prominence of what historian Robert Self has called "breadwinner conservatism" that had emerged in response to women, seeking greater economic equality but threatening a particular vision of the nuclear family, entering the labor market in larger numbers in the 1960s and 1970s.[54] The demographics Reich cited, then, were not surprising, and represented a flowering of the political conflict between "populism and elitism" that Bell foresaw in *The Coming of Post-Industrial Society*.

Pat Buchanan's bid for the Republican nomination in 1996 provides us a window into this growing resentment. Buchanan, a conservative populist who began as a Nixon speechwriter, had made a career mobilizing anti-elite sentiment, pioneering an argument that characterized liberals—especially those with academic credentials—as elites who opposed the needs of the so-called silent majority in the important election of 1968 and during the Nixon presidency.[55] In 1992, Buchanan sought disaffected Republican voters, particularly those hit by the recession in Bush's last year in office. He garnered 38 percent of the vote in New Hampshire by going after Bush on both economic and cultural issues. In his bid to be the party's nominee four years later, Buchanan stressed his opposition to cultural pluralism (following in the footsteps of Bennett), NAFTA, and undocumented immigration.

Buchanan's campaign challenged the inevitability of a "postcapitalist" knowledge society in which nations would be helpless to protect the livelihoods of their citizens from global competition that Drucker, Reich, and others had argued was a force that could not be stopped. In one particularly memorable speech, for instance, Buchanan asked, "What has global competition done for the quality of life of Middle America? What, after all, is an economy for, if not for its people?"[56] Buchanan did not win the nomination, of course, but he garnered almost 3.2 million votes that year. And, arguably, his areas of greatest strength were in states hard hit by the flight of manufacturing capital: Buchanan won the Missouri caucus and 34 percent of the vote in both Michigan and Wisconsin (Dole only won 51 percent and 53 percent, respectively), in contrast to California, for example, where Dole won 64 percent–18 percent. By the 1990s, particularly after Democrats shifted completely away from a capacious version of social democracy and toward free trade and globalism and free markets, the cultural conservativism of many blue-collar whites was no longer constrained by the economic value of voting Democrat.

After the 1996 election, Reich, disappointed, left the president's cabinet. In his second term, Clinton went even further down the road to neoliberalism, passing the Financial Services Modernization Act (1999), which removed the firewall between commercial and investment banking in place since 1933, and the Commodity Futures Modernization Act (2000), which prevented federal regulation of credit default swaps and other high-risk instruments.[57] These laws exacerbated wealth inequality while setting the stage for the economic catastrophe of 2008.

In the 1990s, Clinton and the DLC abetted market-driven education reform in states and school districts across the country, paving the way for the titanic change ushered in by the No Child Left Behind Act in 2001. In the years to come, the education myth would only grow more powerful, reaching its high point less than a year after Clinton left office.

LEFT BEHIND

The Politics of Education Reform and
Rise of the Creative Class

In 2002, Carnegie-Mellon University professor Richard Florida published the best-selling book *The Rise of the Creative Class* (2002). Florida explicitly built on the work of Bell, Drucker, and Reich, but *The Rise of the Creative Class*, however, went even further, arguing that, by the early 2000s, the economy was driven not just by knowledge labor but by the growing number of Americans who were engaged in valuable "creative" work, in his words, the "*decisive* source of competitive advantage." These Americans flocked to cities and valued leisure activities, flexible work hours, and diversity in their occupational and geographic choices. If cities wanted to facilitate economic prosperity, Florida deduced, they should cultivate an attractive creative-class atmosphere, including a "cutting-edge music scene or vibrant artistic community."[1]

For Florida, what distinguished the creative class in the early twenty-first century is that they were increasingly unmoored from the more hierarchical employment relationships that existed when the professional class emerged in the 1970s and 1980s. Indeed, though they didn't yet see themselves as a class, he believed they were connected. "Rather than live in one town for decades," he argued, including himself in the creative class, "we seek places where we can make friends and acquaintances easily and live quasi-autonomous lives." And for Florida, this experience was generalized to "modern life," which was "increasingly defined by contingent commitments. . . . Where people once found themselves bound together by social institutions and formed their identities in groups, a fundamental characteristic of life today is that we strive to create our own identities. It is this creation and re-creation of the self, often in ways that reflect our creativity, that is a key feature of the creative ethos."[2]

This group, however, as had been the case with Reich's "symbolic analysts," represented only about 30 percent of the labor force. Though *The Rise of the Creative Class* was not really a book about education, Florida clearly defined the group as one that was overwhelmingly college educated. Indeed, his "talent index"—which policymakers were encouraged to consult—represented "a simple human-capital measure of the percentage of the population with a bachelor's degree or above." The prosperity of cities, therefore, essentially correlated to the percentage of the population with college degrees. By this logic, the way to create broader prosperity was for cities to develop a "people climate" that supported creativity and would attract talented workers.[3] For the rest of Americans, who lacked college degrees, rootlessness and disruption brought insecurity and despondence—not opportunity and creativity—such as with the working-class Kenoshans after Chrysler closed the AMC plant. A reasonable response to this problem might have been to figure out how to ensure those without college degrees could also have good lives.

Florida did note the growing tension around this inequality. And, to his credit, he also pointed out that in his diversity indices—including immigration and the "gay index"—nonwhites were clearly not benefiting from the new creative-class cities, a development he called "particularly disturbing." In response, however, Florida could only make the case for "tapping the creativity of these people" or at least helping them "share in some of the rewards." While Florida noted the creative class had doubled since 1980, he also pointed out the continued trajectory of what Bell showed in the 1970s: the service sector now made up about 45 percent of the workforce and, of course, the manufacturing sector had been reduced to about 25 percent of workers. Florida noted that many jobs in the service sector, which were becoming less sustainable over time and paid insufficient wages, grew out of necessity, as the growing creative class paid these workers to do the "chores" they needed done in restaurants, homecare, janitorial, and lawn services.[4]

Nothing could be done, however, either to directly create good jobs, provide noncreative class workers more rights, or to "recultivate and rebuild" older forms of community. All of these efforts, according to Florida, were "fruitless, since they fly in the face of today's economic realities." He implored members of the creative class to push their political leaders to invest in human creativity, which included R&D, education, and the arts.[5] Indeed, Florida did little more than reprise the human-capital-as-destiny arguments Clinton, Reich, and Riley had made in the 1990s.

The Rise of the Creative Class, widely read and cited in the 2000s, highlights just how deeply the education myth permeated American culture and politics.[6] There simply were no other serious mainstream possibilities for cultivating either economic security or social esteem for those who lacked the right degree. Democrats, by the end of the 1990s, had emerged as the preeminent champions for the education myth: in a globalizing world, the right education was all it took to give Americans the opportunity for secure lives, and that opportunity represented the common starting point for workers in a supposed meritocracy. Many Democrats still supported some legacy social democratic interventions such as Social Security and Medicare or the very limited supports provided by a reformed welfare system, while many Republicans, of course, wanted to go further in shredding union rights and the social safety net. More and more Republicans, however, in the 1990s, like President George H.W. Bush, Secretary of Education Lamar Alexander, and Wisconsin governor Tommy Thompson also began to embrace human capital as the centerpiece of a conservative argument about how to help workers in this leaner world.

As this chapter makes clear, President George W. Bush (2001–9) did more than any other Republican to elevate the education myth with his work on bipartisan education reform—No Child Left Behind—that assumed education was essential to any shot at a decent livelihood. Even when Republicans and Democrats disagreed over tax cuts, or eventually, the war in Iraq, the notion that investment in education represented the panacea to facilitate equal opportunity in a competitive job market continued to grow from 2001 on. Celebrations of the power of the educated class, such as *The Rise of the Creative Class*, spun deeper and deeper fantasies about the importance of investment in human capital, even arguing that urban economic development required it. All the while, Democrats further embraced market-based education reforms that implicitly viewed education as the commodity every young person must have to succeed. Experts and politicians across the political spectrum now also pushed for "accountability" in higher education, just as they did for K-12, asserting the responsibility for economic opportunity lay with the individual or the school, not the overarching social structure.

The consequences of this path were made tragically evident in 2008 when the economy collapsed after decades of financial deregulation and mounting inequality. In the pivotal election that year, Illinois senator Barack Obama raised expectations that he would lead an effort to reinvigorate a robust American social democracy, running in the Democratic primary against disastrous free trade deals and for union rights, and to hold corporations accountable for their actions in the unfair economic conditions under which Americans worked and accessed social goods like housing. After a resounding victory, however, Obama and congressional Democrats did little to change the course of American politics, instead, bolstering the myth in both rhetoric and policy. By 2010, the first signs

of a political revolt against the education myth—from a growing populism har-
nessed by right-wing reactionaries—were apparent.

No Child Left Behind: The Mountaintop of the Education Myth

By 1996, Bill Clinton had led Democrats to make education reform a key part of
their political brand. Kansas senator Bob Dole, responding to the rightward shift
in the GOP after 1994, took an ultraconservative perspective on human capital,
pushing vouchers and slamming teacher unions as impediments to the reform
necessary to maximize economic opportunity for future American workers.
Dole's resounding defeat by Clinton convinced future Republicans running for
office to accept the principle of federal support for school reform, and this group
prominently included Texas governor George W. Bush. In Congress, this political
shift brought bipartisan increases in education funding—$7 billion in the 1997
budget agreement between the Republican-controlled Congress and Clinton, for
example—and in 1998 and 1999, calls by both Democrats and Republicans for
greater accountability along with this new money.[7]

In states like Wisconsin, Republicans such as Tommy Thompson also further embraced the conservative iteration of the education myth. In Thompson's
1997 State of the State address, for instance, the governor connected the "end"
of welfare with investment in education and job training, arguing, "Not just
in Wisconsin, but in America, if it were not for the bold, visionary and coura-
geous work done here, thousands of families across this country would be sen-
tenced to life in a failed welfare system instead of capitalizing on the freedom to
pursue their dreams." Citing the reduction in welfare rolls during his administration, Thompson argued that investing in education would ensure all those forced
to work could find good jobs, thus also reducing the state's growing number of
incarcerations: "Our goal must be no less ambitious than creating the highest
skilled, most productive workforce in the world, with businesses flocking to Wisconsin for our greatest asset—our people. It is my goal as we march toward the
year 2000 to make education so compelling and relevant to the lives of our youth
that someday we put the Department of Corrections out of business." Bringing
together a number of education themes in the 1990s, Thompson argued, "Parents
must be empowered with more choices; Education must be relevant to the workplace; Schools must be held accountable for their performance; and Technology
must pervade every facet of education." Here Thompson sought to preserve the
market-based Milwaukee School Choice program (then under challenge in the

courts), and, working with Milwaukee activist Howard Fuller, sought to make it easier to charter new schools in the city.[8]

The presidential election of 2000 pitted former Tennessee senator, DLC Democrat, and vice president Al Gore against Texas's governor Bush. Both candidates, propelled by the education myth, campaigned on investing in education and increasing school accountability. After almost twenty years of politicians arguing it was the key to economic opportunity in a global economy, in fact, education had emerged as the number one campaign issue in 2000. For Bush, education reform represented the centerpiece of the slogan "compassionate conservatism," and his campaign, building on a record of supporting accountability, school choice, and increases in education spending as governor, outlined a plan to hold states accountable in exchange for increased federal funding. Bush employed the narrative of the so-called Texas miracle in which test scores had appeared to increase dramatically and dropout rates supposedly decreased during Bush's time as governor, even though the story was misleading at best.[9]

Bush's campaign, indeed, sought to eliminate Democrats' high ground on education, even co-opting the Progressive Policy Institute's plan for performance-based education funding. And Bush, characterizing education policies that did not include accountability as racist, famously cited the "soft bigotry of low expectations" as the reason Latinos and African Americans scored disproportionately lower than whites on standardized tests. In a speech in New Hampshire in November 1999, for instance, the Texas governor linked entrepreneurialism and economic prosperity with public education for all:

> I believe that the next century will be a time of incredible prosperity—if we can create an environment where entrepreneurs like you can dream and flourish. A prosperity sustained by low taxes, unleashed by lighter regulation, energized by new technologies, expanded by free trade. . . . But this hope, in the long-run, depends directly on the education of our children—on young men and women with the skills and character to succeed. So, for the past few months, I have focused on the problems and promise of our public schools. The diminished hopes of our current system are sad and serious—the soft bigotry of low expectations. Schools that do not teach and will not change must have some final point of accountability.[10]

Gore, who earned the endorsement of both the AFT and the NEA, called for even bigger spending increases (more likely since the federal budget deficit had been wiped out under Clinton) to augment teacher salaries and reduce class sizes. Gore also proposed states turn around schools with poor results by shutting them down and reconstituting them with new leadership or as charters (these would be key features of NCLB). Third-party candidates Pat Buchanan and Ralph Nader, in very different ways, attacked the growing neoliberal consensus in the United States. Nader went after the increase of corporate power while Buchanan continued to attack free trade and criticized Bush for proposing to expand the federal role in public education.[11]

In one of the closest elections in American history, Gore won the popular vote but the Supreme Court awarded Bush the presidency.[12] Bush immediately made good on his election promises, as his very first legislative proposal was for a bill called No Child Left Behind, which would be the latest reauthorization of ESEA. The proposal built on many of the shifts in federal education policy pushed by the DLC and enacted in the 1990s under Clinton.[13] But Bush widened the net for reform, working with Democrats, most surprisingly liberal Ted Kennedy, who had long opposed accountability measures.

The negotiations between Republicans and Democrats in Congress and the White House featured a rare level of comity in American politics during that era, since by that time most of the officeholders in both parties had accepted the notion that education was fundamental in economic opportunity. As Connecticut senator and education reformer Joe Lieberman pointed out, both Congress and the White House shared a "common purpose": "We all want to deliver on the promise of equality and opportunity for every child. We all want to increase the supply of highly skilled workers, which we all know is critical to our future economic competitiveness and the long-term prosperity and security of this Nation."[14]

The Business Roundtable and other corporate lobbying groups helped to firm up support for provisions such as mandatory testing some conservatives found unpalatable. The justification reflected two decades of corporate jeremiads about the necessity of building human capital. As Keith Bailey from the Business Coalition for Excellence in Education (BCEE) argued, "The reforms we are seeking cannot be delayed—the world is changing rapidly and we need to ensure that our educational systems can equip our children with the knowledge and skills to meet the challenges they will face."[15]

After passing with huge margins in the House (384–45) and the Senate (91–8) in May and June, respectively, the bills went to conference to reconcile discrepancies in funding proposals (the Senate bill proposed almost twice as much money) and the final accountability measures. Negotiations were contentious, but September 11 helped motivate both sides toward agreement, and the final bill passed by overwhelming margins in both houses.[16]

Congressional debate highlighted the bipartisan nature of the education myth. As the bill came out of committee on May 1, Republican senator Bill Frist (Tennessee) argued, "Those basic skills that we know and that everyone—liberals, conservatives, Democrats, and Republicans—recognizes you have to be equipped with if you are going to live a fulfilling life are increasingly competitive, not just in local towns, communities, States, or regions in this Nation but across this great world in which we live, such as in mathematics."[17] Dale Kildee (D-MI) spoke about the House bill as it left the Committee on Education and the Workforce. "In a time when we are in an increasingly competitive world," he argued, "we can no longer tolerate low-performing schools that place the education of our children at risk."[18] Charles Rangel (D-NY) also asserted the imperative for education reform. "We are going to have to invest in our young people to make certain that we can keep up with foreign technology," he argued. "We hear pleas every day from the medical industry, from the State Department, how important it is for us to train people for these important jobs, and yet we find that if they are not ready to get a decent public school education, how in God's name are they going to be ready for higher education and high tech?"[19]

But even those who critiqued the bill did not challenge the notion that education was essential for a chance at economic security. Kennedy, for example, who argued much more funding was needed for the policy to work, pointed out, "We know that as we move into a global society and economy, that only about 20 percent of the new entrants into the job market have the skills which 60 percent of them need at the present time." The aging liberal highlighted just how much the party had been remade by the DLC: "We are lagging in education and in investing in people and training. The Republicans act as if [Bush's proposed] tax cut is an economic program—it is not. . . . We have to invest in terms of the training, and we have to ask this Nation what its priorities are."[20]

There were few truly dissident voices such as Minnesota's Democratic senator Paul Wellstone. Wellstone pointed to the problem of enhancing accountability without equalizing the conditions under which students learned. "I find it stunning so many Republican colleagues, much less Democratic colleagues, will vote for this," he complained. The bill would mandate that every student be tested every year, but "at the same time, we are quite unwilling to pass a Federal mandate that there will be equality of opportunity for every child to have a good education and to do well and to succeed." Wellstone, one of only five Democrats to vote against the final bill, came the closest in the Senate to pointing out how connecting education and economic opportunity would reinforce inequalities that already existed, arguing that any new mandates should come with full funding for Title I. As Wellstone summed it up, "The White House bill will test the poor against the rich and then announce that the poor are failing. Federally required tests without federal required equity amounts to clubbing these children over the head after systematically cheating them."[21]

The No Child Left Behind Act, signed into law by Bush on January 8, 2002, exchanged increases in federal funding for deliverables from states. States had to adopt academic standards and agree to test all students in math and reading from grades three to eight and at least once in high school. Results had to be publicized and disaggregated by demographic groups and income level. The law also mandated every classroom have a "highly-qualified teacher" for every core subject. Finally, NCLB implemented "accountability" by progressively punishing schools that failed to meet goals: forcing them to pay for the transportation of students who exited their schools; providing students the right to use the school's Title I funds to pay for private tutoring; and requiring schools that did not meet these criteria to hire a different staff or even to transform into a different structure, such as a charter school. (To facilitate the last part, the bill also provided $300 million for states to develop charters.)[22]

No Child Left Behind, however, did not come close to doing what it intended to do. Allowing states to develop their own tests motivated them to calibrate standards and to teach to the tests so they could be seen as making progress. Some principals and teachers, under tremendous pressure to show results, engaged in scandalous behavior such as doctoring students' test answers. In other cases, NCLB metrics caused successful schools to be labeled "failing." The charter industry, however, exploded in the 2000s: from 2001 to 2010, the number of charter schools in the United States more than doubled—from around 2,300 to 5,000.[23]

Opposition to NCLB grew quickly and dramatically. The NEA, for example, did not initially oppose NCLB. Just a year later, however, that changed, and the union argued the law needed serious revision since its "testing provisions, school labels and teacher standards [would] cause chaos."[24] NEA president Reg Weaver argued, rightly, that the law would "force many teachers to do nothing more than teach to the tests."[25] By 2005, the union challenged NCLB in court, arguing it was an "unfunded federal mandate."[26]

At root, the very premise of the bill—that punishing schools for the scores of their students would improve the school's performance—was simply flawed, particularly when school districts did not have the ability to raise students out of poverty or alleviate the trauma of racism. As had been the case with virtually every federal education policy since 1965, NCLB ignored the broader economic structures that might lead a student to succeed or fail in school as well as the relationship between where a student got an education and what jobs would actually be available to them.[27] As political scientist Neil Kraus aptly sums it up, "No Child Left Behind, while ostensibly about extending opportunity to disadvantaged students, was yet another step in exclusively linking economic opportunity solely to the schools one attended."[28]

The most lasting legacy of No Child Left Behind, however, was that it represented the mountaintop of the education myth. Bush's State of the Union in January 2002, for instance, made that clear. The first half of the speech, unsurprisingly, reviewed the US war in Afghanistan and legislative proposals to strengthen "homeland security." But when the president discussed the domestic agenda, education and jobs were inextricably linked, and Bush showed that this commonsense crossed the political aisle. After proposing extending unemployment benefits and tax credits for healthcare costs, Bush pointed out that "American workers want more than unemployment checks—they want a steady paycheck. When America works, America prospers, so my economic security plan can be summed in one word: jobs. Good jobs begin with good schools, and here we've made a fine start. Republicans and Democrats worked together to achieve historic education reform so that no child is left behind."[29] Bush would go on to outline the necessity of energy policy, free trade, and tax reduction, but human capital had become the foundation of any economic opportunity. That notion, indeed, was so commonsensical that almost no one in the mainstream of either party could even imagine challenging it.

The Higher Education Myth

As the number of college graduates continued to grow after the 1970s, American policymakers also began to focus more on postsecondary education and its connection to human capital and economic opportunity. In 1975, almost 22 percent of Americans had completed at least a four-year college degree. After a spike to 24 percent in 1977, the number hovered around 22–23 percent over the course of the 1980s. By the end of the 1990s, however, the percentage of graduates had exploded, reaching 29.1 percent by 2000.[30]

By the 1990s, politicians argued that higher education would not only train new graduates for jobs, but would also facilitate innovation, both through research and development, and also by graduating students who would become innovators themselves. In Wisconsin, Governor Thompson, before joining Bush's cabinet as secretary of health and human services in 2001, emerged as a staunch advocate of this approach. In July 1996, for example, Thompson created the Blue-Ribbon Commission on 21st Century Jobs, tasking the group with explaining "the role the University of Wisconsin System, the Wisconsin Technical College System and Wisconsin's 21 private colleges and universities can play in job development, and examine methods of insuring that job growth is successful in all geographic areas of the state."

In calling for the commission, the governor highlighted national themes we have seen connected to K-12 education. Thompson pointed out both that "technical progress and the imperatives of a global economy have mandated a change in the skill profile of the labor force" and that "Wisconsin must be aggressive and competitive in attracting and keeping high tech jobs."[31] The commission, chaired by the president of the UW System, Katharine Lyall, put together a report that argued there was in Wisconsin an "'underdeveloped' workforce yet to realize its potential" consisting of "chronically un- or under-employed workers who generally lack modern skills and work attitudes." The commission implied these groups were concentrated in "inner-city and rural areas of Wisconsin." And since "higher levels of employee proficiency are required as businesses fight to remain competitive in a global economy" the commission concluded that "worker training and education must be at the heart of Wisconsin's job strategy for the 21st Century."

How would Wisconsin do that? Resurrecting the notion that the university should serve the broad needs of the state, the commission called for a "New Wisconsin Idea for the 21st Century" built on "innovative learning opportunities" for all Wisconsinites, wherever they lived. This education investment was to include "work-based learning" at universities and technical colleges and career planning in high school, in addition to "recogniz[ing] and support[ing] the state's technical colleges and public and private colleges and universities as primary engines of high-quality economic growth." The rising inequality in the state (what the report called the "Two Wisconsins") and lack of jobs for those hit hard by capital flight would thus be met with a holistic plan to tailor the state's education system, particularly in higher education, to the supposed needs of employers and to invest in technology by connecting the resources of the UW System to private industry.[32] This was a much narrower vision of the Wisconsin Idea, one that did not seek to inform broader social democratic possibilities at all, but, instead, sought to ready workers for the supposed realities of a zero-sum global economy.[33]

A purported "shortage of skilled labor" represented the biggest impediment to job growth in the state. But the data on which this argument rested was dubious. Indeed, the commission cited the Forward Wisconsin Survey, which examined why companies moved to Wisconsin from 1992 to 1995. The survey, however, found that 96 percent of companies were either "Very Satisfied" or "Satisfied" with their move. Though employers surveyed believed job training was important and cared deeply about ready access to labor (what employer doesn't?), neither the FWS or either of the other two surveys on which the commission based its work provided any actual evidence employers were not able to fill skilled jobs. Had that been the case, wages would likely have been driven up dramatically. While the report pointed out that a few employers were offering higher wages, the state economic outlook tracked with what Reich had argued was happening nationally at that time: for most workers, wage increases lagged behind the rate of inflation. More likely, other policies in Wisconsin—like employer resistance to unions in new manufacturing or the fact that most job growth occurred in the nonunion service sector, which the report projected would grow to 75 percent of all new jobs by 2005—drove down wages.[34]

Further, while the Governor's Commission acknowledged the lack of jobs in certain parts of the state—particularly in Milwaukee, which had lost thirty thousand manufacturing jobs since 1986—it blamed the culture and lack of education of those in "inner city areas" instead of capital flight. Indeed, the primary culprit was the "alarming numbers" of teenage pregnancies out of wedlock and high school dropout rates. There were few concrete recommendations for bringing jobs to the city that had been decimated by systematic disinvestment.[35] Instead, the report assumed that, as if by magic, better education for Milwaukee residents would create good jobs.

Therefore, the commission sought more education as the solution, and the report's recommendations highlighted just how much the social democratic vision had narrowed to little more than subsidizing the needs of employers in Wisconsin as the education myth choked off other possibilities. As the Blue-Ribbon Commission argued, expanding "opportunities at universities and technical colleges for work-based learning, [and] integrating classroom studies with productive work experience in fields related to the student's career goals" would "provide employers with screened and semi-experienced employees" and improve worker retention. In turn, Wisconsin could become more competitive in the race "to attract and retain firms offering skilled employment."[36]

Thompson, building from the commission's findings, made investment in higher education a major part of his agenda in the 1990s, proudly touting the New Wisconsin Idea and especially the notion that investing in the UW System would yield new high-technology, professional jobs as the state moved beyond traditional manufacturing. Indeed, Governor Thompson did bring billions of dollars in new funding to the UW System, even though his vision represented a far cry from that of John Bascom and Robert La Follette.[37]

By the early 2000s, the importance of higher education—through training college graduates to gain professional skills, become innovators, or even join the creative class à la Richard Florida—was entrenched in the education myth. Even if bringing more Americans into higher education was the right approach to the growing class divide, however, broad, affordable access to colleges and universities would have been essential. And yet, in the 1990s and 2000s, access to universities instead became even more unequal. Economic recessions led states to cut funding for higher education, rationing access to the best colleges and universities in a zero-sum competition supposedly based on merit (very much unlike the 1940s and 1950s). Nationally, state appropriations for colleges and universities fell from about $8.30/$1,000 personal income in 1986 to $6.60/$1,000 in 1998 and between 2001 and 2004, spending per student fell by 15 percent.

Student tuition made up the shortfall, tripling from 1980 to 2010 at public colleges and universities. Federal policies like Pell grants, designed to democratize higher education, failed to keep up, and students relied on a greater percentage of loans to make up the shortfall.[38] These policies, particularly in California, where the university system was forced to significantly weaken affirmative action in the 1990s, led to an even broader racial gap in the construction of the future creative class.[39]

Across the nation, Gary Becker's more conservative version of financing human capital through student loans was gaining ground, even if these loans were not disbursed through strictly private credit markets and instead were guaranteed by the federal government.[40] The result was a growing chasm between wealthy families' ability to send their kids to college (and thus access to the professional class) and that of working families.[41] And from the 1970s on, the gap between students who could access elite universities and those who could not widened considerably. As just one example of this trend, despite critiques of affirmative action for minorities to access a rationed set of slots at elite institutions, the most lasting affirmative action program in American higher education was legacy admissions to elite universities, which reinforce economic and racial inequalities.[42]

Given the push for more higher education combined with growing inequality in access, it is unsurprising that a major Education Department commission in 2006 served as higher education's version of *A Nation at Risk*, arguing both for the necessity of human capital and that the system should better condition its students for the global reality of the job market. The commission was charged by Education Secretary Margaret Spellings, an education reformer in Texas who served as a senior adviser to Bush as governor. As a domestic policy adviser to the president, Spellings played a major role in negotiations between the administration and Congress over NCLB.[43] After Roderick Paige's departure as secretary in 2004, Bush appointed Spellings to fill the position.

The Spellings Commission worked to elevate a conservative version of the education myth. Chaired by private investor Charles Miller, the commission highlighted how much Bush's Education Department saw the function of higher education as serving the direct employment needs of corporations. Of the other seventeen members, four were corporate leaders (from IBM, Microsoft, Kaplan, and Boeing) and another was an executive of the US Chamber of Commerce. Others included education reformers (the director of Education Trust, the chairperson of EduCap Inc., and former North Carolina governor James Hunt), university administrators, and two engineering professors. Arturo Madrid represented the only faculty member from the humanities, and, of course, there were no workers. The report also thanked the Lumina Foundation and Microsoft for their assistance.[44]

Like *ANAR*, the report, entitled *A Test of Leadership: Charting the Future of U.S. Higher Education*, began with anxiety around the competitiveness of American education, only this time with regard to universities: "We may still have more than our share of the world's best universities. But a lot of other countries have followed our lead, and *they are now educating more of their citizens to more advanced levels than we are.* Worse, they are passing us by at a time when education is more important to our collective prosperity than ever" (emphasis in original). For the Spellings Commission, it was obvious why this was a problem: "We have seen ample evidence that some form of postsecondary instruction is increasingly vital to an individual's economic security." The commission pointed to the lack of preparation in high school for postsecondary work, rising costs, a "confusing" financial aid system, and "unacceptable numbers of college graduates [who] enter the workforce without the skills employers say they need in an economy where, as the truism holds correctly, knowledge matters more than ever." In particular, *A Test of Leadership* worried that "the consequences of these problems are most severe for students from low-income families and for racial and ethnic minorities."[45] Clearly the report helped to support the notion that, once again, the failure of working people, especially minorities, to accrue the right human capital was responsible for growing economic inequality.

The Spellings Commission did highlight some of the challenges many students faced in degree attainment. The report rightly pointed out that while more students were going to college, the percentage of students graduating was not increasing at the same rate. Further, a disproportionate amount of these students were minorities and/or lacked economic resources. Still, though the report spoke to some of these inequalities, the recommendations were limited, pushing for better high school standards to "create a seamless pathway between high school and college"; for admitted students to "take [more] responsibility for academic success"; and for "cost-cutting and productivity improvements in U.S. postsecondary institutions" while supporting an overhaul of the byzantine financial aid system and a "significant increase in need-based financial aid." The overarching argument assumed the US system of higher education should become more accountable, just as had been proposed with NCLB, in exchange for any additional funding.[46]

Though *A Test of Leadership* explained how crucial a college education was for economic opportunity, the report's conservative perspective meant the report simply accepted as given that state support would be limited. The Spellings Commission produced staggering numbers: between 1995 and 2005, average tuition and fees at public universities had risen 51 percent, including 30 percent at community colleges as "state funding fell to its lowest level in over two decades." A logical conclusion might have been to call on Congress to provide a massive infusion of funding to support state governments' higher education budgets. The commission did not make this argument, however. *"The bottom line,"* concluded *A Test of Leadership, "is that state funding for higher education will not grow enough to support enrollment demand without higher education addressing issues of efficiency, productivity, transparency, and accountability clearly and successfully. However, based on our commission's review of the education needs of our nation, we encourage states to continue their historic and necessary commitment to the support of public higher education."*[47] Accountability for higher education, just as was the case for K-12, was intended to show that responsibility for economic opportunity lay with the individual or the school, not changing the overarching social structure.

By the end of the Bush administration, prominent scholars were pointing to the inequities that existed in American higher education and arguing to rectify them in order to make the economy more equal. The economists Claudia Goldin and Lawrence Katz, for instance, in their widely cited book *The Race Between Technology and Education* showed the inverse correlation between state support for education and economic inequality over the course of the twentieth century, citing a "race" between the demands of employers to keep up with technological change and the American education system's ability to improve educational attainment. Though some scholars have pointed out that this correlation did not necessarily equate to causation (indeed, it seems equally plausible that greater investment in education stems from widespread economic security), Goldin and Katz at the very least laid out the case for democratizing access to higher education, arguing that while more Americans were responding to the incentive of a higher wage premium by attending college, they were not completing it at the same higher rates. The economists called for greater access to preschool for families with limited resources; reform of K-12 education so more kids would be ready for college (also recommended by the Spellings Commission); and finally, "financial aid sufficiently generous and transparent so that those who are college ready can complete a four-year college degree or gain marketable skills at a community college."[48] Still, just as had been the case with Spellings, the economists did not make the obvious leap: if access to higher education was so crucial to economic success, shouldn't students receive that education as a right, as is the case with K-12 education?

Furthermore, as both Florida and the Spellings Commission failed to do, Goldin and Katz never really addressed the question of what would happen to those American workers who did not go to college, even if all 61 percent of those who attended could graduate. Empirical evidence from the Bureau of Labor Statistics shows that the majority of American jobs have never required college degrees. In 2010, for example, almost 70 percent of jobs in the United States still only required a high school degree or less education. Expanding access to education, then, would seem only to flood the market with more creative-class workers who would be overqualified and underemployed.[49]

But even if we assume that, magically, more educated workers would somehow facilitate such broad prosperity that there would suddenly be enough professional jobs for all college graduates, what would their jobs be like? Florida had fantasized that the creative class had begun to "control the means of production . . . because it is inside their heads; they *are* the means of production."[50] This may have been true for some workers, but the reality for most was that their employers—from rich tech companies like Apple, Microsoft, or Facebook that hired elite graduates all the way down to the regional insurance company that hired graduates from public comprehensive universities—continued to extract profits from the labor of these workers, and they had their own motivations to drive down labor costs.

Indeed, beginning in the 1990s, workers in many sectors of the knowledge economy were finding their relative economic position decline as the wealth of the richest Americans exploded. By that time, many employers had begun using business principles such as "knowledge management," which sought to maximize returns to shareholders by determining which knowledge work created the most value and to reduce the costs of lower-value work as much as possible. In some sectors, employers sought cheaper labor through outsourcing or automating many of the lower end creative-class jobs and by importing the work of cheaper labor elsewhere.[51] The tech industry, in particular, sought to lower costs by pushing Congress to liberalize immigration of workers with training in STEM fields.[52] For those who kept their jobs in the white-collar sector (outside of the work that was high-value "proprietary labor"), the strategy was more surveillance and discipline, and it was no coincidence that this management strategy was similar to the accountability measures put into place for teachers and schools under NCLB and, later, Obama's "Race to the Top." In sum, by the end of the 1990s, the incomes of most college graduates, while still paying a premium above most blue-collar workers, were also starting to stagnate, and many white-collar workers were losing the very discretion that would have made their work "creative."

Even the higher education labor force—a group of workers at the upper echelons of education attainment in the United States and paragons of what Florida called the creative class—was in the midst of a long trend of growing insecurity and deprofessionalization. From 1970 to 2019, as the number of college students in the nation more than doubled, so did the number of college and university instructors. But much of this latter increase was for part-time, nontenure track faculty, which increased by a factor of seven during the same period, from 105,000 to 755,000. The period in which the creative class supposedly began to dominate the American ethos, from the late 1990s to the precipice of the Obama administration, was characterized by a dramatic shift in this direction: the percentage of full-time tenure track faculty from 1997 to 2007 declined from 33.1 percent of the total higher education teaching force (about one-third) to 27.3 percent (just over one-fourth). Part-time faculty increased from 34.1 percent to 36.9 percent. Not only did tenure track status bring higher pay and better benefits and enhanced job security, but not being eligible for tenure, importantly, prevented these workers from having the kind of academic freedom and professional discretion that supposedly marked what Drucker had called "knowledge work" or what Florida called creativity.[53]

Even if Goldin and Katz, then, had been right about the importance of more education, their argument neglected to chart the political decisions needed to re-empower the growing knowledge core of the professional class, not to mention the noncollege-educated workers left behind entirely. Nevertheless, the college premium, coupled with politicians from both parties who turned their back on the livelihoods of those without college degrees, still left going to college as the commonsense solution to economic inequality.[54]

Hope and Change

On February 13, 2008, Illinois senator and presidential candidate Barack Obama spoke in the southern Wisconsin city of Janesville. By that point, the economy was already feeling the impact of a wave of housing foreclosures, and the jobs of the UAW workers at the auto plant there were under threat (major cuts would come later that year, and by 2010, the plant would be completely closed). A candidate for the Democratic nomination, Obama characterized himself as a reformer who would take on the inequality that had grown under twenty years of the DLC at the helm of the nation's oldest political party.

In Janesville, Obama spoke to the promise of secure, blue-collar jobs that many Democrats no longer believed were worth fighting for. "It was nearly a century ago that the first tractor rolled off the assembly line at this plant," he began. "The achievement . . . led to a shared prosperity enjoyed by all of Janesville. Homes and businesses began to sprout along Milwaukee and Main Streets. Jobs were plentiful, with wages that could raise a family and benefits you could count on." Obama contrasted himself with his eventual predecessor George Bush and his two opponents that year, Democratic senator Hillary Clinton and Republican senator John McCain, both of whom he implicitly argued had abetted the recession and the housing crisis in a "failure of leadership and imagination in Washington—the culmination of decades of decisions that were made or put off without regard to the realities of a global economy and the growing inequality it's produced."[55]

In a sharp rebuke to the Clintons, Obama argued this Washington was one "where decades of trade deals like NAFTA and China have been signed with plenty of protections for corporations and their profits, but none for our environment or our workers who've seen factories shut their doors and millions of jobs disappear; workers whose right to organize and unionize has been under assault for the last eight years." The senator from Illinois knew Americans wanted change: "I realize that politicians come before you every election saying that they'll change all this. They lay out big plans and hold events with workers just like this one, because it's easy to make promises in the heat of the campaign. But how many times have you been disappointed when everyone goes back to Washington and nothing changes?" Obama, however, would be different: "When I talk about real change that will make a real difference in the lives of working families . . . it's not just the poll-tested rhetoric of a political campaign. It's the cause of my life. And you can be sure that it will be the cause of my presidency from the very first day I take office."[56]

Though Obama could not extricate himself from the notion that we must "train our workforce for a knowledge economy" by offering up tax credits to college-goers in exchange for community service (an idea the DLC had been pushing since the 1990s) and simplifying the financial aid process (as the Spellings Commission had called to do), his vision for those without college degrees went much further than Democrats had in decades. He pledged to raise the minimum wage substantially, create millions of new green jobs, and provide universal healthcare. In fact, he even criticized Clinton's plan for "requir[ing] the government to force you to buy health insurance." As important, he went after Clinton on trade, attacking her for "go[ing] around talking about how great [NAFTA] was and how many benefits it would bring" and pledging he would "not sign another trade agreement unless it has protections for our environment and protections for American workers." Here Obama spoke to a major political pressure point in Wisconsin, as empirical studies showed that by 2010, NAFTA had cost about 700,000 American manufacturing jobs and China's admittance to the World Trade Organization in 2001, a process of trade normalization begun under Bill Clinton, had cost another two to three million jobs.[57] Though Obama did not talk specifically about labor rights in this speech, elsewhere he pledged to join picket lines and to make labor reform a priority when he took office.

His promises would end up mostly in the same dustbin as those of the politicians he caricatured at Janesville, however. Obama won a massive victory over

McCain as the economy melted down, retaking states like Ohio that had begun to tilt Republican, and Democrats in Congress won a filibuster-proof majority.[58] But the major social democratic reform Obama promised was not forthcoming. For starters, Obama's administration immediately accommodated professionals, particularly in the banking industry. As Thomas Frank has argued, Obama's political instincts were deeply rooted in the notion that America was a meritocracy in which the talented would rise to the top, particularly since his own biography was marked by a rise from obscurity to fame through an Ivy League education. Thus, his administration was run exclusively by elites who had graduated from prestigious universities, especially Wall Street insiders like Timothy Geithner (secretary of treasury) and neoliberal economist Larry Summers (chair of the Council of Economic Advisors).[59]

Obama's legislative agenda in 2009 rightly prioritized preventing greater economic harm and putting demand back into the economy, as he worked with Congress to quickly pass the $800 billion American Recovery and Reinvestment Act (ARRA). Still, given the scale of the crisis, the stimulus package he passed was likely not large enough, as unemployment continued to dog the American economy for years, nor did it prioritize direct job creation, instead spending billions on tax cuts to placate Republicans.[60] Even so, pumping more money to state and local governments did stanch public-sector job losses, particularly for teachers, as about $95 billion of ARRA was used for this purpose.

Obama and his administration's belief in the magic of the education myth, however, limited their commitment to helping those outside the reach of the good-paying jobs of the professional class.[61] After passing ARRA, Obama focused on healthcare, and while the Affordable Care Act (ACA) in 2010 brought some real change—eliminating discrimination based on preexisting conditions, for instance—the law did exactly what Obama had criticized Clinton's proposal for doing: forced people to purchase insurance in private markets instead of offering a single-payer system or even a "public option" that would have made insurers compete with the federal government. The ACA never actually covered all Americans and for those it did, it wasn't always "affordable," either. Obama also put very little effort into badly needed labor law reform, following the legacy of both Carter and Clinton in this regard.[62] Given the work of the AFL-CIO and its member unions to turn out the vote for Obama in 2008, this was a major disappointment for unionized workers.[63]

Whatever moderate advances in social democracy Obama delivered elsewhere, however, in terms of public education, his belief in the magic of human capital continued to cement the nation's commitment to market-based education reform. Obama's community organizing work, just as Lyndon Johnson's teaching experience as a young man in Texas had, seems to have instilled in him a commitment to assist kids from limited means—disproportionately African American and Latino—to access better education.[64]

The intentions of the president's education agenda became immediately apparent when he appointed Arne Duncan instead of Linda Darling-Hammond as secretary of education in 2009. Darling-Hammond, a Stanford professor who many assumed had the inside track on the position as Obama's chief education policy adviser during the campaign, had criticized NLCB for its insufficient funding and narrowing of the curriculum, and she had pointed to the broader inequalities in American education that needed to be rectified instead of blaming teachers and schools.[65] Obama selected Duncan, however, who had been the CEO of Chicago schools from 2001 to 2009. There, Duncan had fought unions for greater flexibility, pushed for more authority for principals, and dramatically expanded the number of charter schools while closing neighborhood public schools. In the words of one scholar, Chicago represented "Arne Duncan's prototype on his national road show to promote school closings and education markets after he was appointed U.S. Secretary of Education in 2008."[66]

Indeed, in Chicago, where hundreds of thousands of blue-collar manufacturing jobs had been lost (including in the steel industry on the south side, where Obama had begun his political career as a community organizer), by the 1990s and 2000s, education reformers like Duncan sought to remake the schools using market fundamentalist ideology. The underlying logic was that students needed schools that could properly equip them with the right human capital to seek economic opportunities in the neoliberal city.[67] By that time, Duncan was hardly alone, as the hedge fund–backed Democrats for Education Reform (DFER) had organized a core of procharter, human capital–focused officeholders like New Jersey mayor Cory Booker.[68] Booker, for instance, with $100 million in funding from tech billionaire Mark Zuckerberg, would soon hand over Newark's schools to corporate consultants in one of the greatest boondoggles in American history.[69]

With Duncan in the fold, the Obama administration got right to work reforming schools. Obama and Duncan used $4.35 billion earmarked from ARRA as leverage to force states to change their education policies. Entitled Race to the Top (RTT), the administration's plan provided funding to a small group of states that won competitive grants in a contest to create more testing, to use that testing to evaluate teachers' supposed added value, and to create more charter schools. While only ten states initially won grants, twenty-three states changed their laws in order to make their applications more competitive, including thirteen that raised caps on charters and eleven tying teacher evaluations to test scores.[70]

Obama's first two years in office, indeed, evidenced a deep belief in the magic of human capital. In his 2010 State of the Union address, for example, the president assessed his administration's first year of efforts to alleviate the economic crisis, pointing to the successful bank bailout, expanded unemployment benefits, and the tax cuts and jobs saved by ARRA. He called on Congress to fund community banks so they could lend money to small businesses, and he also asked for an additional infrastructure bill to create jobs. But the rest of the speech decidedly promised no guarantees. Instead, Obama argued that "the only way to move to full employment is to lay a new foundation for long-term economic growth, and finally address the problems that America's families have confronted for years."

And what were those problems? First and foremost, in the international competition for good jobs, Obama argued that to compete with China, India, and Germany, the United States needed to put "more emphasis on math and science." He concluded by doubling down on the DLC-derived argument about free trade and human capital. Indeed, in a mere two paragraphs, Obama brought together Democratic assumptions—from the Johnson era to the Clinton era—about the connection between reducing poverty and enhancing education, accountability-based school reform, and the creative-class notion that only college degrees could guarantee a decent job:

> Instead of funding the status quo, we only invest in reform—reform that raises student achievement; inspires students to excel in math and science; and turns around failing schools that steal the future of too many young Americans, from rural communities to the inner city. *In the 21st century, the best anti-poverty program around is a world-class education. . . .*
>
> When we renew the Elementary and Secondary Education Act, we will work with Congress to expand these reforms to all 50 states. *Still, in this economy, a high school diploma no longer guarantees a good job.* That's why I urge the Senate to follow the House and pass a bill that will revitalize our community colleges, which are a career pathway to the children of so many working families.[71]

Storm on the Horizon

Obama's presidency, which largely failed to expand social democracy and instead represented yet another Democratic administration that advanced the education myth, would bring a backlash. That backlash was multifaceted, but the response, in which Republican politicians mobilized some of the same forces mobilized by

Nixon, Reagan, Perot, and Buchanan, exploited a growing populist resentment on the right, particularly against the supposed meritocracy in which those outside the professional class were increasingly excluded. But the revolt occurred on the left as well, as disappointment with the high promises set by Obama also cracked open the assumptions at the center of the Democratic Party.

THINGS FALL APART
The Education Myth under Attack

On November 2, 2010, Republicans rode a wave of discontent with President Barack Obama to a resounding win, taking both houses of Congress and huge gains in state offices too. Scott Walker, a Republican from the Milwaukee suburbs running for governor of Wisconsin, perhaps more effectively than any other candidate in the nation ran a campaign that mobilized the resentment of those left out of the economy created by the education myth. Drawing on a path blazed by his two political heroes—Ronald Reagan and Tommy Thompson—Walker trained the resentment on public employees, especially those who worked in public education.[1] Reagan had made hostility to public employees and their unions a key part of his challenge to Gerald Ford in the 1976 Republican primary, and famously, broke the air traffic controllers union during his first year as president in 1981. In Wisconsin, Thompson drew on a reservoir of anger toward public-sector workers in his election campaigns in 1986, 1990, and 1994 as the good manufacturing jobs like those at AMC in Kenosha continued to melt into air.[2] Walker deepened this assault on public employees, and he channeled the disappointment stemming from Obama's failure to save blue-collar livelihoods as he had promised to do in Janesville in 2008.

Walker, in his 2010 campaign, for example, made a major issue of saving manufacturing jobs by arguing he would create the right business climate. The Republican candidate promised that he would prioritize the creation of private-sector, blue-collar jobs, boasting that his agenda would create 250,000 in his first term alone. To do so necessitated lowering taxes, offering corporate incentives, and disciplining the public employee "haves" to help the private sector "have nots."[3]

Further, Walker channeled the discontent of rural Wisconsinites, who by that time, harbored deep resentment against their urban counterparts, equating them to unearned economic prosperity, government resources, and public-sector work. Though rural areas in the state received a fair share of resources, those rural Wisconsinites—the very people left out of Florida's creative class then growing in Madison, the capital city—struggled to secure livelihoods, and took out their frustration on public employees. Further, rural Wisconsinites often believed that the promise of higher education, particularly at the flagship University of Wisconsin-Madison, was outside the reach of their families. Many of these families, as Katherine Cramer's study of rural Wisconsin has shown, believed UW-Madison did not want rural students to succeed there and that high tuition priced them out of that opportunity.[4]

Finally, Walker won in part because African Americans—centered in Milwaukee, and the source of a significant number of votes—did not turn out to vote, as they did not see the Democratic candidate (Milwaukee's own mayor Tom Barrett) making much of an argument to reduce poverty and facilitate good jobs in a city in which male African American workers were hit harder than any other in the nation by capital flight. Indeed, Black turnout in Wisconsin registered one of the steepest declines in states in which African Americans represented an important part of the electorate.[5]

Conservative populists like Walker, bankrolled by deep-pocketed millionaires and billionaires who wanted to utterly decapitate social democracy, exploited the growing discontent over the plight of those without college degrees in states like Wisconsin, Michigan, and Pennsylvania, siphoning white rural and working-class votes in a war against the public sector and leveraging the apathy of African Americans toward Democrats who had done very little to make their lives more economically secure. Walker's agenda, for instance, which never unlinked jobs from education, nonetheless took aim at the liberal version of the myth that asserted that a college degree represented the path to a professional-class job, and the sole path to what Michael Sandel has called "social esteem." Exploiting the growing resentment against the professional class and Democratic policies around trade that had made nonprofessional-class jobs like manufacturing much less secure, Walker undertook a scorched earth attack on public-sector unions and the University of Wisconsin System, asserting that unionized professionals took from blue-collar workers. This effort opened the way for Walker and other reactionary Republicans to further harm all workers, as his promise of a massive number of jobs never materialized, and he also undercut private-sector unions. Walker's approach foreshadowed Donald Trump's in his presidential campaign six years later, as Trump exploited Democrats' support of a supposed meritocracy that favored those with college degrees and the trade policies that had hurt non-professional workers. Much like Walker, Trump's promises would be little more than a mirage.

But in the lead up to 2016, it wasn't only conservatives who were in revolt. Class-based efforts of low-wage workers, like the Fight for $15, and broader anti-corporate movements like Occupy Wall Street, showed that the Obama administration was far from the savior some on the left had expected. Rank-and-file teachers, most prominently in Chicago in the early 2010s, also began to revolt against the education myth, and by making social justice a key part of their organizing, rejected the neoliberal creative-class argument that left African American and Latino working people out of the city's plans. In 2015, the surprising campaign of Vermont senator Bernie Sanders was premised on the idea of rekindling a comprehensive vision for social democracy not seen since the 1930s. Young people in particular, their future increasingly constrained by a grave competition to gain human capital, supported Sanders in large numbers. Though the Vermont senator didn't win, a major area of strength for his campaign, importantly, was the Upper Midwest, where Trump would eke out his victory in the pivotal election of 2016.

The Center Doesn't Hold

While President Obama professed his faith in both an incremental approach to reform and the education myth, conservative political candidates mobilized the growing discontent of those left out of the professional class. In 2010, Republicans in Congress won massive victories two years after the election of a Democratic president, just as had been the case in 1994. This time, Republicans won a net of sixty-three seats (even more than in 1994) to flip the House, and six seats in the Senate, leaving Democrats with a narrow—and easily filibustered—majority. As important as the check on Democrats in Washington, DC, was what happened in the states. Republicans netted six governorships and control of twenty state legislatures. Like any election, this one was complicated, and stemmed, at least in part, from the motivation of those disaffected with the Obama administration—on the failure to hold finance capital accountable for the economic crisis and for the opacity of the ACA—to turn out to vote. Some of this discontent took the form of the Tea Party, which was given oxygen from the ultrawealthy paleoconservative brothers Charles and David Koch.[6] This was also the first election since *Citizens United v. FEC* (2010) opened the floodgates of dark money, disproportionately to Republicans.[7]

The new regimes across the United States were much more conservative than many Republican administrations had been before, and they were also plugged into a corporate, right-wing bill factory, the American Legislative Exchange Council (ALEC). Further, the most conservative shifts took place in the Midwestern states where enormous pressure on blue-collar livelihoods had led to higher-than-average unemployment rates following the economic crisis. Ultraconservative Republican governors Scott Walker, Rick Snyder (MI), Tom Corbett (PA), and John Kasich (OH) were all elected in 2010. In Wisconsin, the legislature also flipped from a Democratic majority to a Republican majority, giving the GOP free rein to remake state politics.

After taking over as governor in 2011, Walker immediately mobilized resentment against the education myth to usher in an ALEC-directed attack on public employees called Act 10. In what had been the first state to guarantee public employee labor rights (in 1959), Walker and the Republican legislature used the pretext of a budget crisis to effectively strip bargaining rights from public employees in the state.[8] Thousands of Wisconsinites demonstrated against the bill and Democratic legislators even left the state to prevent the senate from mustering the quorum needed to take up the bill. Ultimately, however, the GOP was victorious. As a report by Jeffrey Keefe of the Economic Policy Institute pointed out, public employees in Wisconsin were actually underpaid, when factoring in their education level, relative to comparable employees in the public sector. But the adjustment of this calculation for education level speaks volumes. As Keefe pointed out, about 60 percent of public employees had college degrees, while only 30 percent of private-sector workers did. These public employees had health insurance and other benefits that many private-sector workers—after years of capital flight and decimation of private-sector unions—lacked.[9]

Indeed, the Walker agenda clearly targeted the professional-class "winners" of the competition for human capital. Walker's first budget included a massive cut to public education: almost $800 million to K-12, $250 million to the UW System, and $70 million to the state's technical colleges.[10] Here Walker's animus toward public employees departed from Thompson, who was governor at a time when the mainstream of the Republican Party had clearly bought into the mythology around education. In contrast to Thompson, who been a vocal booster for the UW System, Walker in 2015 sought and won another massive budget cut for the UW System—another $250 million—that also eliminated statutory protections for tenure. Walker attempted an even more reactionary change to the mission of the UW System, unsuccessfully trying to extract "the search for truth" and reducing the mission to meeting the state's "workforce needs."[11] On the one hand, shifting the UW System more toward the needs of employers was within the conservative orbit of the education myth, but combined with the assault on tenure, which has had a crushing impact on the national reputation of the UW System, it also represented a clear assault on the professional creative class in the state.

In 2017, Walker desperately sought to fulfill his campaign promise to create more manufacturing jobs by brokering a deal to get the Taiwanese corporation Foxconn to build a factory in Wisconsin. The deal only brought in a negligible number of jobs, and Walker was defeated by superintendent of education Tony Evers in an extremely narrow election in 2018.[12] Nevertheless, Walker's eight years in office realigned Wisconsin politics for the foreseeable future.

Walker was the most successful, but other Midwestern governors mobilized similar resentments. In Ohio, Kasich worked with a Republican legislature to pass that state's version of Act 10.[13] In Michigan, Snyder was able to pass a right-to-work law, primarily targeting teacher unions, that eliminated union security clauses for both public- and private-sector employees, and in Pennsylvania, Corbett, like Walker, ushered in a gargantuan cut to public education.[14] Though Corbett was defeated by a Democrat in 2014, and Ohio's public employee law was repealed through a referendum in November 2011, Kasich and Snyder, like Walker, were reelected to second terms, and these states all went for Trump in 2016.

The left began to take on the education myth during the Obama years too. First, Occupy Wall Street, a protest movement that began in September 2011, elevated the issue of wealth inequality onto the national stage through the public occupation of Zuccotti Park in New York City. Though the demands of Occupy were opaque, the movement rejected the notion that American economic inequality was the legitimate outcome of a meritocratic competition in which those who accrued the right human capital were appropriately rewarded. Further, though the protestors were forcibly ejected in November, Occupy encampments spread to cities across the United States, organizers went on to work in other radical social movements, and Occupy was a factor in social democratic Vermont senator Bernie Sanders's decision to run for president in 2016.[15]

A much more politically sophisticated effort to remake American social democracy emerged through the Chicago Teachers Union (CTU), which made the nation aware of its efforts in a ground-breaking strike against neoliberal austerity in September 2012. It is fitting, given the emergence of Obama and Duncan, that a labor battle in their hometown outlined a new path for American teacher unions. In 2010, an insurgent group of activists called the Caucus of Rank-and-File Educators (CORE) won an election to take the CTU in a different direction. Previous leadership had sought merely to protect teaching jobs in the context of the neoliberal reforms in the city (a defensible goal, to be sure), but CORE officers led the union to organize with other community members in a rejection of the notion that the chance at acquiring human capital was all that was owed to students and that teachers were responsible for the persistent poverty in Chicago.[16]

Indeed, by the early 2010s, after decades of efforts to hold teachers accountable for their students' lack of economic security, there was "broad agreement," in the words of Joanne Barkan, that teachers were responsible for all that was wrong with American schools. Barkan points to a "consensus" that transcended political party and included think tanks, nonprofits, conservative antiunion groups, hedge fund managers, and editorialists who "all concur that teachers, protected by their unions, deserve primary blame for the failure of 15.6 million poor children to excel academically. Teachers also bear much responsibility for the decline of K-12 education overall (about 85 percent of children attend public schools), to the point that the United States is floundering in the global economy." This campaign escalated into attempts to reform public education by finding ways to surveil, discipline, and fire teachers.[17] Indeed, despite the efforts of national union leaders like Shanker and Chase to make unions more palatable by embracing the education myth, ironically, teachers were blamed even more for the inequality abetted by the American political system. Illinois, under a Democratic administration, was one of the first states to change its laws to deepen the connection between student test scores and teacher evaluations to be eligible for additional funding through Race to the Top.

Preparing for contract negotiations in 2012, the CTU developed a vision, called *The Schools Chicago's Children Deserve*, to frame their demands. Though the document did not explicitly reject the economic opportunity associated with public education, it called for broad social democratic change, including smaller class sizes; more nurses, social workers, and psychologists; free public transportation for students; and an end to racial inequities in schools, particularly around disciplinary practices. Importantly, the CTU sought investment in art and music courses, as well as partnering with families to reinvigorate the community connection with schools, asserting that "families are not customers, students are not seats."[18]

As the union's contract expired in September 2012, the school district sought to increase the school day while forcing teachers to contribute more to their benefits, limiting tenure, and connecting teachers' performance even more closely to student test scores. Ninety percent of the city's teachers voted to authorize a strike, and thousands of teachers and their supporters marched downtown during the seven-day strike.[19] Mayor Rahm Emanuel, who had served in both the Clinton and Obama administrations, played hardball with the teachers, but the union's resolve and the support of the community, coupled with the timing of the strike (the September in which Obama sought reelection), turned the tide in the teacher's favor. Emanuel and the school board agreed to raises for the teachers and dropped efforts to curtail tenure and increase the use of test scores to evaluate teachers. Other teachers had resisted efforts at top-down accountability before, but no union had challenged the foundation of the education myth in the spectacular way the CTU did. The effort became a model for other unions across the country.

Still No Guarantees

Following the Tea Party wave in 2010, Obama spent the next two years skirmishing with a Republican Congress over the budget. Going into the 2012 campaign, much of the luster had worn off the social democratic promises Obama made in 2008. His opponent, however, establishment Republican governor Mitt Romney, offered little more than typical platitudes about lowering taxes and free markets. And, Romney's candidacy was tarnished by his connection to Bain Capital, a firm that profited from the destruction of nonprofessional-class jobs.[20]

Romney symbolized just how out of touch he was when he was recorded speaking at a big dollar fundraiser in which he claimed that 47 percent of the country were unproductive parasites who did not pay federal taxes. The former Massachusetts governor walked back his comment, but the Obama campaign took the populist high ground, which gave the incumbent just enough traction to hold off his opponent.[21] Still, the margin of victory was less than resounding: in a lower turnout election than 2008, Obama's popular vote margin fell below 4 percent (from 7.2 percent) and electoral college votes declined to 332 (from 364). Democrats picked up a mere eight seats in the House and two in the Senate. They lost the latter two years later. This was hardly the reelection campaign that reform-oriented Democrats like FDR or LBJ had enjoyed after winning major social democratic reforms.

Obama's second term was a listless four years in which he failed to advance even the rhetoric of a social democratic agenda. The biggest idea he put forward, in fact, was a series of proposals in his 2015 State of the Union address called Middle-Class Economics, which largely consisted of recycled education myth tropes. Despite exploding inequality—that GOP priorities such as smashing unions and cutting taxes were exacerbating—Obama continued to frame the question, not as one of security for working people, but merely a better shot at a decent livelihood. "Will we accept an economy where only a few of us do spectacularly well?" he asked. "Or will we commit ourselves to an economy that generates rising incomes and chances for everyone who makes the effort?" In the speech, Obama highlighted erstwhile waitress Rebekah Erler of Minneapolis, whose husband, a construction worker, struggled following the economic crisis in 2008. The president focused on the role education played in her accessing a decent job and supporting the family as Ben's work dried up: "Rebekah took out student loans, enrolled in community college, and retrained for a new career."[22] One thing was clear: the more restrictive breadwinner model of social democracy— in which the family accessed benefits through the secure job of the male worker— had long passed. Obama lauded the effort of a woman worker to support her family. But this story, in which Rebekah represented one of "the millions who have worked hard, and scrimped, and sacrificed, and retooled" begged the question of how the Democratic agenda had failed to advance a vision in which workers like Rebekah and Ben couldn't simply have a decent livelihood without the struggle and the student debt.

Middle-class economics, then, would not upset the mythologies around education and meritocracy but would provide marginal improvements to "restore the link between hard work and growing opportunity for every American." Regurgitating the line of so many Democrats from Clinton on, Obama argued that "to make sure folks keep earning higher wages down the road, we have to do more to help Americans upgrade their skills." Though he paid lip service to restoring union rights and investment in infrastructure, Obama offered few specific proposals. Instead, he employed a human capital argument to pitch a plan for two years of tuition-free community college: "America thrived in the 20th century because we made high school free, sent a generation of GIs to college, and trained the best workforce in the world. But in a 21st century economy that rewards knowledge like never before, we need to do more." And, though Obama didn't mention it by name, he also offered his support for the Trans-Pacific Partnership— then being negotiated by his administration—in order "protect American workers, with strong new trade deals from Asia to Europe that aren't just free, but fair."[23]

If Obama's first term primarily upheld the education myth by focusing on K-12 education, his second term continued to do so largely in the terrain of higher education and job training. Early on in his first administration, Obama had worked with Congress to expand Pell Grant access, both by increasing the number of students who could receive it (Pell Grant funding is distributed through a first-come, first-serve basis until the budgeted funds run out) and increasing the maximum benefit. Still, the fact that college tuition had increased so dramatically by the 2010s meant that, in the words of one study, "by 2015 federal support for student aid was chiefly in the form of loans, which accounted for almost 60 percent of federal [student aid] spending."[24]

Interventions in Obama's second term focused on the necessity of making colleges and universities more accountable so students could shop for the colleges that would supposedly better position them to get a job. Here, the administration built on an idea from the Spellings Commission, which had argued for such a scheme in 2006.[25] And, in 2013, the administration floated the idea that since "some form of higher education is the surest path into the middle class" while college tuition continued going up, more accountability was needed to keep costs down and insure it would be the best investment possible. As Obama put it, Americans should know "who's offering the best value to students and [ensure] taxpayers get a bigger bang for their buck." Obama's system would focus on student debt and graduation rates and, crucially, the question of "how well do those graduates do in the workforce?"[26] Ultimately, while the president's plan did not include specific numerical rankings, the Education Department published an "Education Scorecard," which asserted as its most important metric a salary range for graduates and average annual cost, challenging Americans to think about the direct connection between higher education and jobs, even if graduates' income level resulted from geography, union rights, family connections, or something else entirely.[27] And no part of the Education Scorecard recognized the importance higher education might play in facilitating the "human potentiality" of civic and political engagement Danielle Allen argues is essential for citizens in a functioning democracy.

Finally, rhetoric about job training as the solution to rising inequality and downward pressure on blue-collar workers found a modest resurgence in Obama's second term. By 2014, unemployment levels, particularly when factoring in the "hidden unemployment" rate, persisted at higher levels than before the economic crisis of 2008 (The Bureau of Labor Statistics does not count long-term unemployed workers in its official unemployment tallies). Corporate leaders and human capital–oriented think tanks explained these numbers not as the long-term consequence of employers' efforts to cut costs, but instead defined them as a "skills gap." On January 4, 2014, for instance, Jamie Dimon, one of the nation's wealthiest investment bankers, and Marlene Seltzer, CEO of Jobs for the Future, authored a piece in *Politico* touting programs like JPMorgan Chase's "New Skills at Work" to close the nation's supposed skills gap. Employing boilerplate language now familiar to readers who have made it this far in this book, Dimon and Seltzer argued, "Today's globalized and technology-driven economy presents serious challenges. But it also offers opportunities and rewards skills. By strategically investing in people, training them in the skills employers in their communities are looking for, we can help drive down unemployment while building the foundation for the broadly shared prosperity we all seek."[28]

The irony of this argument alone makes it worth mentioning, considering that Dimon had just received a huge raise to a $20 million salary in 2013 in spite of the fact that JPMorgan Chase lost money the previous quarter and had had to pay $20 billion in fines for "serious misrepresentations about its mortgage-backed securities."[29] More important, the argument was empirically wrong: as economist Paul Krugman pointed out two months later, chronically unemployed workers in the United States had skills on par with those who had jobs and basically suffered from being outside of the labor market for an extended period of time. In other words, they were unemployed because they were unemployed, not because they were unemployable. Further, as Krugman pointed out, if there were huge gaps in skills, employers would have been bidding up wages, which certainly was not happening.[30]

But empirical realities didn't stop the Obama administration from furthering this narrative. On July 22, 2014, Obama signed into law the Workforce Innovation and Opportunity Act, effectively the replacement for Reagan's JTPA, which had been replaced by Clinton's Workforce Investment Act of 1998. The bill was bipartisan, and as part of the effort, Obama had tasked Vice President Joe Biden with developing a "roadmap" for "how to keep and maintain the highest-skilled workforce in the world." As Biden explained in his remarks on the bill, Americans were more than willing to "learn the new skills of the 21st century that the workforce requires." The bill would not do anything to ensure Americans had jobs, of course, but it would "empower job seekers and employers with better data on what jobs are available and what skills are needed to fill those jobs." Biden suggested job training could help unemployed Americans better access professional-class jobs such as computer coding and petroleum engineering. For those who did not or could not reinvent their lives through job training, as Biden capped thirty years of this argument, entry to the middle-class was restricted: "The mission is to widen the aperture to be able to get into the middle class by expanding opportunity. No guarantees, just expanding opportunity to American men and women."[31]

Doomsday: Election of 2016

In April 2015, former secretary of state Hillary Clinton announced she was running for president. Clinton, of course, was the First Lady from 1993 to 2001, and then served as senator for New York. She ran for president in 2008, finishing second to Obama and then joined his administration. Clinton's campaign, as had her spouse's campaigns in the 1990s, continued to assert that America was a meritocracy in which making education more accessible represented one of the small changes necessary to make the United States more prosperous for everyone.

In her campaign launch in June, Clinton invoked the legacy of Franklin D. Roosevelt by giving her speech on Roosevelt Island at Four Freedoms Park in New York City. In the speech, Clinton criticized the growing inequality and the unfairness of the economy. Unlike FDR, however, Clinton's vision for change centered on helping Americans acquire education to advance in the meritocracy. Her ultimate pitch was, like Obama, to open up the middle-class to more Americans who worked hard and made the right choices in the human capital marketplace: "Just weeks ago," Clinton began, "I met . . . a single mom juggling a job and classes at community college, while raising three kids. She doesn't expect anything to come easy. But she did ask me: What more can be done so it isn't quite so hard for families like hers? I want to be her champion and your champion."[32]

In addition to being closely connected to two of the most prominent Democrats advancing the education myth—Bill Clinton and Barack Obama—Hillary Clinton was also connected to two free trade deals that signified Democrats' lack of attention to the livelihoods of those without college degrees: NAFTA, and the TPP, which Obama had begun negotiating during Clinton's tenure as secretary of state. In the latter role, Clinton had praised TPP dozens of times, referring to it as the "gold standard" of deals.[33]

The TPP was a free trade agreement struck between the most important economies in the Pacific Rim. Though the Obama administration signed onto the treaty in 2016, it was never ratified by Congress and so the agreement was never actually binding. Based on the history of NAFTA, many Americans were unenthused about the deal's possibility for upholding workers' rights and environmental protections. Economists critical of the deal argued it would, like NAFTA, cost Americans jobs, particularly in the Midwest. One study asserted that trade deficits with TPP countries already cost the United States 40,000 jobs in Wisconsin, 215,000 in Michigan, and 113,000 in Ohio in 2015 and would only exacerbate losses were the deal ratified.[34] Senator Bernie Sanders called the TPP "NAFTA on steroids." Sanders's argument, reminiscent of Perot's in 1993, was that the trade deal would further incentivize American corporations to shift production to countries like Vietnam or Malaysia where workers made extremely low wages and toiled with few labor protections.[35]

In May 2016, Sanders announced his campaign as a social democratic alternative to Clinton and the neoliberal course of the Democratic Party. An independent first elected to the House in 1990, Sanders caucused with Democrats in that chamber as well as the Senate after getting elected there in 2006. As a representative, Sanders helped to form the Progressive Caucus, walked the picket line in opposition to NAFTA, and became known as a prominent advocate of workers' rights. He was also one of the few representatives to vote against No Child Left Behind in 2002. In the Senate, Sanders successfully advocated to include community health centers in the ACA, fought to protect Social Security, and gave a long filibuster in 2010 in which he opposed Obama's deal to extend Bush tax breaks to wealthy Americans.[36]

Sanders's launch speech in May 2015 called for a "political revolution" against the corporate interests he argued were responsible for the crisis of economic inequality and putting the nation on the precipice of environmental catastrophe. While promising a $1 trillion jobs program (though not a guarantee), Sanders hit Clinton on trade deals: "For decades, presidents from both parties have supported trade agreements which have cost us millions of decent paying jobs as corporate America shuts down plants here and moves to low-wage countries. As president, my trade policies will break that cycle of agreements which enrich at the expense of the working people of this country." He also called for a guarantee of healthcare through Medicare-for-all.

Even though Sanders used human capital language to make the argument, he also advocated for tuition-free public higher education.[37] Further, while Sanders fought to make human capital more broadly accessible, he also, fundamentally, rejected the notion that college would be the only avenue toward economic security, and that other economic interventions were necessary. In his campaign memoir he made clear, "Not everybody wants to go to college, and not everybody needs to go to college. This country needs a large supply of carpenters, plumbers, welders, bricklayers, ironworkers, mechanics, and many other professions that pay workers, especially those with unions, good wages for doing very important, skilled work."[38]

Sanders was initially written off as a protest candidate by beltway insiders, but he gained traction quickly, highlighting the growing thirst among many Democrats for a broadly social democratic vision. Indeed, Robert Reich, who was perhaps the most vocal advocate for the education myth in the Clinton administration, had moved far from his argument in the early 1990s that upskilling workers and increasing access to college would unleash broad prosperity among Americans. In his 2016 book *Saving Capitalism: For the Many, Not the Few*, Reich now referred to the "meritocratic myth" that workers were rewarded for their "worth" in the marketplace, instead pointing out that exploding income inequality was "largely the consequence of how power has been allocated and utilized." The former labor secretary specifically pointed to the growing power of corporations, the weakening of unions, and the enactment of trade deals to explain what was happening. *Saving Capitalism* was a particularly stark turnaround from Reich's account of NAFTA in *Locked in the Cabinet*, as he admitted in 2016 that he had harbored objections he could not make public as secretary of labor. Indeed, Reich, pointing out that even the wages of most college graduates had stagnated in the years after Clinton left office, concluded with a mea culpa: "I was wrong in believing that college degrees would deliver steadily higher wages and a larger share of the economic pie."[39]

Mobilizing many of the Americans whom Reich had pointed out were struggling, Sanders fared well in early state competitions, coming within a percentage point of winning Iowa and handily winning New Hampshire. Clinton ran up huge margins in southern states and delegate-rich liberal states with large professional-class populations like New York and California. Sanders's surprise showing, which included the majority of young Democratic voters, garnered more than thirteen million votes and 46 percent of the total pledged delegates, this in spite of Clinton having most of the party structure behind her, including the endorsement of almost 80 percent of the so-called superdelegates.[40] Importantly, Sanders also won victories in states such as Wisconsin, Michigan, and Ohio that had been decimated by blue-collar job loss and reactionary policies from Republican governors since 2011. Further, much of his appeal stemmed from separating his candidacy from Hillary Clinton's on trade. In Wisconsin, Sanders won by thirteen points overall, including every single county except for one.[41] It wasn't enough to win the nomination, however, and even though Sanders had pulled Clinton left—forcing her to publicly oppose TPP, for instance—she faced a tough race from the Republican nominee.

On June 16, 2015, Donald Trump, the self-proclaimed billionaire and television celebrity, announced he was running for the Republican nomination for president.[42] Though Trump had no experience in government nor had ever won elected office, it wasn't his first foray into politics. In 2000, he considered a third-party candidate run with Ross Perot's Reform Party (Pat Buchanan won the nomination instead) and flirted with running for the GOP nomination in 2012. In 2015, he entered a crowded field that eventually included almost twenty candidates.

Much like the reaction of establishment Democrats to Sanders in the Democratic primary, both the established Republican officeholders and media pundits gave Trump little chance at winning. But the real estate mogul quickly captivated Republican voters and media attention by making spectacular and typically false claims while tapping into resentment against the nation's political dynasties.

Trump skewered the political establishment and upended the niceties that defined electoral politics. He cast aspersions against undocumented Mexican immigrants and pledged to build a wall between the United States and Mexico. He caricatured critiques of racism and sexism as political correctness. It is easy enough to point to the absurdity of Trump's campaign, as well as the bold-faced lies he spun to gain media attention. Any reasonable person should, indeed, condemn the white supremacy and schadenfreude that motivated many of his followers in the primary, and the for-profit media bears a good deal of responsibility for elevating Trump, whose performances were excellent for ratings. But amidst all these phenomena, we should not lose sight that there was a rejection of an education myth in which politicians, especially Democrats, had brokered trade deals eliminating manufacturing jobs while lecturing workers to go back to school and learn new skills. In powerful ways, Trump campaigned, on a national and much more fantastical scale, as governors like Walker had done in states like Wisconsin.

In an obviously more vulgar manner, Trump, like Obama in 2008, campaigned on the security of blue-collar jobs. He began his launch speech, for instance, by arguing:

> Our country is in serious trouble. We don't have victories anymore. We used to have victories, but we don't have them. When was the last time anybody saw us beating, let's say, China in a trade deal? They kill us. I beat China all the time. All the time. When did we beat Japan at any-thing? They send their cars over by the millions, and what do we do? When was the last time you saw a Chevrolet in Tokyo? It doesn't exist, folks. They beat us all the time. When do we beat Mexico at the border? They're laughing at us, at our stupidity. And now they are beating us economically. They are not our friend, believe me. But they're killing us economically.

After calling Mexican immigrants "rapists," Trump argued, in marked contrast to Clinton, whose speech argued the United States was tweaks away from broad prosperity,

> Our labor participation rate was the worst since 1978. But think of it, GDP below zero, horrible labor participation rate. And our real unem-ployment is anywhere from 18 to 20 percent. Don't believe the 5.6. Don't believe it. That's right. A lot of people up there can't get jobs. They can't get jobs, because there are no jobs, because China has our jobs and Mex-ico has our jobs. They all have jobs. But the real number, the real number is anywhere from 18 to 19 and maybe even 21 percent, and nobody talks about it, because it's a statistic that's full of nonsense.[43]

Here Trump spoke to a reality many Americans were facing. They had been told about the improving American economy, but they knew that lower unemploy-ment rates were not equating to higher wages or more job security.

Trump, however, promised change. "We have people that have no incentive to work. But they're going to have incentive to work [when I am president], because the greatest social program is a job," he argued. "And they'll be proud, and they'll love it, and they'll make much more than they would've ever made . . . I will be the greatest jobs president that God ever created. I tell you that. I'll bring back our jobs from China, from Mexico, from Japan, from so many places." Trump did not have any actual plan to do any of these things. His stream-of-consciousness remarks concluded with an assertion that he would jawbone the heads of cor-porations into moving manufacturing back to the United States. But for some working people, in states like Wisconsin, who had heard Democratic politicians retreat from big social democratic ideas that could help them make their lives more secure, Trump's argument likely seemed a welcome alternative, even if it came with unsavory attacks on undocumented immigrants.

The New Yorker dominated the delegate count and easily won the GOP nomination with a commanding plurality of the total votes cast (about 45 percent, while Senator Ted Cruz, who had the second most, got 25 percent). In the general election, Clinton faced several unfair critiques, including a false equivalency between her use of a private email server while secretary of state and Trump's history of corrupt business practices, failure to disclose his financial records, and celebration of sexual assault in a 2005 *Access Hollywood* interview. Still, Clinton made plenty of mistakes in framing the question of blue-collar livelihoods. For instance, in a CNN town hall in March 2016, Clinton promised to "put a lot of coal miners and coal companies out of business" in the context of shifting toward green energy future. Miners, many of them Trump supporters, protested her speaking events in Appalachia, and this gaffe likely played a role in Sanders's commanding win in the West Virginia primary.[44]

Further, at a fundraiser in September 2016, Clinton called half of Trump's supporters a "basket of deplorables. . . . racist, sexist, homophobic, xenophobic, Islamophobic—you name it" arguing that many of them were "irredeemable." Clinton did point out that the other half of Trump's supporters "feel that the government has let them down, the economy has let them down, nobody cares about them, nobody worries about what happens to their lives, and they're just desperate for change."[45] Still, the recent history of mainstream Democrats, who for decades pitched the notion that upgrading workers' human capital was the only shot for an economic livelihood in a changing world, left many workers who feared for the future of their manufacturing jobs with little confidence in the party. Further, a comment like this—replayed incessantly on right-wing media — fed into the notion that Democrats seemed to hold Republican voters in low social regard. Trump, on the other hand, promised to save jobs like those at the Carrier HVAC factory in Indiana, which had announced it would shift production to Mexico but reversed course after a conversation with Trump.[46]

Coal mining may have been dangerous and work at plants like Carrier may not have represented the creative-class work Florida celebrated in the many iterations of his book. And, even without Democratic support for trade deals speeding up the process, blue-collar livelihoods would have undoubtedly been under duress over the past several decades. But the education myth—treating living people as fungible assets who should upgrade their skills and seek new jobs where they were plentiful—neglected the humanity of these workers. Some of them were at points of their lives in which they didn't want to go to college or retrain. Some simply might not want to go to school at all and nonetheless felt entitled to economic security. Many more were rooted in communities and didn't want to move away from where they lived. All of these realities were missing from the creative-class assumptions that Clinton and other national Democratic leaders had relied on for so long.

Trump made a major issue of trade deals that had put downward pressure on blue-collar livelihoods, and he went hard—and effectively—after Clinton for her support of NAFTA and TPP. He promised to bring back jobs and the dignity that seemed to be attached to them, and for some Americans, particularly in places in which manufacturing jobs had been lost, those promises, even if unlikely to be true, were better than hearing about the need to get the right education yet again.

With these winds at his back, Trump was elected president of the United States. Trump won the electoral college by narrowly capturing the so-called rust-belt states of Wisconsin, Michigan, and Pennsylvania. Though many Democrats rightly pointed out that Trump handily lost the popular vote, the geographic distribution of this vote was meaningful: subtract the state of California, and Trump would have won by 1.4 million. Subtract New York, too, and Trump would have received over 3 million more than Clinton.

American presidential elections are never the consequence of one development. But there are a few statistics that, as we attempt to understand both Trump and the broader political divisions that elevated him to the presidency, require greater attention. Whites without college degrees voted for Trump in overwhelming numbers, while fewer minority voters went to the polls compared to previous presidential elections. Further, despite overwhelming support for Clinton from the labor movement, many individual union members voted for Trump, as the supposed billionaire won a greater percentage of the union household vote (43 percent) than either Romney (40 percent) or McCain (39 percent). When third-party votes were factored in, the result was even more pronounced: Obama had won 61 percent of this demographic in 2008, while Clinton only won 53 percent eight years later.[47] These represented hundreds of thousands of votes, which likely made a significant difference in states like Wisconsin and Michigan.

It is true that Trump voters, on the whole, were wealthier than Obama voters, and that not having a college degree doesn't necessarily mean that one does not own a thriving business or have a high-paying job.[48] Clearly, plenty went for Trump because they wanted lower taxes, because they valued religious ideology above all else, or because they simply wanted to protect the advantages whites had historically enjoyed in the United States. Trump, however, won somewhere in the range of 6.7 million to 9.2 million Obama voters from 2012, which represented between 11–15 percent of Trump's total.[49] The Obama-Trump voters, many of them almost certainly union households, represented the margin that swung the election. And many of these voters went for Trump because, just as they had bet on Obama after his promises all the way back in Janesville, they saw the New York real estate mogul as more likely to restore the livelihoods—and the social esteem—of noncollege-educated workers.[50]

The Point of No Return

The numbers for Trump, indeed, spoke to a fear that Richard Florida had out-lined in 2002 as he concluded *The Rise of the Creative Class*:

> I fear we may well be splitting into two distinct societies with differ-ent institutions, different economies, religious orientations and politics. One is creative and diverse—a cosmopolitan admixture of high-tech people, bohemians, scientists, and engineers, the media and the profes-sions. The other is a more close-knit, church-based, older civic society of working people and rural dwellers. The former is ascendant and likely to dominate the nation's economic future. Not only are these places richer, faster growing and more technologically savvy, they are also attracting people. The reason is simple: These places are open and easy to enter. They are where people can most easily find opportunity, build support structures and be themselves.[51]

This was a version, of course, of what sociologist Daniel Bell had predicted back in the 1970s. In the case of Florida's prediction, however, Trump's election high-lighted that, even after the development of these two distinct societies, the elec-toral college's outsized support for smaller, more rural states meant that those outside the creative class could not be ignored, even if some Democrats wanted to.

Obama ran as the president to bridge this divide: he argued he could provide prosperity for the creative class, the manufacturing working class, and the service sector. He would reject free trade deals and empower working people, while also enhancing diversity and opportunity for the creative class. In office, Obama dou-bled down on mythological thinking, however, pushing market-based education reform and hawking access to college as the opportunity equalizer. In this sense, he largely sided with the professional class as president, mostly turning his back on the working people who elected him. Hillary Clinton's campaign, with its con-nections to the last two Democratic administrations, was a fitting symbol of the recent history of the party in 2016. Both Sanders and Trump, from the left and from the right, represented a revolt against the assumptions of the education myth.

A Social Democratic Future?

Education is one of the few common experiences that truly binds Americans together. Virtually everyone today has spent at least some time in an institution of education, and many of us for a long part of our lives: almost 90 percent of young people who attend high school now graduate, and about half of Americans aged twenty-five to twenty-nine have at least an associate degree.[1] Most of us spend a lot of time in the education system, and by choice or by necessity, we see the value of it.

But why do we value education and what do we hope to get out of it? Because our institutions change so slowly—one's experience in, say, elementary school, is not that different than that of one's children's—public education can seem to have a timeless quality, as if we have always valued it for the same reasons. But as *The Education Myth* has shown, the reasons American politicians, policymakers, intellectuals, and working people have advocated for more investment in public education has changed dramatically over time.

In the nation's first century, republican-minded leaders like Thomas Jefferson sought public education to help develop political independence. Though their vision was far from universal, they nonetheless expanded the circle of democracy, and they viewed education as providing the training to help do that. Social reformers like Horace Mann sought investment in education to cultivate dispositions to help working people navigate the rising inequality brought on by market capitalism, but public education as job training was mostly an afterthought. Republicans like Abraham Lincoln supported investment in colleges and universities to provide both "liberal and practical" education, and union activists such as Margaret Haley in the Progressive Era saw public education as teaching students to build industrial democracy. Though more working people did begin to view public education in terms of economic opportunity, the boldest and most dramatic efforts to expand social democracy in the first half of the twentieth century, such as social security, strong collective bargaining rights, and minimum wage laws had little to do with public education. While New Deal social democracy never fulfilled its promise of fundamentally guaranteeing universal economic security by establishing the right to a job, it nonetheless left in place high expectations for the postwar nation.

Investment in higher education after World War II (through the GI Bill and state support for public education) began to emphasize individual economic opportunity, particularly as the more complex American Cold War economy required more professional labor. But even so, developing citizenship, as evidenced by the Truman Commission recommendations in 1949 and state missions like that of the University of Wisconsin System in 1971, continued to be a twin goal of higher education.

By the 1960s, however, the economists Theodore Schultz and Gary Becker were at the forefront of an intellectual argument emphasizing the importance of investing in human capital. Neither was wrong to assert the importance of improving worker capabilities in American economic growth. Their arguments, however, elevated a call for investing in education at the expense of the other social democratic interventions that had put the United States on a path to greater economic security, even if that security was premised on a breadwinner model that saw women as ancillary partners and excluded many minorities. The Johnson administration, in the last great reform effort of the twentieth century, sought to rectify past racial injustices and went to war on poverty, but its main weapon in the fight was human capital instead of the broader changes, represented by A. Philip Randolph and Bayard Rustin's Freedom Budget, that could have taken meaningful steps toward fulfilling the promise of New Deal social democracy.

From there, the seeds of the education myth grew into a fast-growing and ubiquitous weed that increasingly choked off the promise of any broad social democratic possibilities in the future. In the 1970s, there were reform proposals in the political mainstream with broad social backing that could have changed this trajectory. The best example of this effort was the version of Humphrey-Hawkins that would have finally guaranteed the right to a job, thereby giving the United States its best chance of moving toward a true multiracial democracy. Instead, a new generation of Democrats, led by Jimmy Carter, elevated public education in the federal bureaucracy while withholding support from broader social democratic reforms. This generation of officeholders, seeing themselves as representing the growing number of professional-class college graduates, increasingly imagined the nation as a meritocracy in which not everyone deserved to do well.

By the 1980s, the education myth was prominently advocated by Republicans, too, as even Ronald Reagan's Education Department advanced the specious argument that the decline of economic security for American workers stemmed from the supposed decline of public education. Major political figures in both parties—including both George Bushes and Bill Clinton—built entire campaigns around the importance of investing in public education so that America's future workers could compete in a global marketplace. Crucially, the agenda of both parties also made that competition more cutthroat by negotiating trade deals that empowered American manufacturers to seek cheaper nonunion labor elsewhere. In contrast to earlier proponents of human capital investment, however, these politicians also sought to make teachers and schools more "accountable" for the supposed failure of their students to overcome the poverty and lack of economic options in an increasingly unequal nation.

Intellectuals such as Robert Reich and Richard Florida fancifully pushed to create as many symbolic-analyst or creative-class lifeboats as possible, but by 2008, the economic crash showed in stark relief that investing in human capital was failing to make most Americans, even many college graduates, more economically secure. In the election of 2008, Barack Obama mobilized a coalition built on the premise of improving the lives of professional-class, service-sector, and manufacturing workers, but broad social democratic interventions, if he ever intended to support them, lost out to efforts to mollify finance capital, more bromides about the importance of education, and market-based reform. Right-wing populists, building on the protean efforts of Reagan, Patrick Buchanan, and Ross Perot, seized the opportunity to exploit anger caused by economic insecurity, the loss of social esteem for many Americans outside the professional class, and false notions of meritocracy. Though Donald Trump perfected this strategy in 2016, he built on the groundwork laid by reactionary populists like Wisconsin governor Scott Walker who came to power in 2010. On the left, for the first time in decades, serious social democratic demands moved once again into the political mainstream through insurgent teacher unions and once-marginal politicians like Bernie Sanders.

So, the way we think about public education is once again changing. Though the process is slow, I am hopeful the education myth *is* falling. Most Americans—even those who have voted for reactionary populists like Walker or Trump—continue to view education as important. But whether it is as simple as trade policy to prioritize American nonprofessional-class jobs, or as transformative as the notion of a federal jobs guarantee, the growing prominence of other political ideas shows that fewer politicians, across the political spectrum, view education as able, as if by magic, to ensure broad economic opportunity. Further, savvy politicians in both parties seem to be recognizing the perniciousness of taking for granted noncollege-educated voters.

If we can fully dismantle the education myth, the bigger question moving forward is what will replace it at the center of our politics? Will we transcend it by ensuring the broad economic security, social respect, and civic capability all working Americans deserve? The future of our democracy hinges on this question, and the answer is very much uncertain. One direction is false concern for those damaged by the myth while advancing reactionary policies and corporate power. Assuming the presidency in January 2017, for example, Trump acted symbolically in the interests of Americans left out of the supposed creative class, but he largely neglected them in favor of the corporate right. Indeed, Trump clearly privileged the latter in his cabinet, appointing Steve Mnuchin (Goldman Sachs) to Treasury, Rex Tillerson (Exxon-Mobil) as secretary of state, and Betsy DeVos (Amway) to head the Department of Education. Trump threw red meat to anti-immigrant populist politicians like Alabama senator Jeff Sessions by empowering Immigration and Customs Enforcement (ICE) to raid communities of undocumented but otherwise law-abiding immigrants, and he continued to talk big about building a border wall. The single most consequential policy of his single term, however, was the Tax Cuts and Jobs Act of 2017, which, while minimally reducing taxes for many working Americans, dramatically slashed the top rates for wealthy Americans and corporations. For those Americans left out of the knowledge economy, the tax cut did little to help them, however, instead encouraging stock buybacks and gargantuan executive bonuses.[2]

Trump also deeply diminished the civic and democratic capabilities of Americans in an astoundingly short amount of time. Appointing the controversial DeVos represented a major threat to the democratic promise of public education. Indeed, DeVos was not shy about her overarching goal to completely privatize the nation's schools by allowing families to use vouchers to study at any kind of school they would like, including religious institutions.[3] During her tenure as secretary, she sought to advance that agenda at every turn.[4] Even worse than that, Trump's repeated fabrications about voter fraud falsely cast doubt on the very integrity of American democracy and culminated in the stunning effort by some of his supporters on January 6, 2021, to stage a coup and overturn the results of the 2020 presidential election.

The president did undertake efforts to restore American sovereignty in the global economy, particularly exploiting Democrats' failure to provide any vision to ensure good jobs for Americans outside the professional class. For starters,

Trump immediately pulled the United States out of the TPP, which he had crudely called a "continuing rape of our country" on the campaign trail.[5] He also renego-tiated NAFTA, creating the US-Mexico-Canada-Agreement (USMCA). Though the effort hardly remade international trade, it did create tighter requirements that American manufacturers employ American labor, and AFL-CIO Presi-dent Richard Trumka called it a "huge win for working people."[6] Trump further incited a trade war with China, which arguably hurt American manufacturers and, especially farmers, more than it helped. Still, his supporters remembered Democrats' support for NAFTA and liberalized relationships with China that empirical evidence has shown cost blue-collar jobs and supported Trump's hard line on trade.[7]

Finally, Trump sought to make good on his promise to directly bring back American manufacturing, even if it meant dependence on foreign employers. The best example of this effort, which coincided with Scott Walker's desper-ate campaign move, was the ill-fated deal to bring the Taiwanese manufacturer Foxconn to Wisconsin. Calling it the "eighth-wonder of the world," Walker and Trump posed with billionaire CEO Terry Gou in the summer of 2018 to break ground on a factory that would supposedly create thirteen thousand jobs producing LCD screens.[8] Both the state and local government in Mt. Pleasant, Wisconsin, invested millions in infrastructure upgrades, local government invoked eminent domain to give Foxconn the land of homeowners, and the state promised billions in subsidies. To date, virtually no jobs have been produced.[9] Both Walker and Trump lost by nearly identical margins in Wisconsin (Walker lost in 2018 by thirty thousand votes and Trump in 2020, by twenty thousand). But each also won more total votes than in 2014 and 2016, respectively.

In contrast to reactionary populism, the other alternative is a robust social democracy that finally includes all American working people across the lines of race, gender identity, sexuality, and immigration status. Sanders's defeat in 2016 to a candidate who then lost to Trump only emboldened the reemergence of social democracy on the left. Massive teacher uprisings occurred in surprising places in 2018: first in West Virginia, then Kentucky, Oklahoma, Arizona, and North Carolina. Many of these activists, in West Virginia and Arizona, especially, had been inspired by the Sanders campaign.[10] Insurgent social democratic can-didates Alexandria Ocasio-Cortez (NY), Ayanna Pressley (MA), Rashida Tlaib (MI), and Ilhan Omar (MN) also won seats in Congress after campaigning for bold ideas such as eliminating student debt and have since supported visionary ideas such as the Green New Deal and a federal jobs guarantee. More main-stream Democrats—including some prominent presidential candidates—like Cory Booker and Kristin Gillibrand also began supporting at least limited ver-sions of transformative social democratic policies like a jobs guarantee.[11] By the time states held primary votes in 2020, other Democrats with relatively large followings such as the tech entrepreneur Andrew Yang promised dramatic policies like his version of Universal Basic Income: a "freedom dividend" for all Americans.[12]

In 2019, more insurgent teacher unions followed the model of the CTU and pushed for broad social democratic changes such as more social workers and mental health services for students and caps on charter schools in attention-grabbing strikes in Los Angeles and elsewhere.[13] The CTU upped the stakes even further in fall 2019, striking again for a social worker and a nurse in every school, reducing class size, protections for undocumented students, and resources for homeless students.[14] Like teachers in LA, the CTU also fought, largely unsuccessfully, to force the city to provide affordable housing. The United Teachers of Los Angeles (UTLA) endorsed Sanders in the next presidential election, and while the CTU didn't officially do so, its top leadership did.[15]

Entering 2020, Sanders was the front-runner, winning the popular vote in the first three contests of Iowa, New Hampshire, and Nevada. Establishment Democrats closed ranks around former vice president Joe Biden, however, as Obama reportedly interceded to get Mayor Pete Buttigieg, at that point with a viable candidacy, to withdraw before Super Tuesday.[16] Biden's campaign represented a human capital throwback (recall his enthusiasm for Obama's job-training policy in the last chapter), explaining to Black families how their kids faced education deficits because they listened to "records" rather than reading and advising unemployed miners to learn to code.[17] Even so, the growing social democratic wing, which had led a majority of Americans to support Medicare-for-all, pushed Biden to the left. As a result, Biden promised to "build back better" at the conclusion of the COVID crisis with a major infrastructure program and nonchalantly promised a fifteen dollar an hour minimum wage (unthinkable before the years of organizing by the Fight for $15 movement) in his final debate with Trump. Though Sanders ultimately lost, his huge margins among young Democratic voters spoke to a growing resistance to the education myth among young people shut out of an economy marked by ever greater inequality.[18]

In an election with record-breaking turnout, Biden beat Trump by a sizable overall margin of six million votes, and by almost the same electoral college margin by which Trump had defeated Clinton. Even so, Trump won millions more votes in 2020 than he did in 2016 and lost by very thin margins in the "rust-belt" states that gave him victory four years earlier. A major takeaway from the election of 2020 is that as economic inequality continues to increase, livelihoods for those without college degrees is a major political problem to which neither party has, until very recently, paid enough attention.[19]

Nationally, many of Biden's gains came at the expense of Trump in the suburbs, and in Wisconsin, suburban professionals breaking for Biden represented the margin of victory as many working-class whites voted for Trump and many working-class African Americans sat the election out.[20] Elsewhere, votes among minorities, particularly Latinos, actually increased for Trump in 2020.[21] Nationally, twenty-five million voters, about one-third of Trump's total, made less than fifty thousand dollars a year, and though Biden won that demographic by around 10 points, that was a large drop from the 22-point margin with which Obama had won low-income voters in 2012.[22] In Florida, the state's voters elected Trump while also, by a very large margin, supporting an increase in the minimum wage to fifteen dollars per hour.[23]

Indeed, the politics of Trumpism is far from over. The Biden administration has moved beyond the assumptions of the education myth in some important ways, prioritizing infrastructure for its significance in creating jobs and expanding child tax credits to include cash payments that will reduce poverty, for example. Still, broad, transformative social democratic changes—a jobs guarantee, labor reform, universal childcare—have remained off the agenda, or as of this writing, stand stymied by Democrats' unwillingness to eliminate the filibuster to overcome Republican intransigence. There do seem to be a growing number of Democrats who understand a broader social democratic promise has to be at the center of any long-term political movement capable of defeating Trumpism. The future of democracy in the United States depends on the success of this path, and it is a narrow one. If Democrats (or anyone else for that matter) are going to prevent an ever more mendacious version of reactionary populism in the future, how they approach the connection between education and economic security is vital. No longer can we privilege those with college degrees, and we must ensure that our politics centers life, liberty, and the pursuit of happiness for *everyone* through an empowering vision of economic and social rights, including the right to a job, high-quality healthcare, good housing, a livable environment, and yes, an education. Whoever can do that can realign American politics for a long time, and for the better.

Acknowledgments

Although there is only one name on the byline of this book, I could not have written it without the solidarity and support of many family, friends, and colleagues. If you found this one valuable, you should know that all the people below helped in ways I won't be able to acknowledge well enough. But I will try anyway.

First, I thank the National Academy of Education and the support of their generous postdoctoral fellowship, funding which they extended multiple times as it was disrupted by the COVID-19 pandemic. Also essential was the support of a summer fellowship from the UW-Green Bay Research Council. Without funding from each of these sources, this book probably wouldn't have happened.

Though COVID prevented me from doing all the archival research I would have liked, the help of several archives was essential in producing this book. I thank the staff, especially Vakil Smallen, at the NEA Archives at George Washington University, as well as the staff of the Walther Reuther Library, especially Dan Golodner, whose help has been integral for two books now. Thanks also to the one-and-only Deb Anderson and the rest of the staff at the UW-Green Bay Area Research Center.

At UW-Green Bay, I owe more debts than I can count. Our campus truly is a community of scholars and teachers, and I deeply treasure all the support and insights over the years from my colleagues. For friendship and support, thanks very much to Gaurav Bansal, David Coury, Tara DaPra, Christin DePouw, Mike Draney, Adam Gaines, Georgette Heyrman, Doreen Higgins, J. P. Leary, Ryan Martin, Rebecca Nesvet, Cristina Ortiz, Courtney Sherman, Heidi Sherman,

Christine Smith, Patricia Terry, David Voelker, Aaron Weinschenk, and Brian Welsch. Thanks also to Dean Chuck Rybak for his support of this project. My home department, Democracy and Justice Studies, is the best academic department anyone could ask for, and I offer my deepest gratitude to Andrew Austin, Nolan Bennett, Jillian Jacklin, Katia Levintova, Eric Morgan, Kaden Paulson-Smith, Kim Reilly, and Alison Staudinger. I can't thank our administrative assistant, Lorri Kornowski, enough for her help and support.

In addition to anything I've taught them, my students over the years have taught me just as much, particularly about the topic of this book. I've continued to learn from many of these students after they've graduated, and I thank my friends Elyza Ahrens, Evan Ash, Tresavoya Blake, Dan Buckley, Nate Fiene, Ben Freeman, Guillermo Gomez, Marcus Grignon, Casey Hicks, Rachel Kaschak, Lorenzo Lones, Greg Lutz, Anastasia McCain, Chad Osteen, Chris Parker, Sierra Spaulding, Joey Taylor, and Linnea Zintman. For this book, in particular, I'd like to thank the students of two upper-division senior seminars at UWGB that took up the topic of the political economy of education, especially Kwynn Carter, Shane Kanneberg, Kylie Olson, and Sergei Sutto.

In my work as a union activist, I've been blessed with brothers and sisters across the state who have become like a second family. Thanks to Melanie Cary, Andy Felt, Chad Goldberg, Peter Hart-Brinson, John Heppen, Doug Margolis, Peter Meyerson, Nerissa Nelson, Anya Paretskaya, Chris Ramaekers, David Simmons, and Paul Van Auken. Thanks also to former American Federation of Teachers-Wisconsin staff Rob Henn and Dan Suarez, and special thanks to AFT-W program director John Yaggi and President Kim Kohlhaas, both of whom have taught me more about solidarity than I can put into words. Then there are my comrades in the Wisconsin Labor History Society. Thanks to Steve Cupery, Ken Germanson, Judy Gatlin, Jaclyn Kelly, and the rest of the Board of Directors for their support and friendship.

A number of generous scholars and authors have either read drafts, given me feedback that prevented me from heading in a disastrous direction, or just provided important encouragement. Thanks to Mahasan Chaney, Ansley Erickson, Patricia Graham, Tina Groeger, Jeff Helgeson, Dan Kaufman, Joe McCartin, Adam Mertz, Bill Reese, Kate Rousmaniere, Cam Scribner, Eleni Schirmer, Naomi Williams, and Lane Windham. Thanks also to the other members of the "Lighthouse Nine," Cathleen Cahill, Chris Florio, Frederick Gooding, Will Jones, Fran Ryan, Katie Turk, Eric Yellin, and Amy Zanoni, for our conversations on public-sector work. I'll never be able to stop thanking my graduate school mentors Saverio Giovacchini and David Freund, both of whom continue to support my work these many years after I've left the University of Maryland, College Park. And my graduate school adviser, Julie Greene, has never stopped mentoring me to this day. She's the best. Finally, Jerry Podair continues to be a great friend and confidant, and I relish our conversations about history and baseball.

Speaking of friends, I want to thank my friends in Green Bay and elsewhere for all their support over the past few years: Eric and Emily Genrich, Eli Helman, Lorna Kaye, Jamie Lynch, Adam Parrillo, Tim Sharma, David Siegel, and Ira Wigley. I also want to acknowledge three friends, in particular, who have shaped my thinking on this project more than anyone else: Stephen Duncan, who continues to read just about everything I write and never fails to help me figure out what I am trying to do; Neil Kraus, whose conversations with me about what Americans have gotten so wrong about education have made this book much, much better; and especially, Harvey Kaye, who has helped me truly understand why the case for social democracy is so essential. If I weren't friends with Harvey, this book simply wouldn't be here.

Thanks to Sarah Grossman, my editor at Cornell University Press, as well as the two anonymous reviewers whose feedback, at several stages, improved this book immensely. And I thank Tracy Steffes and Jon Zimmerman, the two series editors for CUP's Histories of Education. Before I had a publisher, Jon pitched this series to me, and I'm so glad I decided to go with Cornell. Jon has given me tough but compassionate feedback at many stages along the way, and both he and Tracy have consistently pushed me to ensure this book made the argument I wanted to make. I couldn't have asked for better guidance.

Finally, over the past couple years, the support of family has never been more important. Thank you to Tom and Tina Sandherr, Evan Sandherr and Elodie Ontala, Justin and Stephanie Sandherr, and the extended Sandherr and Vasko families. I can't thank my father Keith Shelton or my siblings, Angi, Arryn, and Stephen, enough for their support over the years. Thanks also to Teresa Banks, and to my uncle Steve Shelton for his constant encouragement. My grandparents, Lester and Erline Shelton, to whom this book is dedicated, continue to be my role models. Finally, to Sara, Keith, and Kristina: much of this book was written as we were all living together 24/7 in close quarters. I appreciate the three of you sharing that space with me as the love in our family only grew stronger. To write a book during that time was only a bonus.

Notes

PREFACE

1. Danielle Allen, *Our Declaration: A Reading of the DECLARATION of INDEPENDENCE in Defense of Equality* (New York: Liveright, 2014), 145.
2. Malcolm Harris, *Kids These Days: Human Capital and the Making of Millennials* (New York: Little, Brown, 2017).

INTRODUCTION

1. On the meaning of FDR's Economic Bill of Rights, see Harvey Kaye, *The Fight for the Four Freedoms: What Made FDR and the Greatest Generation Truly Great* (New York: Simon and Schuster, 2014), 114–47.
2. Nancy Beadie, *Education and the Creation of Capital in the Early American Republic* (Cambridge: Cambridge University Press, 2010). Michael Katz, *The Irony of Early School Reform: Educational Innovation in Mid-Nineteenth Century Massachusetts* (Cambridge, MA: Harvard University Press, 1968).
3. Tracy Steffes, *School, Society, & State: A New Education to Govern Modern America, 1890–1940* (Chicago: University of Chicago Press, 2012). W. Norton Grubb and Marvin Lazerson, *The Education Gospel: The Economic Power of Schooling* (Cambridge, MA: Harvard University Press, 2004).
4. Cristina Groeger, *The Education Trap: Schools and the Remaking of Inequality in Boston* (Cambridge, MA: Harvard University Press, 2021).
5. David Labaree, *Someone Has to Fail: The Zero-Sum Game of Public Schooling* (Cambridge, MA: Harvard University Press, 2010).
6. I build on the work of W. Norton Grubb and Marvin Lazerson, who compare this development to religious faith. See *The Education Gospel.*
7. Michael Sandel, *The Tyranny of Merit: What's Become of the Common Good?* (New York: Farrar, Strauss, and Giroux, 2020), especially chapter 4.
8. Danielle Allen, *Education and Equality* (Chicago: University of Chicago Press, 2017), 5–18.
9. Lane Windham, *Knockin' on Labor's Door: Union Organizing in the 1970s and the Roots of a New Economic Divide* (Chapel Hill: University of North Carolina Press, 2017). Gabriel Winant, *The Next Shift: The Fall of Industry and the Rise of Health Care in Rust Belt America* (Cambridge, MA: Harvard University Press, 2021).
10. I use the terms *neo-liberal* and *neoliberal* differently in this book. *Neo-liberal*, a term coined by Randall Rothenberg, refers to a specific historical movement of Democrats in the 1980s, which I explain in chapter 5. *Neoliberal* is a broader analytical term that refers to a political economic philosophy built on privatizing public services, making workers more flexible by reducing or eliminating worker protections, and facilitating private capital accumulation. Most scholars view the latter as emerging in the 1970s and gaining wider purchase in American politics from that point until the recent past or even the present.
11. By this point, there are scores of empirical studies highlighting the continued growth of inequality, both in terms of income and in wealth, from about 1980 to the present. Most Americans have seen their wages stagnate or only grow a little since that time,

while the wealthiest 10 percent, 1 percent, and 0.1 percent, respectively, have all enhanced their wealth dramatically, and exponentially so the higher up in the wealth distribution. For an aggregation of some of this evidence, see Juliana Menasce Horowitz, Ruth Igielnik, and Rakesh Kochnar, "Trends in Income and Wealth Inequality," *Pew Research Center*, https://www.pewsocialtrends.org/2020/01/09/trends-in-income-and-wealth-inequality/. See also Emmanuel Saez and Gabriel Zucman, "Wealth Inequality in the United States Since 1913: Evidence from Capitalized Income Tax Data," *National Bureau of Economic Research Working Paper Series*, Oct. 2014, https://eml.berkeley.edu/~saez/saez-zucman NBER14wealth.pdf; and Saez and Zucman, "Trends in Income and Wealth Inequality: Revising after the Revisionists," *NBER Working Paper Series*, Oct. 2020, file:///C:/Users/sheltonj/Downloads/w27921.pdf. Though their argument puts too much stock in building individual human capital as the solution to economic inequality, Nicholas Kristof and Sheryl WuDunn highlight, qualitatively, what life looks like for many Americans who lack college degrees. See *Tightrope: Americans Reaching for Hope* (New York: Alfred A. Knopf, 2020).

12. For the failed promise of human capital to pay off for many college graduates, see Phillip Brown, Hugh Lauder, and Sin Yi Cheung, *The Death of Human Capital? Its Failed Promise and How to Renew It and an Age of Disruption* (New York: Oxford University Press, 2020), chapters 4 and 5. For the single best treatment of how students from limited means fare in college, see Sara Goldrick-Rab, *Paying the Price: College Costs, Financial Aid, and the Betrayal of the American Dream* (Chicago: University of Chicago Press, 2016).

13. Sandel, *Tyranny of Merit*, 25.

14. Ashitha Nagesh, "US Election 2020: Why Trump Gained Support among Minorities," *BBC News*, Nov. 22, 2020, https://www.bbc.com/news/world-us-canada-54972389.

15. T. H. Marshall has referred to these "social rights" as the right to a certain level of economic security that is "not proportionate to the market value of the claimant." See "Citizenship and Social Class," in *Citizenship and Social Class*, ed. Marshall and Tom Bottomore (London: Pluto Press, 1993), 28.

16. "Biden's Electoral Win Was Narrow in the 'Tipping Point' State," *The Conversation*, Nov. 15, 2020, https://theconversation.com/bidens-electoral-college-win-was-narrow-in-the-tipping-point-state-labor-surges-in-victoria-150143.

17. Bryan Caplan, *The Case against Education: Why the Education System is a Waste of Time and Money* (Princeton: Princeton University Press, 2018).

CHAPTER 1. FROM INDEPENDENCE TO SECURITY

1. Merle Curti and Vernon Carstensen, *The University of Wisconsin: A History, 1848–1925*, vol. 1 (Madison: University of Wisconsin Press, 1949), 275–95, 508–25. On the Wisconsin Idea, see Gwen Drury, "The Wisconsin Idea: The Idea that Made Wisconsin Famous," https://www.ssc.wisc.edu/soc/wiscidea/wp-content/uploads/2017/08/496-week-2-Rq1-and-RC1.pdf; Chad Alan Goldberg, "The University's Service to Democracy," in *Education for Democracy*, ed. Goldberg (Madison: University of Wisconsin Press, 2020), 3–52; and Charles McCarthy, *The Wisconsin Idea* (New York: MacMillan, 1912).

2. Dan Kaufman, *The Fall of Wisconsin: The Conservative Conquest of a Progressive Bastion and the Future of American Politics* (New York: W. W. Norton, 2018), 25–26; Robert Ozanne, *The Labor Movement in Wisconsin: A History* (Madison: Wisconsin Historical Society Press, 1984), 129–33.

3. On the role of reformers' attempts to use of public education during the Progressive Era, see Steffes, *School, Society, & State*.

4. Danielle Allen, *Our Declaration*.

5. See Harold Hyman, *American Singularity: The 1787 Northwest Ordinance, the 1862 Homestead and Morrill Acts, and the 1944 G.I. Bill* (Athens: University of Georgia Press, 1986).

6. See Jefferson's Second Draft of the Virginia Constitution, before June 13, 1776, https://founders.archives.gov/documents/Jefferson/01-01-02-0161-0003.

7. As Steve Fraser has pointed out, Jefferson was joined by Benjamin Franklin and James Madison, among others, who feared what dispossession from land would mean for the future of American democracy. See *The Age of Acquiescence: The Life and Death of American Resistance to Organized Wealth and Power* (New York: Little, Brown), 70–74.

8. Thomas Paine, "Agrarian Justice, Opposed to Agrarian Law, and to Agrarian Monopoly, Being a Plan for Meliorating the Condition of Man," 1797.

9. Harvey Kaye, *Thomas Paine and the Promise of America* (New York: Hill and Wang, 2005), 132–39.

10. Johann Neem, *Democracy's Schools: The Rise of Public Education in America* (Baltimore: Johns Hopkins University Press), 6–12.

11. Thomas Jefferson, "A Bill for the More General Diffusion of Knowledge," June 18, 1779, https://founders.archives.gov/documents/Jefferson/01-02-02-0132-0004-0079.

12. "Comparing them by their faculties of memory, reason, and imagination," Jefferson argued, "it appears to me, that in memory [African Americans] are equal to the whites; in reason much inferior, as I think one could scarcely be found capable of tracing and comprehending the investigations of Euclid; and that in imagination they are dull, tasteless, and anomalous." *Notes on the State of Virginia* (New York: Penguin, 1999), 146.

13. "Land Ordinance of 1785," https://www.in.gov/history/2478.htm; "An Ordinance for the Government of the Territory of the United States Northwest of the River Ohio, 1787," https://www.ourdocuments.gov/doc.php?flash=false&doc=8&page=transcript.

14. Benjamin Rush, *Thoughts upon Female Education Accommodated to the Present State of Society, Manners, and Government, in the United States of America: Addressed to the Visitors of the Young Ladies' Academy in Philadelphia, 28 July, 1787, at the Close of the Quarterly Examination* (Philadelphia: Prichard & Hall, 1787).

15. Labaree, *Someone Has to Fail*, 72–73. "In the antebellum period, this meant expanding government to provide canals, turnpikes, and railroads; penitentiaries, hospitals, asylums, and poorhouses; common schools and normal schools. This amounted to a huge increase in the role of the state."

16. Julie Reuben, "Patriotic Purposes: Public Schools and the Education of Citizens," in *The Public Schools*, ed. Susan Fuhrman and Marvin Lazerson (Oxford: Oxford University Press, 2005), 7–8.

17. William Reese, *America's Public Schools: From the Common School to "No Child Left Behind"* (Baltimore: Johns Hopkins University Press, 2011), 10–44. Other important reformers who sought to advance public education for this purpose included Unitarian pastor Charles Brooks, Massachusetts congressman Joseph Richardson, Pennsylvania representative Thaddeus Stevens, and educator Henry Barnard. See Donald Warren, *To Enforce Education: A History of the Founding Years of the United States Office of Education* (Detroit: Wayne State University Press, 1974), 30–47.

18. Horace Mann, "Means and Objects of Common School Education," *Lectures and Annual Reports on Education* (Boston: Rand and Avery, 1867), 39–88, 41. Italics in original quotation.

19. Mann, "The Necessity of Education in a Republican Government," in *Lectures and Annual Reports*, 150.

20. Horace Mann, *Fifth Annual Report of the Board of Education, Together with the Fifth Annual Report of the Secretary of the Board, Covering the Year 1841* (Boston: Dutton and Wentworth, State Printers, 1842), 70, 82.

21. Mann, *Fifth Annual Report*, 86–120, 86, 89, 120.

22. Mann, *Twelfth Annual Report* (1849).

23. Helen Sumner, "Rise and Growth in Philadelphia," in *History of Labour in the United States*, vol 1, ed. John Commons and Associates (New York: MacMillan, 1926),

169–230, 224, 225. As Katznelson and Weir point out, there has long been a history of working-class support for education throughout American history. See *Schooling for All: Class, Race, and the Decline of the American Ideal* (New York: Basic Books, 1985).

24. Neem, *Democracy's Schools*, 24.

25. Michael Katz, *The Irony of Early School Reform: Educational Innovation in Mid-Nineteenth Century Massachusetts* (Cambridge: Harvard University Press, 1968), 21–112.

26. Hilary Moss, *Schooling Citizens: The Struggle for African American Education in Antebellum America* (Chicago: University of Chicago Press, 2009), 8–9.

27. Lloyd Jorgensen, "The Origins of Public Education in Wisconsin," *Wisconsin Magazine of History* 33 (September 1949): 16, 21.

28. Curti and Carstensen, *The University of Wisconsin*, 13–14.

29. Curti and Carstensen, *The University of Wisconsin*, 22.

30. Howard Peckham, edited and updated by Margaret Steneck and Nicholas Steneck, *The Making of the University of Michigan, 1817–1992* (Ann Arbor: University of Michigan Press, 1994), 1–15.

31. Curti and Carstensen, *The University of Wisconsin*, 64.

32. Curti and Carstensen, *The University of Wisconsin*, 75–76.

33. David Wilmot, speech in the House of Representatives, 1847.

34. Abraham Lincoln, "Address on the Kansas-Nebraska Act," 1854.

35. Lincoln, "Annual Address to Congress," December 1861.

36. "An Address by Abraham Lincoln Before the Wisconsin State Agricultural Society in Milwaukee, Wisconsin," Sep. 30, 1859, https://www.nal.usda.gov/topics/lincolns-milwaukee-speech

37. Harold Holzer and Norton Garfinckle, *A Just and Generous Nation: Abraham Lincoln and the Fight for American Opportunity* (New York: Basic Books, 2015), 41–50.

38. Holzer and Garfinckle, *A Just and Generous Nation*, 88.

39. Hyman, *American Singularity*, 36.

40. The promise of the Morrill Act was significantly expanded later, through the Morrill Land-Grant Act of 1890, as well as the creation of the USDA Cooperative Extension Service with the Smith-Lever Act (1914). See Christopher Loss, *Between Citizens and the State: The Politics of American Higher Education in the 20th Century* (Princeton: Princeton University Press, 2012), 57–60.

41. Warren, *To Enforce Education*, 58–76. Quotation in Bernard Steiner, "Life of Henry Barnard, The First United States Commissioner of Education, 1867–1870," Department of the Interior Bureau of Education, Bulletin, 1919, No. 8. (Washington: Government Printing Office, 1919). National Education Association Collection, George Washington University, Box 2244, Folder 4.

42. Hyman, *American Singularity*, 46–47.

43. See, for example, "Letter from Henry Bram, Ishmael Moultrie, and Yates Sampson to the Commissioner of the Freedmens' Bureau, Oct. 1865," https://herb.ashp.cuny.edu/items/show/2621.

44. Eric Foner, *A Short History of Reconstruction*, Updated ed. (New York: Harper Perennial, 2015).

45. James Anderson, *The Education of Blacks in the South, 1860–1935* (Chapel Hill: University of North Carolina, 1988), 28, 148–85.

46. Rosanne Currarino, *The Labor Question in America: Economic Democracy in the Gilded Age* (Urbana: University of Illinois Press, 2011); Lawrence Glickman, *A Living Wage: American Workers and the Making of Consumer Society* (Ithaca: Cornell University Press, 1997).

47. The best synthetic account is Fraser's *The Age of Acquiescence*.

48. Carlos Schwantes, *Coxey's Army: An American Odyssey* (Moscow, ID: University of Idaho Press, 1994).

49. Fraser, *Age of Acquiescence*, 97–102.

50. Shelton Stromquist, *Reinventing "The People": The Progressive Movement, the Class Problem, and the Origins of Modern Liberalism* (Urbana: University of Illinois Press, 2006).

51. Katznelson and Weir, *Schooling for All*, 75–76, 150–77. Groeger, *The Education Trap*, 111–22.

52. Groeger, *The Education Trap*, especially chapters 2 and 4.

53. Groeger, *The Education Trap*, chapters 3–4.

54. Harvey Kantor and Robert Lowe, "The Price of Human Capital: The Illusion of Equal Educational Opportunity," in *Public Education Under Siege*, ed. Michael Katz and Mike Rose (Philadelphia: University of Pennsylvania Press, 2013), 77.

55. Reese, *America's Public Schools*, 182.

56. Claudia Goldin and Lawrence Katz, *The Race between Education and Technology* (Cambridge, MA: Harvard University Press), 87.

57. Labaree, *Someone Has to Fail*, 11.

58. Reuben, "Patriotic Purposes," 12; and Jaroslav Pelikan, "General Introduction: The Public Schools as an Institution of American Constitutional Democracy," in *The Public Schools*, ed Susan Fuhrman and Marvin Lazerson, xviii.

59. John Dewey, *Democracy and Education: An Introduction to the Philosophy of Education* (New York: Free Press, 1916), 86–87.

60. Kate Rousmaniere, *Citizen Teacher: The Life and Leadership of Margaret Haley* (Albany: State University of New York Press, 2005), 59–91, 158.

61. Margaret Haley, "Why Teachers Should Organize," National Education Association, *Journal of Proceedings and Addresses of the Forty-Third Annual Meeting*, June 27–July 1, 1904.

62. Jon Shelton, ed., "Why Teachers Should Organize," study guide for "Teaching Labor's Story" project, http://www.lawcha.org/wp-content/uploads/7-2-Why-Teachers-Should-Organize-FINAL.pdf.

63. Patricia Aljberg Graham, *Schooling America: How the Public Schools Meet the Nation's Changing Needs* (New York: Oxford University Press, 2005), 7–35.

64. Mae Ngai, *Impossible Subjects: Illegal Aliens and the Making of Modern America* (Princeton: Princeton University Press, 2004).

65. Reuben, "Patriotic Purposes," 13.

66. *The Towner-Sterling Bill: An Analysis of the Provisions of the Bill; A Discussion of the Principles and Policies Involved; And a Presentation of FACTS AND FIGURES Relating to the Subject* (Washington, DC: The National Education Association, 1923), National Education Association Collection, George Washington University, Box 2255, Folder 14.

67. *The Towner-Sterling Bill*, NEAC, Box 225, Folder 14.

68. The quest for a federal department of education did not die with the failure of Towner-Sterling. In 1928, the NEA lobbied for yet another bill to elevate public education to a cabinet-level position, the Curtis-Reed Bill. The AFT, a much smaller organization with about ten thousand members, also supported it. *Hearing before the Committee on Education, House of Representatives, Seventieth Congress, First Session on H.R. 7, A Bill to Create a Department of Education and for Other Purposes* (Washington, DC: US Government Printing Office, 1928), 2–4.

CHAPTER 2. TO SECURE THESE RIGHTS

1. Michael Bennett, *When Dreams Came True: The GI Bill and the Making of Modern America* (Washington: Brassey's, 1996), 1–30.

2. Steffes, *School, Society, & State*, 83–117.

3. Peter Drucker, from the vantage point of 1993, argued the GI Bill "signaled the shift to the knowledge society." See *Post-Capitalist Society* (New York: Harper Business, 1993), 3. "Future historians," he predicted, "may well consider it the most important event of the twentieth century."

4. Nelson Lichtenstein, *State of the Union: A Century of American Labor* (Princeton: Princeton University Press, 2002), 20–53.

5. Kaye, *The Fight for the Four Freedoms*; Lizabeth Cohen, *Making a New Deal: Industrial Workers in Chicago, 1919–39* (Cambridge, MA: Cambridge University Press, 1990), chapter 6; Alan Brinkley, *The End of Reform: New Deal Liberalism in Recession and War* (New York: Vintage Books, 1995); and David Kennedy, *Freedom from Fear: The American People in Depression and War, 1929–45* (New York: Oxford University Press, 1999), chapters 9–10.

6. Transcript of National Labor Relations Act (1935), https://www.ourdocuments. gov/doc.php?flash=false&doc=67&page=transcript.

7. Steven Attewell, *People Must Live by Work: Direct Job Creation in America, from FDR to Reagan* (Philadelphia: University of Pennsylvania Press, 2018), chapters 1–3.

8. Brinkley, *The End of Reform*, 245–46.

9. Adolph Reed Jr., "The New Deal Wasn't Intrinsically Racist," *The New Republic*, Nov. 26, 2019, https://newrepublic.com/article/155704/new-deal-wasnt-intrinsically-racist.

10. On the meaning of FDR's Economic Bill of Rights, see Harvey Kaye, *The Fight for the Four Freedoms*, 114–47.

11. Franklin D. Roosevelt Address to the National Education Association, June 30, 1938, https://www.presidency.ucsb.edu/documents/address-before-the-national-education-association-new-york-city.

12. Kathleen Frydl, *The GI Bill* (Cambridge: Cambridge University Press, 2009), 81. Bennett, *When Dreams Came True*, 80–81.

13. Bennett, *When Dreams Came True*, 90–91.

14. Kaye, *The Fight for the Four Freedoms*, 134–36.

15. *The Veteran's Guide* (New York: Prentice-Hall, 1944).

16. Hyman, *American Singularity*, 65–66.

17. Loss, *Between Citizens and the State*, 91–120; Suzanne Mettler, *Soldiers to Citizens: The G.I. Bill and the Making of the Greatest Generation* (New York: Oxford University Press, 2005), 22–23, 89–92.

18. Statement of Mr. Philbin, *Congressional Record*, Jan. 1944, 357.

19. Extension of Remarks of Hon. Marion T. Bennett of Missouri, Jun 15, 1944, *Congressional Record: Proceedings and Debates of the 78th Congress, Second Session, Appendix, Volume 10—Part 10*, A3046.

20. Extension of Remarks of Hon. Dean Gillespie of Colorado, June 13, 1944, in *Congressional Record . . . Appendix*, A3082.

21. "Statement of Mr. O'Hara," *Congressional Record*, Jan. 1944, 357–58.

22. "Extension of Remarks of Hon. Samuel A. Weiss," *Congressional Record . . . Appendix*, June 13, 1944, A3008.

23. Michael Bennett, *When Dreams Came True*, 86–88. All veterans under the age of twenty-four who were in school two years before being drafted were automatically eligible for the education provisions of the GI Bill.

24. Hyman, *American Singularity*, 69. Enrollment of veterans in college exploded from about 88,000 in 1945 to over a million by 1946, over 40 percent of the college-age population. See Bennett, *When Dreams Came True*, 18. On social mobility, see Mettler, *Soldiers to Citizens*, 48–53.

25. Mettler, *From Soldiers to Citizens*, 7–8.

26. Bennett, *When Dreams Came True*, 155–59.

27. Frydl, *The GI Bill*, 333.

28. Lizabeth Cohen, *A Consumer's Republic: The Politics of Mass Consumption in Postwar America* (New York: Vintage Books, 2004), 138.

29. Alice Kessler-Harris, *In Pursuit of Equity: Women, Men, and the Quest for Economic Citizenship in 20th-Century America* (New York: Oxford University Press, 2001), chapter 3.

30. Cohen, *A Consumer's Republic*, 138.

31. Mettler, *From Soldiers to Citizens*, 55.

32. Ira Katznelson, *When Affirmative Action Was White: An Untold History of Racial Inequality in Twentieth-Century America* (New York: Norton, 2005); Frydl, *The GI Bill*, 7.

33. Katznelson, *When Affirmative Action Was White*, 128–33; and Mettler, *From Soldiers to Citizens*, 74–75.

34. Katznelson, *When Affirmative Action Was White*, 121.

35. As *The Veteran's Guide* pointed out, "Your former employer is required by law to reinstate you in your former position or to a position of like seniority, status, and pay if your circumstances meet the qualifications set forth in the law" (28).

36. Stephen Bailey, *Congress Makes a Law: The Story behind the Employment Act of 1946* (New York: Vintage Books, 1964), 42.

37. Attewell, *People Must Live by Work*, chapter 4.

38. "Statement of Hon. Robert F. Wagner," *Full Employment Act of 1945 Hearings before a Subcommittee of the Committee on Banking and Currency United States Senate* (Washington, DC: US Government Printing Office, 1945), 1–3.

39. The Grange was typical of opposition in the Senate, and later, the House: "The Government's chief role in a free enterprise system is to see that it is free—that its citizens are protected from physical or economic aggression or interference, so that each may develop his talents in his own way according to his capacity, energy, and ingenuity, just long as his activities do not interfere with the rights of others." See *Full Employment Act of 1945 Hearings*, 589.

40. "Statement of the Most Reverend Bernard J. Sheil, D.D., Auxiliary Bishop of Chicago, and Director of the Catholic Youth Organization, Archdiocese of Chicago," *Full Employment Act of 1945 Hearings*, 611–12.

41. "Statement of Walter White, Secretary, National Association for the Advancement of Colored People," *Full Employment Act of 1945 Hearings*, 615–21, 617, 616.

42. "Statement of Paul G. Hoffman, President, Studebaker Corp., and Chairman of the Board of Trustees of the Committee for Economic Development," *Full Employment Act of 1945 Hearings*, 706.

43. "Statement of Francis J. Brown, Consultant, American Council on Education," *Full Employment Act of 1945 Hearings*, 770–71.

44. Murray alone issued twenty-five statements between January 1945 and February 1946, and authored publications ranging from *American Political Science Review* to the *International Teamster* to *The New Republic*. See Bailey, *Congress Makes a Law*, 69–76, 81–98.

45. Harry Truman, "Special Message to the Congress Presenting a 21-Point Program for the Reconversion Period," September 6, 1945, https://www.trumanlibrary.gov/library/public-papers/128/special-message-congress-presenting-21-point-program-reconversion-period.

46. On the reserve army argument, see Michal Kalecki, "Political Aspects of Full Employment," *Political Quarterly* 14 (1943): 3. For other arguments against the more robust version of the bill, see Bailey, *Congress Makes a Law*, 130–78. And for a convincing argument of the radical implications of full employment see Michael Dennis, "The Idea of Full Employment: A Challenge to Capitalism in the New Deal Era," *LABOR: Studies in Working-Class History* 14, no. 2 (May 2017): 69–93.

47. "Statement of George Terborgh of the Machinery and Allied Products Institute," *House Hearings on H.R. 2202*, 614, quotation in Bailey, *Congress Makes a Law*, 165.

48. Hugh Norton, *The Employment Act and the Council of Economic Advisers, 1946–1976* (Columbia: University of South Carolina Press, 1977), 99.

49. Margaret Weir, *Politics and Jobs: The Boundaries of Employment Policy in the United States* (Princeton: Princeton University Press, 1992), xiii.

50. Jack Metzgar, *Striking Steel: Solidarity Remembered* (Philadelphia: Temple University Press, 2000), 26–27.

51. Letter to Wagner from Walter Reuther, *Full Employment Act of 1945 Hearings*, 1186–87.

52. Nelson Lichtenstein, *Walter Reuther: The Most Dangerous Man in Detroit* (New York: Basic Books, 1995), 280.

53. Winant, *The Next Shift*, 10.

54. Metzgar, *Striking Steel*, 39.

55. Kaufman, *The Fall of Wisconsin*, 25–26; Ozanne, *The Labor Movement in Wisconsin*, 129–33.

56. Ozanne, *The Labor Movement in Wisconsin*, 60–70, 136–39; Darryl Holter, "Labor Law: Wisconsin's 'Little Wagner Act' and the Road to Taft-Hartley," in *Workers and Unions in Wisconsin: A Labor History Anthology*, ed. Darryl Holter (Madison: State Historical Society of Wisconsin, 1999), 186–91.

57. Goldin and Katz, *The Race between Technology and Education*, 196.

58. Frydl, *The GI Bill*, 308.

59. Goldin and Katz, *The Race between Technology and Education*, 269.

60. "Table 33—Current Fund Revenue of Institutions of Higher Education, by Source of funds, 1889–90–1989–90," *National Center for Education Statistics, 120 Years of American Education: A Statistical Standpoint, 1993*, 89, https://nces.ed.gov/pubs93/93442.pdf.

61. Goldin and Katz, *The Race between Technology and Education*, 250–52. Women born in 1955 began to attend college at higher rates than men born at the same time, a trend that continues to this day.

62. The committee also included, for example, the future president's brother Milton Eisenhower, then president of Kansas State University; Nobel Prize–winning nuclear physicist and Washington University of St. Louis chancellor Arthur Compton; Ball State president John Emens; New School philosopher Horace Kallen; and corporate executive Murray Lincoln.

63. Harry Truman, "Letter of Appointment of Commission Members, Washington, D.C., July 15, 1946," in *Higher Education for American Democracy: A Report of The President's Commission on Higher Education*, https://archive.org/stream/in.ernet.dli.2015.89917/2015.89917.Higher-Education-For-American-Democracy-A-Report-Of-The-Presidents-Commission-On-Higher-Education-Vol-I---Vi_djvu.txt.

64. Truman Commission, *Higher Education for American Democracy*, 1–2.

65. Truman Commission, *Higher Education for American Democracy*, 8, 14.

66. Truman Commission, *Higher Education for American Democracy*, 27, 10.

67. Truman Commission, *Higher Education for American Democracy*, 30, 36–46.

68. Loss, *Between Citizens and the State*, 117.

69. Mettler, *From Soldiers to Citizens*, 136–43.

70. Majority Opinion, *Brown v. Board of Education of Topeka*, 347 U.S. 483 (1954).

71. Labaree, *Someone Has to Fail*, 30.

CHAPTER 3. EDUCATION'S WAR ON POVERTY IN THE 1960S

1. For an excellent account of the intellectual development of human capital theory, see Brown, Lauder, and Cheung, *The Death of Human Capital?* especially chapter 2.

2. Edward Baptist, *The Half Has Never Been Told: Slavery and the Making of American Capitalism* (New York: Basic Books, 2014).

3. On the differences between Becker and Schultz, see Melinda Cooper, *Family Values: Between Neoliberalism and the New Social Conservatism* (Brooklyn, NY: Zone Books, 2017), 219–27. On the Chicago school more generally, see Daniel Rodgers, *Age of Fracture* (Cambridge, MA: Belknap Press, 2011), 63–68.

4. Theodore Schultz, "Investment in Human Capital," Presidential Address at the Seventy-Third Annual Meeting of the American Economic Association, St. Louis, December 28, 1960, reprinted in *The American Economic Review* 51, no. 1 (1961): 1.

5. Becker, *Human Capital,* 12.

6. Schultz, "Investment in Human Capital," 3.

7. Becker, *Human Capital,* 16.

8. Schultz, "Investment in Human Capital," 15.

9. Joshua Zeitz, *Building the Great Society: Inside Lyndon Johnson's White House* (New York: Viking, 2018), 47–57.

10. Cooper, *Family Values,* 221–22

11. Attewell, *People Must Live By Work,* 180–84.

12. Schultz, "Investment in Human Capital," 14.

13. Lyndon B. Johnson, "State of the Union Address," Jan. 8, 1964.

14. Guian McKee, *The Problem of Jobs: Liberalism, Race, and Deindustrialization in Philadelphia* (Chicago: University of Chicago Press, 2010), 8.

15. Lyndon Johnson, "Remarks at the University of Michigan," May 22, 1964, https://millercenter.org/the-presidency/presidential-speeches/may-22-1964-remarks-university-michigan.

16. See, for example, Doxey Wilkerson, "Federal Aid to Education: To Perpetuate or Diminish Existing Educational Inequalities?" AFT Publications, AFT Collection, Walter Reuther Archives, Wayne State University, Box 2, folder 17.

17. Title I, "The National Defense Education Act, 1958," https://www.govinfo.gov/content/pkg/STATUTE-72/pdf/STATUTE-72-Pg1580.pdf.

18. Sandel, *Tyranny of Merit,* 156–63.

19. Graham, *Schooling America,* 107.

20. *House of Representative Hearings before a Sub-committee of the Committee on Education and Labor,* 85th Congress (Washington DC: US Government Printing Office, 1958). Quotation in Lee Anderson, *Congress and the Classroom: From the Cold War to "No Child Left Behind"* (University Park: Pennsylvania State University Press, 2007), 46.

21. Reese, *America's Public Schools,* 235–38.

22. Weir, *Politics and Jobs,* 64.

23. Annelise Orleck, "Introduction," in *The War on Poverty: A New Grassroots History, 1964–1980,* ed. Annelise Orleck and Lisa Gayle Hazirjian (Athens, GA: University of Georgia Press, 2011), 10.

24. Guian McKee, "'This Government Is with Us': Lyndon Johnson and the Grassroots War on Poverty" in *The War on Poverty,* ed. Orleck and Hazirjian, 38.

25. Anderson, *Congress and the Classroom,* 61–62.

26. Zeitz, *The Great Society,* 146–51.

27. Graham, *Schooling America,* 136–37. About 90 percent of school districts would receive some federal funding.

28. The shift was profound: before ESEA, only about 1 percent of school budgets came from the federal government, most of which came in the form of money for vocational education and other minor programs. Reese, *America's Public School,* 241.

29. Lyndon Johnson State of the Union Address, Jan. 4, 1965, https://millercenter.org/the-presidency/presidential-speeches/january-4-1965-state-union.

30. "Message from the President of the United States Transmitting Education Program," Jan. 12, 1965, Subcommittee on Education for the Committee on Labor and Public Welfare, US Senate, *Elementary and Secondary Education Act of 1965 Background Material with Related Presidential Recommendations* (Washington, DC: US Government Printing Office, 1965), 11–12.

31. "Message from the President," *Elementary and Secondary Education Act*, 14.

32. House of Representatives, *Report from the Committee on Education and Labor to the Whole House on the Elementary and Secondary Education Act* (Washington, DC: US Government Printing Office, 1965), 1–2.

33. United States Senate, *Elementary and Secondary Act Hearings before the Subcommittee on Education of the Committee on Labor and Public Welfare* (Washington, DC: US Government Printing Office, 1965), 631.

34. Committee on Labor and Public Welfare, *Elementary and Secondary Education Act Report together with Minority Views and Individual Views* (Washington, DC: US Government Printing Office, 1965), 81–88, 87.

35. As Harvey Kantor and Robert Lowe put it, "By institutionalizing the idea that poverty and income insecurity were chiefly matters of education . . . the Great Society actually increased expectations about what education could accomplish. As a result the federal commitment to education and its role in social policy remained firmly in place despite the backlash against the Great Society's own educational programs." See "Educationalizing the Welfare State and Privatizing Education," in *Closing the Opportunity Gap: What America Must Do to Give Every Child and Even Chance*, ed. Prudence Carter and Kevin Welner (New York: Oxford University Press, 2013), 32.

36. Aaron Bady and Mike Konczal, "From Master Plan to No Plan: The Slow Death of Public Higher Education," *Dissent* (fall 2012), https://www.dissentmagazine.org/article/from-master-plan-to-no-plan-the-slow-death-of-public-higher-education.

37. Cooper, *Family Values*, 227–28.

38. The Pell Institute for the Study of Opportunity in Higher Education, "State Investment and Disinvestment in Higher Education: 1961 to 2015," *Postsecondary Education Opportunity* 272 (February 2015): 17–24.

39. Coordinating Committee for Higher Education, *A Comprehensive Plan for Higher Education in Wisconsin* (1965), 3.

40. Betty Brown, *University of Wisconsin-Green Bay: From the Beginning* (Green Bay: University of Wisconsin-Green Bay, 2000), 27–28.

41. Brown, *University of Wisconsin-Green Bay*, 30–32. "Report of the Ad Hoc Committee of the Report of the Committee of Twenty-Five on Organization for Higher Education," CCHE #83, 1964 Working Paper, October 1964.

42. Coordinating Committee for Higher Education, *A Comprehensive Plan for Higher Education in Wisconsin* (1966), 5.

43. Coordinating Committee for Higher Education, *A Comprehensive Plan for Higher Education in Wisconsin*, 9, 18, 27.

44. Loss, *Between Citizens and the State*, 156–60. About 1.5 million students used NDEA student loans to go to college between 1959–69.

45. Lyndon Johnson, "Special Message to Congress: Toward Full Educational Opportunity," Jan. 12, 1965, https://www.presidency.ucsb.edu/documents/special-message-the-congress-toward-full-educational-opportunity.

46. Becker, *Human Capital*, 121. Contemporaries of Becker, Paul Baran and Paul Sweezy had a different view of the function of expanding access to higher education. Under monopoly capitalism, they pointed out, it was not really possible for enterprising young Americans to start businesses. So, "a substitute mechanism has been found in the educational system. Through low-tuition state universities, scholarships, loans, and

the like, boys and girls who are really able and ambitious (desirous of success, as society defines it) can move up from the inferior part of the educational system. From there the road leads through the corporate apparatus or the professions into integration into the upper-middle, and occasionally, the higher, strata of society." See *Monopoly Capital: An Essay on the American Economic and Social Order* (New York: Monthly Review Press, 1966), 172.

47. On "supply curves," see Becker, *Human Capital*, 138.

48. "Statement of Hon. Winston Prouty, a US Senator from the State of Vermont," *United States Senate, Hearings before the Subcommittee on Education of the Committee on Labor and Public Welfare, Part I* (Washington, DC: US Government Printing Office, 1965), 96–97.

49. William Jones, *The March on Washington: Jobs, Freedom, and the Forgotten History of Civil Rights* (New York: W. W. Norton, 2013), 121–61.

50. Jerald Podair, *Bayard Rustin: American Dreamer* (Lanham, MD: Rowman and Littlefield, 2009), 37–41.

51. Transcript of A. Philip Randolph speech at the March on Washington for Jobs and Freedom, August 28, 1963.

52. On capital flight in American cities and its implications, see Jefferson Cowie, *Capital Moves: RCA's Seventy-Year Quest for Cheap Labor* (Ithaca: Cornell University Press, 1999); Robert Self, *American Babylon: Race and the Struggle for Postwar Oakland* (Princeton: Princeton University Press, 2003); Thomas Sugrue, *The Origins of the Urban Crisis: Race and Inequality in Postwar Detroit*, 2d ed. (Princeton: Princeton University Press, 2005); and Winant, *The Next Shift*.

53. Bayard Rustin, "From Protest to Politics: The Future of the Civil Rights Movement," *Commentary*, Feb. 1, 1965.

54. Daniel Levine, *Bayard Rustin and the Civil Rights Movement* (New Brunswick, NJ: Rutgers University Press, 2000), 188–89.

55. "A Freedom Budget for All Americans" (1967), text in Jerald Podair, *Bayard Rustin*, 140.

56. "Hearings of Sen. Abraham Ribicoff Subcommittee on Executive Reorganization," Dec., 1966, quoted in Daniel Levine, *Bayard Rustin and the Civil Rights Movement*, 191.

57. Paul Le Blanc and Michael Yates, *A Freedom Budget for All Americans: Recapturing the Promise of the Civil Rights Movement in the Struggle for Economic Justice Today* (New York: Monthly Review Press, 2013), 145–79.

58. The commission, officially titled the *Report of the National Advisory Commission on Civil Disorders*, was charged on July 29, 1967. It was bipartisan, including Republican mayor John Lindsay (vice chairman), United Steelworkers president I. W. Abel, and the NAACP's Roy Wilkins, among others.

59. *Report of the National Advisory Commission on Civil Disorders*, 1.

60. Rustin argued, "We have gone far enough to arouse expectations but not to satisfy them—and that is a dangerous thing to do." "The Report of the National Advisory Committee on Civil Disorders, An Analysis by Bayard Rustin," AFT Office of the President Collection (AFTOPC), 1960–1974, Box 1, Folder 2.

61. *Report of the National Advisory Commission on Civil Disorders*, 1.

62. *Report of the National Advisory Commission on Civil Disorders*, 4–7.

63. See, for example, Melvyn Dubofsky, *We Shall Be All: A History of the Industrial Workers of the World*, Abridged ed., ed. Joseph McCartin (Urbana: University of Illinois Press, 2000); Annelise Orleck, *Common Sense and a Little Fire: Women and Working-Class Politics in the United States, 1900–1965* (Chapel Hill: University of North Carolina Press, 1995); and Thomas Reid Andrews, *Killing for Coal: America's Deadliest Labor War* (Cambridge, MA: Harvard University Press, 2008). Among the many primary documents the

Kerner Commission could have consulted: Jacob Riis's photo-essay *How the Other Half Lives* (1890); Upton Sinclair's novel *The Jungle* (1905); and the findings of Basil Manly's report for the United States Commission on Industrial Relations (1915).

64. *Report of the National Advisory Commission on Civil Disorders,* 11.

65. *Report of the National Advisory Commission on Civil Disorders,* 11–12.

66. "The Report of the National Advisory Committee on Civil Disorders, An Analysis by Bayard Rustin," AFTOPC.

67. Weir, *Politics and Jobs,* 62–98.

68. On the rise of white Americans' anxieties about "law and order," see Jon Shelton, "Letters to the Essex County Penitentiary: David Selden and the Fracturing of America," *Journal of Social History* 48 (2014): 135–55.

69. Weir, *Politics and Jobs,* 93.

CHAPTER 4. NEW POLITICS

1. Daniel Bell, *The Coming of Post-Industrial Society: A Venture in Social Forecasting* (New York: Basic Books, 1976), ix–xv. Italics in original quotation. Bell pointed out that the number of teachers in the United States increased from about 1.3 million in 1954–55 to 2.1 million by 1964–65 and to 2.8 million in 1970 (215).

2. Bell, *The Coming of Post-Industrial Society,* xvi–xviii.

3. Bell, *The Coming of Post-Industrial Society,* 44.

4. Kevin Phillips, *The Emerging Republican Majority* (New Rochelle, NY: Arlington House, 1969).

5. Rick Perlstein, *Nixonland: The Rise of a President and the Fracturing of America* (New York: Scribner, 2009).

6. Kenneth Baer, *Reinventing Democrats: The Politics of Liberalism from Reagan to Clinton* (Lawrence: University of Kansas Press, 2000), 13.

7. US Census Bureau, "CPS Historical Timetables: Years of School Completed by People 25 Years and Over, by Age and Sex: Selected Years, 1940 to 2019," https://www.census.gov/data/tables/time-series/demo/educational-attainment/cps-historical-time-series.html accessed 5/29/2020. As Daniel Bell characterized it in *The Coming of Post-Industrial Society,* this was a "democratization of higher education on scale that the world has never seen before. No society has ever attempted to provide formal education for the bulk of its youth through age nineteen or twenty (the junior college level) or through age twenty-two, yet this has now become the explicit policy of the United States" (216).

8. Burton Kaufman and Scott Kaufman, *The Presidency of James Earl Carter,* 2d ed. (Lawrence: University of Kansas Press, 2006), 26.

9. Charles Clotfelter, *Unequal Colleges in the Age of Disparity* (Cambridge, MA: Belknap Press, 2017), 97.

10. Iver Peterson, "'New Vocationalism' Now Campus Vogue," *New York Times,* Dec. 25, 1973.

11. Hearing One Transcript, Dec. 8, 1970; Office of the Governor-Elect Press Release, Dec. 4, 1970; and "Suggested Press Release on Budget Hearings," *Wisconsin Governor Patrick Lucey Records, 1971–77,* University of Wisconsin Archives and Records Management, Series 2419, Box 184, Folder 39.

12. Letter from Lucey to Joseph Sobek, Apr. 22, 1971, and Lucey letter to Ed Weidner, Apr. 30, 1971. *Lucey Records,* Series 2419, Box 185, Folder 14. In background preparation for hearings in December 1970, the administration pointed out that "society demands of the individual both employable skills and a liberal arts background to adjust and operate in today's complex world." See "Section 4—Reducing Limitations of the Two-Year Technical Education Effort," Lucey Transition team hearing preparation document, also in Box 185, Folder 14.

13. "Mission of the University of Wisconsin System," https://www.wisconsin.edu/about-the-uw-system/. As business analyst and futurist Peter Drucker points out, the increasing use of the term *human resources* was coeval with the growth of human capital and the advent of the knowledge society. See *Post-Capitalist Society,* 66.

14. Lily Geismer, *Don't Blame US: Suburban Liberals and the Transformation of the Democratic Party* (Princeton: Princeton University Press, 2015), 1–16, 71–95, 95.

15. Joyce Baugh, *The Detroit School Busing Case:* Milliken v. Bradley *and the Controversy over Desegregation* (Lawrence: University of Kansas Press, 2011), 165.

16. According to Randall Rothenberg, "The Class of '74 was one of the largest freshman classes in congressional history. Scholars and professionals, they were well-educated men and women who had been fired up by John and Robert Kennedy." See *The Neo-Liberals: Creating the New American Politics* (New York: Simon and Schuster, 1984), 41. See also Judith Stein, *Pivotal Decade: How the United States Traded Factories for Finance in the Seventies* (New Haven: Yale University Press, 2010), 152.

17. Barbara and John Ehrenreich, "The Professional-Managerial Class," *Radical America*, March–April 1977, 7–31, 9.

18. Ehrenreich and Ehrenreich, "The Professional-Managerial Class," 11–17.

19. Barbara and Ehrenreich, "The New Left: A Case Study in Professional-Managerial Class Radicalism," *Radical America* 11, no. 3 (May–June 1977), 8. As they went on to argue, "The commonly held attitudes of the working class, are as likely to be anti-PMC as they are to be anti-capitalist—if only because people are more likely, in a day-to-day sense, to experience humiliation, harassment, frustration, etc. at the hands of the PMC than from members of the actual capitalist class" (19).

20. On American policymakers' failure to develop an industrial policy, see Stein, *Pivotal Decade*, in chapters 7–8. On the decline of manufacturing, see Windham, *Knockin' on Labor's Door,* 107–27; and Ira Magaziner and Robert Reich, *Minding America's Business: The Decline and Rise of the American Economy* (New York: Harcourt Brace Jovanovich, 1982), 1–2.

21. Windham, *Knockin' on Labor's Door,* especially 1–81.

22. Weir, *Politics and Jobs,* 66–67.

23. National Commission on Technology, Automation, and Economic Progress, *Technology and the American Economy*, vol. 1 (Washington, DC: US Government Printing Office, 1966), xii, 9.

24. Automation Commission's Report on Technological Development," *Monthly Labor Review*, Mar. 1, 1966, 274–77. In fact, Reuther believed the right to a job was even more urgent than the commission report, arguing in a footnote for "productive employment and adequate incomes for all who are willing and able to work" (276n1).

25. Weir, *Politics and Jobs,* 107–10.

26. "Unemployment Rate, Labor Force Statistics from the Current Population Survey," U.S. Bureau of Labor Statistics, https://data.bls.gov/timeseries/LNS14000000 extracted Aug. 16, 2021.

27. Weir, *Politics and Jobs,* 114–19.

28. "Unemployment Rate, Labor Force Statistics from the Current Population Survey," U.S. Bureau of Labor Statistics, https://data.bls.gov/timeseries/LNS14000000 extracted Aug. 16, 2021.

29. "Statement of Eli Ginzberg, Chairman, National Commission for Manpower Policy," October 3, 1974, *The Emergency Jobs Act: Hearings before the Select Subcommittee on Labor of the Committee on Education and Labor, House of Representatives Ninety-Third Congress, Second Session* (1974), quotation on 73.

30. "Statement of Nathaniel Goldfinger, Director, Department of Research, AFL-CIO," October 10, 1974, *The Emergency Jobs Act* (1974), 149–50.

31. Weir, *Politics and Jobs,* 120–23.

32. In a letter from January 1976, George Caudelle, secretary-treasurer of the North Georgia Building and Construction Trades Council, asserted that "for the best part of his four-year term as Governor, Carter did little in support of Labor's programs. You can trace his interest in, and support of, Labor issues to his decision to go national. . . . I would characterize his term in office as a period of smiles and broken promises." Further, in 1971, Carter wrote the National Right to Work Committee that he opposed repealing the state's right-to-work law. See "Labor Voter Facts on Jimmy Carter," AFT President's Office: Albert Shanker Collection (AFTPOASC), Reuther Archives, Wayne State University, Box 49, Folder 14.

33. AFL-CIO General Board Statement, Aug. 28, 1976, AFTPOASC, Box 49, Folder 14.

34. Wayne Urban, *Gender, Race, and the National Education Association: Professionalism and Its Limitations* (New York: RoutledgeFalmer, 2000), 171-209.

35. "Educators Help Carter/Mondale to Victory," *NEA Now,* Nov. 8, 1976.

36. Diana D'Amico Pawlewicz, *Blaming Teachers: Professionalization Policies and the Failure of Reform in American History* (New Brunswick, NJ: Rutgers University Press, 2020).

37. Jon Shelton, *Teacher Strike! Public Education and the Making of a New American Political Order* (Urbana: University of Illinois Press, 2017); and Jon Shelton, "Teacher Unions and Associations," in *Handbook of Historical Studies in Education: Debates, Tensions, and Directions,* ed. Tanya Fitzgerald (London: Springer, 2020).

38. Stein, *Pivotal Decade.*

39. Albert Shanker, "Where We Stand: Equal Rights for Public Employees," *New York Times,* Feb. 20, 1977.

40. David Stein, "Why Coretta Scott King Fought for a Jobs Guarantee," *Boston Review,* May 17, 2017, https://bostonreview.net/articles/david-stein-why-coretta-scott-king-fought-job-guarantee/.

41. Robert Self, *All in the Family: The Realignment of American Democracy since the 1960s* (New York: Hill and Wang, 2012). Cooper, *Family Values,* 21. Windham, *Knockin' on Labor's Door.*

42. Marisa Chappell's work has shown that while the fight over full employment ultimately led to a bill with "breadwinner" bias, both feminists and civil rights activists had pushed to establish a true "right to a job" for everyone. See *The War on Welfare: Family, Poverty, and Politics in Modern America* (Philadelphia: University of Pennsylvania Press, 2010), 125-38. In my view, a meaningful version of Humphrey-Hawkins, even the more limited version that still privileged breadwinners, could nevertheless have set expectations on which future activists could have further dismantled the version of American social democracy that privileged whites and privileged men.

43. Weir, *Politics and Jobs,* 131-40.

44. David Chappell, *Waking from the Dream: The Struggle for Civil Rights in the Shadow of Martin Luther King, Jr.* (New York: Random House, 2014), 66-68; Weir, *Politics and Jobs,* 134-35; Stein, *Pivotal Decade,* 140.

45. Stein, *Pivotal Decade,* 118-22. As Stein describes him, "Humphrey was the one candidate who had his eyes on the changes in the American economy, as well as the support of constituency groups that made liberalism a majoritarian political project. . . . He abstained from the emotionally satisfying anticorporatism, critiqued conventional Keynesianism, and offered social democratic solutions to repair the racial divisions in the party" (138).

46. *Full Employment and Balanced Growth Act of 1976, Hearings before the Committee on Banking, Housing, and Urban Affairs,* May 20, 21, and 25, 1976 (Washington, DC: US Government Printing Office, 1976), 6.

47. Letter from Coretta Scott King to Full Employment Action Council Board Member Albert Shanker, Mar. 5, 1976, AFT President's Office Al Lowenthal Collection, Box 3, Folder 1. See also Chappell, *Waking from the Dream*, 68–70.

48. Andrew Levison, *The Full Employment Alternative* (New York: Coward, McCann, and Geoghegan, 1980), 157; Helen Ginsburg, "Historical Amnesia: The Humphrey-Hawkins Act, Full Employment and Employment as a Right," *Review of Black Political Economy* 39 (March 2012): 121–36, especially 130.

49. Michael Honey, *Going Down Jericho Road: The Memphis Strike, Martin Luther King's Last Campaign* (New York: W. W. Norton, 2008).

50. Jeff Greenfield, "What Makes Hubert Not Run?" *New York Times*, April 4, 1976.

51. "Statement of Hubert Humphrey," *Full Employment and Balanced Growth Act of 1976, Hearings*, 132, 137.

52. "Statement of Augustus F. Hawkins, Representative in Congress from the State of California," *Full Employment and Balanced Growth Act of 1976, Hearings*, 142.

53. In addition to the discussion here, see Jefferson Cowie, *Stayin' Alive: The 1970s and the Last Days of the Working Class* (New York: New Press, 2010), 275–76; and Attewell, *People Must Live By Work*, 226–39.

54. "Statement of Carl Madden, Chamber of Commerce of the United States of America; Accompanied by Richard S. Landry, Staff Executive, Banking and Monetary-Fiscal Policy Committee," in *Full Employment and Balanced Growth Act of 1976, Hearings*, 214.

55. Soma Golden, "Democrats Put Focus on Jobs," *New York Times*, May 22, 1976; Greenfield, "What Makes Hubert Not Run?"

56. Weir, *Politics and Jobs*, 138.

57. Greenfield, "What Makes Hubert Not Run?"

58. Attewell, *People Must Live by Work*, 248.

59. "1976 Democratic Party Platform," July 12, 1976, https://www.presidency.ucsb.edu/documents/1976-democratic-party-platform.

60. Charles Mohr, "Udall Calls Carter Evasive on Jobs Bill," *New York Times*, Apr. 2, 1976. At a conference organized by the FEAC, Carter called the bill "laudable" but did not endorse it. He later endorsed it "at the prodding of labor and black groups," according to journalist John Lee, but "his heart doesn't seem to be into it." See John Lee, "The Economic Scene: Prices, Jobs, and Voters," *New York Times*, Aug. 22, 1976.

61. "Jimmy Carter on the Issue of: Jobs and Unemployment" undated campaign material, in AFTPOASC, Box 49, Folder 14.

62. Chappell, *Waking from the Dream*, 74–76.

63. Ginsburg, "Historical Amnesia," 131. See also Kaufman and Kaufman, *The Presidency of James Earl Carter*, 134–35.

64. Weir, *Politics and Jobs*, 124–29.

65. Kim Phillips-Fein, *Invisible Hands: The Businessmen's Crusade against the New Deal* (New York: W. W. Norton: 2009), 185–212.

66. Weir, *Politics and Jobs*, 136–37.

67. Stein, "Why Coretta Scott King Fought for a Job Guarantee."

68. Jimmy Carter, "State of the Union Address," Jan. 19, 1978, https://millercenter.org/the-presidency/presidential-speeches/january-19-1978-state-union-address.

69. "Full Employment and Balanced Growth Act" (Humphrey-Hawkins Act), Public Law 95–523, https://fraser.stlouisfed.org/title/full-employment-balanced-growth-act-humphrey-hawkins-act-1034.

70. "Statement of F. Ray Marshall, Secretary, Department of Labor," *Full Employment and Balanced Growth Act of 1976, Hearings*, 180–84. Early in the Carter administration,

Marshall had advocated for guaranteed public service jobs for welfare recipients, so this stance appears to have been pushed by Carter. See Burton Kaufman and Scott Kaufman, *The Presidency of James Earl Carter,* 65–66.

71. "Statement on the Full Employment and Balanced Growth Act (S.50) before the Senate Committee on Banking, Housing and Urban Affairs for the Chamber Commerce for the United States," by Dr. Jack Carlson, May 8, 1978. *Full Employment and Balanced Growth Act of 1978, Hearings before the Committee on Banking, Housing, and Urban Affairs, United States Senate* (Washington, DC: US Government Printing Office, 1978), 42. Questioning of panelists by Senate committee, *Full Employment and Balanced Growth Act of 1978, Hearings,* 156.

72. *Full Employment and Balanced Growth Act of 1978, Hearings,* 229–30.

73. Windham, *Knockin' on Labor's Door,* 57–81.

74. On the right's efforts to stop labor law reform in 1978, see Cowie, *Stayin' Alive,* 288–96; Stein, *Pivotal Decade,* 180–90; and Jon Shelton, "'Compulsory Unionism' and Its Critics: The National Right to Work Committee, Teacher Unions, and the Defeat of Labor Law Reform in 1978," *Journal of Policy History* 29, no. 3 (2017): 378–402. On Carter, see Martin Halpern, *Unions, Radicals, and Democratic Presidents: Seeking Social Change in the Twentieth Century* (Westport, CT: Praeger, 2003), 123–26.

75. David Stein, "Full Employment and Freedom," *Jacobin,* May 25, 2018, https://www.jacobinmag.com/2018/05/full-employment-humphrey-hawkins-inflation-jobs-guarantee.

76. Stein, *Pivotal Decade,* 192–204, 225–337. As David Stein points out, "In 1979, only a year after the law was passed, under Federal Reserve chairman Paul Volcker, the hearings bordered on farcical, with Volcker asserting that controlling inflation should continue to take precedence over the Fed's employment mandate—a direct contravention of the NCFE/FEAC's goals. The infamous 'Volcker Shock' then raised interest rates to heretofore-unfathomable levels and helped bring rates of unemployment for Black workers to as high as 19.5 percent in 1983." See "Full Employment and Freedom."

77. Kim Moody, *An Injury to All: The Decline of American Unionism* (London: Verso, 1988), 152–56.

78. "Jimmy Carter on the Issue of: Education," Undated Campaign literature, AFTPOAS, Box 49, Folder 14. See also, "Statements by President Jimmy Carter on a Separate U.S. Department of Education," NEAC, Box 2246, Folder 4.

79. Eisenhower message to Congress, "Reorganization Plan No. 1 of 1953," https://uscode.house.gov/view.xhtml?req=granuleid:USC-prelim-title5a-node84-leaf134&num=0&edition=prelim.

80. Zeitz, *Building the Great Society,* 153.

81. AFT Press Release, "AFT Outlines Early Childhood Drive in Campaign Manual," Mar. 31, 1976; and AFT Press Release, "Battle Over Day Care Sponsorship to Headline AFT QuEST Consortium '75," April 24, 1975, in AFTPOASC, Box 49, Folder 3.

82. Carter Education Task Force First Meeting note, June 15, 1976, AFTOPASC, Box 49, Folder 14.

83. "A State Department of Education—Issues," sent to the HEW Team Transition Planning Group, Dec. 8 1976, AFTOPASC, Box 49, Folder 15.

84. "Citizens Committee Asks for White House Meeting to Seek Support for Cabinet-Level Education Post," NEAC, Sep, 23, 1977, Box 2246, Folder 4.

85. The NEA publication, *The NEA Reporter* asked teachers to send letters to Carter. See "Teacher—It's Time for You to Talk to Jimmy Carter," *NEA Reporter* 15, no. 6 (Sept 1977): 1; Letter from Gerry McDonough to Jimmy Carter, Oct. 20, 1977; and Letter from Marilyn Parnell, Sep. 20, 1977, NEAC, Box 2246, Folder 1. There are six folders of letters alone in Box 2246.

86. Carter, "State of the Union Address," Jan. 19, 1978, https://millercenter.org/the-presidency/presidential-speeches/january-19-1978-state-union-address.

87. "Statement of Hale Campion, Under Secretary, Department of Health, Education, and Welfare before the Committee on Governmental Affairs, United States Senate, May 17, 1978," NEAC, Box 2244, Folder 1. Califano, however, also likely sought to hamstring the proposal by calling to include a number of programs he knew loud constituencies would oppose: Head Start, Indian Education, and CETA training programs. See "Califano Launches Drive to Keep the 'E' in HEW," *National Journal*, Feb. 25, 1978.

88. "NEA Hits 'Dancing Around Philosophical Outskirts' of Education Department Issue before Senate Committee," Oct. 13, 1977, NEAC Box 2247, Folder 1. See also, "Statement of John Ryor, President of the National Education Association," House Hearings, HR 13443, 55–67.

89. "Statement Adopted by the Twelfth Constitutional Convention, AFL-CIO," December 1977, House Hearings 1978, 320–21. Public Employee Department, AFL-CIO, "Opposition to a Federal Department of Education," Sep. 21, 1977 and "Resolution for AFL-CIO Industrial Union Department Convention on a Separate Department of Education," NEAC, Box 2247, Folder 1.

90. "Pro and Con: Should There Be a Separate U.S. Department of Education?" *Times Herald* (Port Huron, MI), Dec. 4, 1977.

91. "Statement of Hon. Shirley Chisolm, a Representative in Congress from the State of New York," *House Hearings*, 380.

92. "Education Department Opponents Force Bill Off House Schedule," *Congressional Quarterly*, Oct. 7, 1978, 2752; Harrison Donnelly, "Education Department Survives by One Vote in House Committee," *CQ*, May 5, 1979, 836; Harrison Donnelly, "Education Department Passes House, 210–206," *CQ*, Jul. 14, 1979, 1411; Harrison Donnelly, "Conferees Drop House's Controversial Education Department Amendments," *CQ*, Sept. 15, 179, 2026; Harrison Donnelly, "Education Department Wins Final Approval," *CQ*, Sept. 29, 1979, 2112; Anderson, *Congress and the Classroom*, 125.

93. Vice President Walter Mondale, "Remarks at Meeting of Ad Hoc Committee on a Cabinet Department of Education," Jan. 24, 1979. NEAC, Box 2247, Folder 5.

94. News release on the Department of Education Organization Act, Oct. 17, 1979. NEAC, Box 2472, Folder 4.

95. Bell, *The Coming of Post-Industrial Society*, 424–75, 451.

96. Philip Shabecoff, "Kennedy Offers Broad Health Plan and Challenges Carter to Support It," *New York Times*, May 15, 1979; and Hedrich Smith, "Kennedy Declares His Candidacy, Vowing New Leadership for Nation," *New York Times*, Nov. 8, 1979. See also, Attewell, *People Must Live by Work*, 259.

97. Stein, *Pivotal Decade*, 271.

CHAPTER 5. "AT RISK"

1. "How Groups Voted in 1976," https://ropercenter.cornell.edu/how-groups-voted-1976; "How Groups Votes in 1980," https://ropercenter.cornell.edu/how-groups-voted-1980.

2. As Judith Stein has pointed out, the evidence shows that Reagan beat Carter because Americans wanted to see change, not because Reagan was a conservative. See *Pivotal Decade*, 262–63.

3. Charles Holden, Zach Messitte, and Jerald Podair, *Republican Populist: Spiro Agnew and the Origins of Donald Trump's America* (Charlottesville: University of Virginia Press, 2019). Rick Perlstein, *Nixonland: The Rise of a President and the Fracturing of America* (New York: Scribner, 2008), and *The Invisible Bridge: The Fall of Nixon and the Rise of Reagan* (New York: Simon and Schuster, 2014).

4. On the increasing prominence of the conservative version of human capital in the 1970s, see Cooper, *Family Values*, 226.

5. Ronald Reagan Inaugural Address, Jan. 20, 1981, https://www.reaganlibrary.gov/research/speeches/inaugural-address-january-20-1981.

6. Gordon Lafer, *The Job Training Charade* (Ithaca: Cornell University Press, 2002), 162.

7. Donald Critchlow, *The Conservative Ascendancy: How the GOP Right Made Political History* (Cambridge, MA: Harvard University Press, 2007), 186–91.

8. Adam Nelson, "The Federal Role in Education: A Historiographical Essay," in *Rethinking the History of American Education*, ed. William Reese and John Rury (New York: Palgrave MacMillan, 2008), 268.

9. "Federal Education Funding," *Classroom Agenda for the Education Summit*, NEAC, Series 7, Subseries 12, Box 2542, Folder 18. In inflation-adjusted dollars, this represented $3 billion less in FY 1989 than FY 1979. See also Richard Kahlenberg, *Tough Liberal: Albert Shanker and the Battles over Schools, Unions, Race, and Democracy* (New York: Columbia University Press, 2007), 233–34; and Maris Vinovskis, *The Road to Charlottesville: The 1989 Education Summit* (A Publication of the National Educational Goals Panel, September 1999), 8, https://govinfo.library.unt.edu/negp/reports/negp30.pdf

10. Cooper, *Family Values*, 232–41.

11. "Statement of the National Education Association on the Confirmation of Secretary of Education-Designate Terrel Bell before the Senate Committee of Labor and Human Resources, Presented by Willard McGuire of the National Education Association," NEAC Collection, Series 7, Subseries 8, Box 2244, Folder 5.

12. Pat Ordovensky, "Bell, Home Again, Opens Fire," *Idaho Statesmen*, Feb. 3, 1985.

13. "Introduction," *A Nation at Risk: The Imperative for Educational Reform, A Report to the Nation and the Secretary of Education*, National Commission on Excellence in Education, April 1983.

14. "A Nation at Risk," *ANAR*.

15. "The Risk," *ANAR*.

16. Magaziner and Reich, *Minding America's Business*.

17. Diane Ravitch, *Reign of Error: The Hoax of the Privatization Movement and the Danger to America's Public Schools* (New York: Alfred A. Knopf, 2013), 38–39. See also David Berliner and Bruce Biddle, who referred to *ANAR* as a deliberate "misinformation campaign" in *The Manufactured Crisis: Myths, Fraud, and the Attack on America's Public Schools* (Reading, MA: Addison-Wesley, 1995), 3. Finally, the Energy Department's Sandia Report in 1989 showed the methodology used by *ANAR* was deeply problematic, scores on neither the SAT nor the NAEP were declining, and claims of a skills gap were simply false. Deputy Education Secretary David Kearns, however, buried the report, and the government never issued it. See Deborah Duncan Owens, *The Origins of the Common Core: How the Free Market Became Public Education Policy* (New York: Palgrave Macmillan, 2015), 98–103, 128–29.

18. "Table 222.85, Average National Assessment of Educational Progress (NAEP) Mathematics Scale Score, by Age and Selected Student Characteristics: Selected Years, 1973–2012," National Center for Education Statistics, *Digest of Education Statistics*, https://nces.ed.gov/programs/digest/d18/tables/dt18_222.85.asp. As Deborah Duncan Owens points out, *ANAR* relied on SAT scores as their only longitudinal test, and the SAT was far from representative. Further, declining SAT scores actually resulted from more students taking the test in the 1970s. See *The Origins of the Common Core*, 7–17.

19. "Hope and Frustration," *ANAR*.

20. "Excellence in Education," *ANAR*.

21. "Recommendations A-E," *ANAR*.

22. Graham, *Schooling America*, 168–71.

23. Michael Oreskes, "Shanker Urges Teachers to Aid School Reforms," *New York Times,* May 1, 1983.

24. Kahlenberg, *Tough Liberal,* 272–80, 272.

25. Urban, *Gender, Race, and the National Education Association,* 264.

26. National Education Association, "An Open Letter to American on Schools, Students, and Tomorrow," National Education Association, 1984, AFTOPASC. Box 51, Folder 9.

27. Shelton, *Teacher Strike!* 48.

28. Joseph McCartin, *Collision Course: Ronald Reagan, the Air Traffic Controllers, and the Strike That Changed America* (New York: Oxford University Press, 2010). On PATCO as precedent for other strikes, see Stein, *Pivotal Decade,* 267.

29. Stein, *Pivotal Decade,* 267–70; Nicholas Lemann, *Transaction Man: The Rise of the Deal and the Decline of the American Dream* (New York: Farrar, Strauss, and Giroux, 2019), 136–81.

30. Critchlow, *The Conservative Ascendancy,* 216.

31. Adam Mertz, "Growing Realignment: Land, Labor, Taxes, and the Decline of Wisconsin's Democratic Majority," PhD diss., University of Illinois-Chicago, 2019, chapter 8.

32. Michael Rosen and Charlie Dee, "Briggs & Stratton's Demise: Greed, Mismanagement, Blaming Others," *Wisconsin Examiner,* Sept. 28, 2020, https://wisconsinexaminer.com/2020/09/28/briggs-strattons-demise-greed-mismanagement-blaming-others/.

33. Lafer, *The Job Training Charade,* 156–89.

34. Lafer, *The Job Training Charade,* 1–2.

35. Lola Fadulu, "Why Is the U.S. So Bad at Worker Retraining?" *The Atlantic,* Jan. 4, 2018.

36. Lafer, *The Job Training Charade,* 1–3.

37. Lafer, *The Job Training Charade,* 1–3; 157.

38. On the connection between labor reform and the Panama Canal treaty, see Halpern, *Unions, Radicals, and Democratic Presidents,* 157.

39. Julie Greene, *The Canal Builders: Making America's Empire at the Panama Canal* (New York: Penguin Press, 2009), 373–77. See also, Reagan in debate over the canal on *Firing Line* on Jan. 13, 1978, https://www.c-span.org/video/?154034-1/firing-line-panama-canal-treaties.

40. Department of Education briefing document on Bennett, NEAC, Box 2244, Folder 6.

41. Letter from Bennett to Clarence Thomas, Jan. 16, 1984, and NEA Memo "William Bennett Nomination," Jan. 14, 1985, GWU, Box 2244, Folder 6

42. As Christopher Newfield puts it, the culture wars were actually "economic wars," which represented "a kind of intellectual neutron bomb, eroding the social and cultural foundations of a growing, politically powerful, economically entitled, and racially diversifying middle class, while leaving its technical capacities intact." See *Unmaking the Public University: The Forty-Year Assault on the Middle Class* (Cambridge: Harvard University Press, 2011), 5–6.

43. John Podhoretz, "William Bennett, the Idea Warrior," *Washington Times,* Jun. 11, 1984.

44. Ronald Brownstein, "In Person . . . William Bennett," *National Journal,* Nov. 17, 1984.

45. William Bennett, *To Reclaim a Legacy: A Report on the Humanities in Higher Education* (National Endowment for the Humanities, 1984), 1–2.

46. Allan Bloom, *The Closing of the American Mind: How Higher Education Has Failed Democracy and Impoverished the Souls of Today's Students* (New York: Simon and Schuster, 1987).

47. Newfield, *The Unmaking of the Public University,* 51–52.

48. Reese, *America's Public Schools,* 249.

49. Bennett Speech to Colorado Association of Commerce and Industry, May 14, 1985. NEAC, Box 2244, Folder 7.

50. Bennett Speech to Conference on Civic Virtue and Educational Excellence, Apr. 19, 1985, NEAC, Box 2244, Folder 7.

51. See, for instance, "Bennett Offers Revised School Voucher Plan," *Los Angeles Times,* Mar. 16, 1987.

52. Bennett speech at the National Catholic Education Association Annual Convention, Apr. 10, 1985, NEAC, Box 2244, Folder 7.

53. "Bill Bennett Finally Turns Republican," *Washington Post,* June 27, 1986.

54. Rothenberg, *The Neo-Liberals.*

55. The literature on neoliberalism is vast. See, for instance, David Harvey, *A Brief History of Neoliberalism* (New York: Oxford University Press, 2004) and Jamie Peck, *Constructions of Neoliberal Reason* (Oxford: Oxford University Press, 2010).

56. Rothenberg, *The Neo-liberals,* 23–27.

57. Charles Peters, "A Neoliberal's Manifesto," *The Washington Monthly,* May 1983, 10–11.

58. On the "Atari Democrats" see Rothenberg, *The Neo-liberals,* 79–91.

59. Peters, "A Neoliberal's Manifesto," 11–12.

60. Rothenberg, *The Neo-Liberals,* 87–90.

61. Rothenberg, *The Neo-Liberals,* 139, 193–94.

62. Gary Hart, *A New Democracy* (New York: Quill, 1983), 20–21.

63. Hart, *A New Democracy,* 83–84.

64. Hart, *A New Democracy,* 92–93.

65. According to an NEA analysis in 1982, the bill was introduced in the House "at the request of the National Education Association." See "Analysis of Legislative Proposals Affecting Science, Mathematics, and Engineering Education," Sep. 15, 1982. NEAC, Box 2255, Folder 5.

66. National Education Association, "National Defense Education Act: An NEA Policy Paper," Feb. 1983, 2, NEAC, Box 2255, Folder 5.

67. Text of the High Technology Morrill Act, introduced to the US Senate by Sen. Paul Tsongas, NEAC, Box 2255, Folder 5.

68. Hart, *A New Democracy,* 102–4.

69. "1984 Democratic Primary Debate," Mar. 18, 1984.

70. Baer, *Reinventing Democrats,* 64–68.

71. Baer, *Reinventing Democrats,* 81.

72. Al From with Alice McKeon, *The New Democrats and the Return to Power* (New York: Palgrave Macmillan, 2013), 2.

73. Baer, *Reinventing Democrats,* 78.

74. Baer, *Reinventing Democrats,* 64–119.

75. Geismer, *Don't Blame Us,* 251–79.

76. William Galston and Elaine Kamarck, *The Politics of Evasion: Democrats and the Presidency* (Progressive Policy Institute, 1989), 18, https://www.progressivepolicy.org/wp-content/uploads/2013/03/Politics_of_Evasion.pdf.

CHAPTER 6. "WHAT YOU EARN DEPENDS ON WHAT YOU LEARN"

1. Vinovskis, *The Road to Charlottesville,* 23.

2. Patrick McGuinn, *No Child Left Behind and the Transformation of Federal Education Policy, 1965–2005* (Lawrence: University Press of Kansas, 2006), 52–57, 53. See also "The Basic Speech: George Bush," *New York Times,* Feb. 4, 1988.

3. Critchlow, *The Conservative Ascendancy*, 221–23.

4. Thomas Frank, *Listen, Liberal: Or What Ever Happened to the Party of the People?* (New York: Henry Holt, 2016).

5. Committee for Economic Development, *Investing in Our Children: Business and the Public Schools* (1985), 2. Citation and context in Vinovskis, *The Road the Charlottesville*, 6.

6. William Johnston and Arnold Packer, eds., *Workforce 2000: Work and Workers for the 21st Century* (Indianapolis, IN: Hudson Institute, 1987), xiii–xvii, https://files.eric.ed.gov/fulltext/ED290887.pdf.

7. Johnston and Packer, *Workforce 2000*, xiv, xxiv.

8. Becker, *Human Capital*, 18.

9. Chris Pipho, "Governors Push Better Schools Coalition," *Phi Delta Kappan* (October 1986), 101.

10. Vinovskis, *The Road to Charlottesville*, 17–18, 17.

11. NBC News, *Meet the Press*, May 18, 1986. Reuther Archives, AFT Collection: Educational Issues (AFTCEI), Box 51, Folder 9.

12. Brent Cebul, "Supply-Side Liberalism: Fiscal Crisis, Post-Industrial Policy, and the Rise of the New Democrats," *Modern American History* 2 (2019), 139–64.

13. Vinovskis, *The Road to Charlottesville*, 23–36; Maris Vinovskis, *From A Nation at Risk to No Child Left Behind: National Education Goals and the Creation of Federal Education Policy* (New York: Teachers College Press, 2009), 23–24.

14. Keith Geiger, President, National Education Association, "Opening Statement," Sept. 20, 1989, News Conference. NEAC, Box 2542, Folder 12.

15. Vinovskis, *The Road to Charlottesville*, 28.

16. "The Summit Conference on Education Working Groups," AFTCEI, Box 51, Folder 6.

17. The President's Education Summit with Governors, University of Virginia, September 27–28, 1989, "Joint Statement," AFTCEI, Box 51, Folder 6. See also Vinovskis, *Road to Charlottesville*, 38–39.

18. George H.W. Bush State of the Union address, Jan. 31, 1990, https://millercenter.org/the-presidency/presidential-speeches/january-31-1990-state-union-address.

19. White House Press Release, July 31, 1990, AFTCEI, Box 51, Folder 6.

20"Welcome Remarks by James D. Hayes, Publisher, *Fortune Magazine*," Fortune Annual Education Summit, 1990, AFTCEI, Box 115, Folder 19.

21. Address of Vartan Gregorian, President, Brown University, *Fortune Magazine* education summit, 1990, AFTCEI, Box 115, Folder 19.

22. George H.W. Bush, "Address to the Nation on the National Education Strategy," Apr. 18, 1991. George H.W. Bush Presidential Library and Museum Archives, https://bush41library.tamu.edu/archives/public-papers/2895; Patrick McGuinn, *No Child Left Behind*, 65–69.

23. "The Summit Conference on Education Working Groups," AFTCEI, Box 51, Folder 6.

24. Milton Friedman, "The Role of Government in Education" (1955), https://la.utexas.edu/users/hcleaver/330T/350kPEEFriedmanRoleOfGovttable.pdf.

25. Jim Carl, *Freedom of Choice: Vouchers in American Education* (New York: Praeger, 2011), chapters 1–3; *Free to Choose*, episode 6, "What's Wrong with Our Schools?" directed by Peter Robinson (Video Arts Production, 1980); Jon Shelton, *Teacher Strike!* 186–90.

26. John Chubb and Terry Moe, *Politics, Markets, and America's Schools* (Washington, DC; Brookings Institution, 1990), 3–9.

27. Chubb and Moe, *Politics, Markets, and America's Schools*, 190.

28. Chubb and Moe, *Politics, Markets, and America's Schools*, 33.

29. Chubb and Moe, *Politics, Markets, and America's Schools*, 219.

30. Patrick Jones, *The Selma of the North: Civil Rights Insurgency in Milwaukee* (Cambridge, MA: Harvard University Press, 2010).

31. James Nelsen, *Educating Milwaukee: How One City's History of Segregation and Struggle Reshaped Its Schools* (Madison: Wisconsin Historical Society Press, 2015), 126.

32. Jack Dougherty, *More Than One Struggle: The Evolution of Black School Reform in Milwaukee* (Chapel Hill: University of North Carolina Press, 2004), 167–93.

33. Carl, *Freedom of Choice,* 105–7; Dougherty, *More Than One Struggle,* 189–91; Nelsen, *Educating Milwaukee,* 131–33.

34. Carl, *Freedom of Choice,* 87, 116. For the full program, see GOPAC's *American Opportunities Workshop* 1990, https://www.youtube.com/watch?v=8lPJ-2O-E4g.

35. Carl, *Freedom of Choice,* 88.

36. Mertz, "Growing Realignment," chapter 8.

37. Carl, *Freedom of Choice,* 118–19.

38. Nelsen, *Educating Milwaukee,* 147–49; Carl, *Freedom of Choice,* 119–23.

39. Nelsen, *Educating Milwaukee,* 149.

40. Carl, *Freedom of Choice,* 87–88, 117–75.

41. Matt Pommer, "Rep Jolting School Powers," *The Capital Times* (Madison, WI), June 18, 1990.

42. McGuinn, *No Child Left Behind,* 69.

43. George H.W. Bush, "Remarks Announcing Proposed Legislation to Establish a 'GI Bill for Children,'" June 25, 1992, https://bush41library.tamu.edu/archives/public-papers/4488.

44. "Remarks of President Bush at the New Education Choice Initiative Ceremony," June 25, 1992. Bush speech quoted in McGuinn, *No Child Left Behind,* 68.

45. "Statement by National Education Association President Keith Geiger on the New Educational Choice Initiative, June 26, 1992," NEAC Box 2542, Folder 11.

46. "Statement by Keith Geiger," NEAC, Box 2541, Folder 18.

47. The PPI's most important initial backer was the New York hedge fund manager Michael Steinhardt, who in exchange for agreeing to donate $1.5 million over three years was made chairman of the PPI Board of Trustees. Baer, *Reinventing Democrats,* 137.

48. "Back to School," *New Democrat,* Sept. 1991, 2.

49. "Recess," *New Democrat,* Dec. 1991, 2.

50. Seymour Martin Lipset, "The Real Civil Rights Debate," *New Democrat,* Sept. 1991, 13, 14.

51. David Kurapka, "Crime and Bushment," *New Democrat,* Dec. 1991, 16–18.

52. See, for example, Sugrue, *The Origins of the Urban Crisis.*

53. "Editor's Note to excerpt from David Osborne and Ted Gaebler, *Reinventing Government,*" *New Democrat,* Mar. 1992, 4.

54. David Osborne and Ted Gaebler, *Reinventing Government: How the Entrepreneurial Spirit Is Reinventing the Public Sector* (New York: Addison-Wesley, 1992), xv, xvi–xvii, 17, 172. On Deming, see Mary Walton, *The Deming Management Method* (New York: Perigee, 1986), a book blurbed by Robert Reich: "W. Edwards Deming is to management what Benjamin Franklin was to the Republican conscience—a guide, a prophet, and instigator." Xerox executive David Kearns, appointed deputy secretary of the Department of Education by George H.W. Bush, argued that failing schools could be turned around by using TQM as early as 1989. See Owens, *The Origins of the Common Core,* 91–93.

55. Osborne and Gaebler, *Reinventing Government,* 1, 17, 94.

56. Osborne and Gaebler, *Reinventing Government,* 94.

57. Ron Sachs, "Florida Rebounds" (12–13); David Kurapka, "The Second City?" (13–14); and Elaine Kamarck, "The Philadelphia Story" (14–16), *New Democrat,* Mar. 1992.

58. Al From, "Reinventing the Democratic Party," *New Democrat*, Mar. 1992, 32.

59. Cebul, "Supply-Side Liberalism," 16.

60. See, for example, "Arkansas Overhauling Its Education System," *New York Times*, Nov. 20, 1983; and William Schmidt, "Teachers Up in Arms Over Arkansas's Skills Test," *New York Times*, Jan. 17, 1984.

61. Michael Tomasky, *Bill Clinton* (New York: Henry Holt and Company, 2017), 7–11. David Maraniss, *First in His Class: A Biography of Bill Clinton* (New York: Simon and Schuster, 1995), 409–18. See also McGuinn, *No Child Left Behind and the Transformation of Federal Education Policy*, 79–80.

62. Baer, *Reinventing Democrats*, 163–65, 174–77, 177.

63. Bill Clinton, "What We Believe," *The New American Choice Resolutions*, 3–4.

64. Clinton, "What We Believe," 5, 9. Emphasis in original.

65. "Restoring America's Competitive Edge, Part Two: Meeting the Global Challenge," *The New American Choice Resolutions*, 17. Emphasis in original.

66. Kate Bronfenbrenner, "No Holds Barred: The Intensification of Employer Opposition to Organizing," *Economic Policy Institute*, Briefing Paper #235, May 20, 2009.

67. "Restoring America's Competitive Edge," *New American Choice Resolutions*, 18.

68. Baer, *Reinventing Democrats*, 187.

69. "Restoring America's Competitive Edge, Part Two," *New American Choice Resolution*, 35.

70. Magaziner and Reich, *Minding America's Business*, 1–8.

71. Geismer, *Don't Blame Us*, 268–69. Robert Reich, *Locked in the Cabinet* (New York: Vintage, 1988), 17.

72. Osborne and Gaebler, *Reinventing Government*, xi.

73. Drucker, *Post-Capitalist Society*, 4–9.

74. Magaziner and Reich, *Minding America's Business*, 106.

75. National Center on Education and the Economy, *America's Choice: High Skills or Low Wages*, 2–3, http://www.ncee.org/wp-content/uploads/2013/09/Americas-Choice-High-Skills-or-Low-Wages.pdf.

76. National Center on Education and the Economy, *America's Choice*, 3.

77. Johnston and Packer, *Workforce 2000*, 3.

78. Drucker, *Post-Capitalist Society*, 4.

79. Robert Reich, *The Work of Nations: Preparing for 21st Century Capitalism* (New York: Vintage, 1991), 177–80.

80. *The New American Choice Resolutions*, 23–25, 40–41. Indeed, the DLC cited Chubb and Moe's *Politics, Markets, and America's Schools*.

81. See, for instance, "We're All DLCers Now," *New Democrat*, Mar. 1992, 1. Harkin, in fact, referred to himself as the only "real Democrat" in the race. See Judith Miller, "Tom Harkin's Old-Time Religion," *New York Times Magazine*, Feb. 9, 1992.

82. Becker, *Human Capital*, xix.

83. Bill Clinton and Al Gore, *Putting People First: How We Can All Change America* (New York: Times Books, 1992), 6. As Reich pointed out in his memoir, "I've burdened Bill with every one of my books and articles, and urged *him* to run. And he *did*. And he *used* my ideas." *Locked in the Cabinet*, 9.

84. Clinton and Gore, *Putting People First*, 9.

85. As Michael Sandel has pointed out, Clinton publicly employed a version of the phrase "what you earn depends on what you learn" at least thirty times during his presidency. *Tyranny of Merit*, 86.

86. Clinton and Gore, *Putting People First*, 17–19.

87. Bill Clinton, "A New Covenant": Address to the Democratic National Convention, Jul. 16, 1992.

88. John Judis, *The Populist Explosion: How the Great Recession Transformed American Politics and European Politics* (New York: Columbia Global Reports, 2016), 46–51.

89. 96 percent of the electorate in 1992 believed that the Bush administration had either made the economy worse or done nothing to make it better. See Kenneth Baer, *Reinventing Democrats*, 207.

CHAPTER 7. PUTTING SOME PEOPLE FIRST

1. "First Inaugural Address of William J. Clinton," Jan. 20, 1993, https://avalon.law.yale.edu/20th_century/clinton1.asp.

2. Jeremy Rosner, "Take Two Aspirin," *New Democrat*, Dec. 1991.

3. Reich, *Locked in the Cabinet*, 28–31.

4. As Thomas Frank points out, the professional-managerial class, particularly academic economists, supported the claims of NAFTA despite the fears of many unions that it would lead to the loss of hundreds of thousands of blue-collar manufacturing jobs. See *Listen, Liberal*, 86–89.

5. "1993 NAFTA Debate: Al Gore vs. Ross Perot," Nov. 9, 1993, *CNN.com*, https://www.cnn.com/videos/politics/2016/09/02/nafta-debate-1993-al-gore-ross-perot-entire-larry-king-live.cnn/video/playlists/larry-king-live-interviews/.

6. Timothy Minchin, *Labor under Fire: A History of the AFL-CIO since 1979* (Chapel Hill: University of North Carolina Press, 2017), 195–206.

7. Kathryn Marie Dudley, *The End of the Line: Lost Jobs, New Lives in Postindustrial America* (Chicago: University of Chicago Press, 1994).

8. On Clinton's development agenda, see, for instance, Brent Cebul, "Supply-Side Liberalism," 158–62.

9. Reich, *Locked in the Cabinet*, 66.

10. Reich, *Locked in the Cabinet*, 66–70.

11. Reich, *Locked in the Cabinet*, 66–70, 93–95, 133–34.

12. Vinovskis, *The Road to Charlottesville*, 19–20.

13. Vinovskis, *From A Nation at Risk to No Child Left Behind*, 114–16.

14. "Statement of Hon. Richard Riley, Secretary of Education," *Hearings on H.R. 1804—Goals 2000: Educate America Act* (Washington, DC: US Government Printing Office, 1993), 4–5.

15. "Statement of Hon. Richard Riley," 5–6.

16. "Statement of Hon. Robert Reich, Secretary of Labor" *Hearings on H.R. 1804*, 45–46.

17. "Statement of Hon. Robert Reich," 45–48.

18. "Statement of Hon. Robert Reich," 55.

19. William Celis, "Schools to Get Wide License on Spending Federal Money under New Education Law," *New York Times*, Oct. 19, 1994; Anderson, *Congress and the Classroom*, 149–50; McGuinn, *No Child Left Behind*, 95–97.

20. Department of Education Analysis of School-to-Work Opportunities Act of 1994, https://www2.ed.gov/pubs/Biennial/95-96/eval/410-97.pdf

21. Minchin, *Labor under Fire*, 209–10.

22. Anderson, *Congress and the Classroom*, 154–55.

23. Sean Wilentz, *The Age of Reagan: A History, 1974–2006* (New York: Harper Collins, 2009).

24. Bill Clinton, State of the Union address, Jan. 23, 1996.

25. Cooper, *Family Values*, especially chapter 2.

26. Bruce Reed, "The Parent Trap," *Mainstream Democrat*, Sept. 1991, 18–21.

27. Johnston and Packer, *Workforce 2000*, xxvi.

28. Carol Jouzaitis, "Welfare Reform: Now It's Up to States," *Chicago Tribune*, Sept. 30, 1996.

29. Wilentz, *The Age of Reagan*, 364–67.

30. William Julius Wilson, *When Work Disappears: The World of the New Urban Poor* (New York: Vintage Books, 1997).

31. Luke Shaefer and Kathryn Edin, "What Is the Evidence of Worsening Conditions among American's Poorest Families with Children?" Mar. 2, 2016, http://static1.squarespace.com/static/551caca4e4b0a26ceeee87c5/t/56d9f10f1bbee030291fedce/1457123600812/Shaefer-Edin-SIPP-WorseningConditions3-2-16.pdf; Lafer, *The Job Training Charade*, 191.

32. McGuinn, *No Child Left Behind*, 80.

33. Bob Dole, "Acceptance of the Republican Party Nomination for President," Aug. 15, 1996.

34. Quotation in Kahlenberg, *Tough Liberal*, 333.

35. "Minutes of the Tenth Meeting of the President's Education Policy Advisory Committee, Jan. 22, 1992, AFTPOAS, Box 49, Folder 32.

36. Kahlenberg, *Tough Liberal*, 334–46. Albert Shanker, "Where We Stand: Two Kinds of Equity," *New York Times* (paid advertisement), Jun. 13, 1993.

37. Bob Chase, "Education Reform: Into the New Millenium," Education International Roundtable of Teacher Organizations, Dec. 1996, NEAC, Box 2443, Folder 8.

38. Urban, *Gender, Race, and the National Education Association*, 271–75.

39. Bill Clinton, "State of the Union Address," Feb. 4, 1997.

40. Clinton, "State of the Union Address," Feb. 4, 1997.

41. Clinton, "State of the Union Address," Feb. 4, 1997.

42. Kahlenberg, *Tough Liberal*, 373–74.

43. Bob Chase, "The New NEA: Reinventing Teacher Unions for a New Era," Before the National Press Club, Feb. 5, 1997, NEAC, Box 2541, Folder 8.

44. *Investing in Public Education: The Importance of Schools in the New Global Economy* (1999), NEAC, Box 2540, Folder 13.

45. *Investing in Public Education*.

46. Bill Clinton, "Foreword," in Al From, *The New Democrats and the Return to Power*, x.

47. Rothenberg, *The Neo-Liberals*, 245–46.

48. Reich, *Locked in the Cabinet*, xiii.

49. Goldin and Katz, *The Race Between Technology and Education*, 93.

50. Charles Petersen, "Serfs of Academe," *New York Review of Books*, Mar. 12, 2020.

51. Frank, *Listen, Liberal*, 92–94, 111–15.

52. Reich, *Locked in the Cabinet*, 193–206.

53. Bell, *The Coming of Post-Industrial Society*, xvii.

54. Robert Self, *All in the Family: The Realignment of American Democracy since the 1960s* (New York: Hill and Wang, 2012), 6.

55. Holden, Messitte, and Podair, *Republican Populist*, 70–134.

56. Quotation in Judis, *The Populist Explosion*, 51–53.

57. Stein, *Pivotal Decade*, 288; Lemann, *Transaction Man*, 165–78.

CHAPTER 8. LEFT BEHIND

1. Richard Florida, *The Rise of the Creative Class: And How It's Transforming Work, Leisure, Community and Everyday Life* (New York: Basic Books, 2002), 5, 55. Italics in original.

2. Florida, *The Rise of the Creative Class*, 7–8.

3. Florida, *The Rise of the Creative Class*, 252, 283.

4. Florida, *The Rise of the Creative Class*, 10, 70–72. 263.

5. Florida, *The Rise of the Creative Class*, 12, 320.

6. See for example, the *New York Times* feature story by Emily Eakin, "The Cities and Their New Elite," Jun. 1, 2002, as well as Herbert Muschamp, "Who Gets IT?" *New York Times*, May 18, 2003; and David Leonhardt, "In Most of the U.S., A House Is a Home But Not a Bonanza," *New York Times*, Aug. 6, 2003. For useful critical retrospectives of Florida's influence, see Oliver Wainwright, "'Everything Is Gentrification Now,' but Richard Florida Isn't Sorry," *The Guardian*, Oct. 26, 2017, https://www.theguardian.com/cities/2017/oct/26/gentrification-richard-florida-interview-creative-class-new-urban-crisis; and Jonathan O'Connell, "This Guy Convinced Cities to Cater to Tech-Savvy Millennials. Now He's Reconsidering," *Washington Post*, April 17. 2017, https://www.washingtonpost.com/news/digger/wp/2017/04/17/as-the-creative-class-divides-america-its-inventor-richard-florida-reconsiders/.

7. McGuinn, *No Child Left Behind*, 105–45.

8. Gov. Tommy Thompson, "State of the State Address," Jan. 29, 1997.

9. Owens, *The Origins of the Common Core*, 136–38; Jack Jennings, *Fatigued by School Reform* (Lanham, MD: Rowman and Littlefield, 2020), 53.

10. "Full Text of Bush's Campaign Speech on Education," *New York Times*, Nov. 2, 1999.

11. McGuinn, *No Child Left Behind*, 146–64.

12. Guy Stuart, "Databases, Felons, and Voting: Errors and Bias in the Florida Felons Exclusion List in the 2000 Presidential Elections," *John F. Kennedy School of Government, Harvard University, Faculty Research Working Papers Series*, September 2002, https://poseidon01.ssrn.com/delivery.php?ID=546004070078007088024111111300 112708906805101708701104803001702902411311901302103103004116007120119127 097117120026025047076079123115103007126030123027090076023086014023005017 120124095070085112004117095028001023004127114107086099098029001 069077&EXT=pdf; Wade Payson-Denney, "So, Who Really Won? What the Bush v. Gore Studies Showed," CNN.com, Oct. 31, 2015. https://www.cnn.com/2015/10/31/politics/bush-gore-2000-election-results-studies/index.html.

13. McGuinn, *No Child Left Behind*, 101.

14. Joseph Lieberman Statement, *Congressional Record* (hereafter referred to as CR), May 2, 2001, S4147.

15. Keith Bailey, "Testimony before the Committee on Education and the Workforce, U.S. House of Representatives," quoted in McGuinn, *No Child Left Behind*, 175.

16. McGuinn, *No Child Left Behind*, 165–76; Owens, *Origins of the Common Core*, 133–34.

17. Bill Frist statement on the Better Education for Students and Teachers Act, *CR*, May 1, 2001, S4056.

18. Dale Kildee statement, *CR*, May 21, 2001, H2396.

19. Charles Rangel statement, *CR*, June 13, 2001, H3080.

20. Statement of Ted Kennedy, *CR*, May 1, 2001, S4063.

21. Statements of Paul Wellstone, *CR*, May 1, 2001, S4060 and S4075–76.

22. McGuinn, *No Child Left Behind*, 177–83; 107th Congress, Public Law 110. https://www.congress.gov/bill/107th-congress/house-bill/1/text.

23. Diane Ravitch, *Reign of Error: The Hoax of the Privatization Movement and the Danger to America's Public Schools* (New York: Alfred A. Knopf, 2013), 11–13; William Reese, *America's Public Schools*, 332.

24. Ben Feller, "NEA Political Targets Education Law, Mulls Presidential Endorsement," *Associated Press*, July 3, 2003.

25. NEA Press Release, "NEA President Rallies Members for Great Public Schools for Every Child," NEA Collection, NEAC, Box 2540, Folder 1.

26. Vinovskis, *From A Nation at Risk to No Child Left Behind,* 189–90.

27. Kantor and Lowe, "The Price of Human Capital," 81.

28. Neil Kraus, *The Fantasy Economy,* forthcoming manuscript. Or, as Lee Anderson argues, "By 2001, no one challenged the antipoverty rationale of No Child Left Behind." See *Congress and the Classroom,* 22.

29. George W. Bush State of the Union Address, Jan. 29, 2002, https://georgewbush-whitehouse.archives.gov/news/releases/2002/01/20020129-11.html.

30. CPS Historical Time Series Tables, Table A-1, "Years of School Completed by People 25 Years and Over, by Age and Sex: Selected Years 1940 to 2019," https://www.census.gov/data/tables/time-series/demo/educational-attainment/cps-historical-time-series.html.

31. "Executive Order #289, Relating to the Creation of the Governor's Blue-Ribbon Commission on 21st Century Jobs," in Governor's Blue-Ribbon Commission on 21st Century Jobs, *The New Wisconsin Idea: 'The Innovative Learning State,'* July 1997, i.

32. "Executive Summary," Governor's Blue-Ribbon Commission, *The New Wisconsin Idea,* 1–4.

33. For a critique of the "New Wisconsin Idea," see Chad Goldberg, "The University's Service to Democracy," 11.

34. Governor's Commission, *The New Wisconsin Idea,* 7–17, Attachment A, and Attachment C.

35. Governor's Commission, *The New Wisconsin Idea,* 7, 9, 22.

36. Governor's Commission, *The New Wisconsin Idea,* 33.

37. Marc Eisen, "What Would Tommy Do?" *Isthmus,* Apr. 14, 2016, https://isthmus.com/news/cover-story/a-republican-governor-was-once-uws-greatest-champion/.

38. Clotfelter, *Unequal Colleges in the Age of Disparity,* 97–102; Suzanne Mettler, *Degrees of Inequality: How the Politics of Higher Education Sabotaged the American Dream* (New York: Basic Books, 2014), 10–11.

39. Newfield, *Unmaking the Public University,* 9, 80–88.

40. Cooper, *Family Values,* 225.

41. See, for example, the declining support per student for public funding for higher education: https://shef.sheeo.org/report/. As the 2006 Spellings Commission pointed out, "Unmet financial need among the lowest-income families (those with incomes below $34,000 annually) grew by 80 percent from 1990 to 2004 at four-year institutions, compared with seven percent for the highest-income families" (11).

42. Clotfelter, *Unequal Colleges in the Age of Disparity,* 170–72; Richard Reeves, *Dream Hoarders: How the American Upper Middle Class Is Leaving Everyone Else in the Dust, Why That is a Problem, and What to Do about it* (Washington, DC: Brooking Institution, 2017), 107–13.

43. McGuinn, *No Child Left Behind,* 176.

44. Neil Kraus has highlighted the role of foundations in purveying the erroneous assumption that education is responsible for labor market outcomes during this era; see *The Fantasy Economy,* forthcoming, MS in possession of the author.

45 *A Test of Leadership: Charting the Future of U.S. Higher Education,* A Report of the Commission Appointed by Secretary of Education Margaret Spellings, Pre-Publication Copy, September 2006, vi–vii, https://www2.ed.gov/about/bdscomm/list/hiedfuture/reports/pre-pub-report.pdf.

46. *A Test of Leadership,* 1–5.

47. *A Test of Leadership,* 9. Italics in original.

48. Goldin and Katz, *The Race between Education and Technology,* 323–26, 350. For a compelling critique of Goldin and Katz's argument regarding causation, see David Labaree, *Someone Has to Fail,* 203–5.

49. BLS numbers are from 2012, cited in Neil Kraus, *Fantasy Economy.*

50. Florida, *The Rise of the Creative Class,* 37.

51. Newfield, *Unmaking the Public University,* 129–38.

52. Michael Anft, "The STEM Crisis: Reality or Myth?" *Chronicle of Higher Education,* Nov. 11, 2013, https://www.chronicle.com/article/the-stem-crisis-reality-or-myth/.

53. Herb Childress, *The Adjunct Underclass: How America's Colleges Betrayed Their Faculty, Their Students, and Their Mission* (Chicago: University of Chicago Press, 2019), 23; American Federation of Teachers, *American Academic: The State of the Higher Education Workforce 1997–2007,* 5–11, AFT Collection—Publications, Box 2, Folder 36.

54. Charles Clotfelter, *Unequal Colleges in the Age of Disparity,* 80–81.

55. Barack Obama, "Remarks in Janesville, Wisconsin: 'Keeping America's Promise,'" Feb. 13, 2008, https://www.presidency.ucsb.edu/documents/remarks-janes ville-wisconsin-keeping-americas-promise.

56. Barack Obama, "Remarks in Janesville, Wisconsin."

57. Kaufman, *Fall of Wisconsin,* 185; Scott, "Heading South: US-Mexico Trade and Job Displacement after NAFTA," May 3, 2011, https://www.epi.org/publication/heading_south_u-s-mexico_trade_and_job_displacement_after_nafta1/.

58. Obama won the popular vote 52.9 percent to 45.7 percent and the electoral college by a rout: 365–173.

59. Frank, *Listen, Liberal* 20–43.

60. Frank, *Listen, Liberal,* 143–47.

61. Frank, *Listen, Liberal,* 29–36.

62. Mike Elk, "Abandoning EFCA Is Obama's Political Suicide: Lessons from Three Presidents on Workers' Rights," *Huffington Post,* May 25, 2011, https://www.huffpost.com/entry/abandoning-efca-is-obamas_b_414209.

63. Minchin, *Labor under Fire,* 286–96.

64. Robert Maranto and Michael McShane, *President Obama and Education Reform: The Personal and the Political* (New York: Palgrave MacMillan, 2012), 51–55.

65. Linda Darling-Hammond, "Evaluating No Child Left Behind," *The Nation,* May 21, 2007, https://www.thenation.com/article/archive/evaluating-no-child-left-behind/.

66. Pauline Lipman, *The New Political Economy of Urban Education* (New York: Routledge, 2011), 19.

67. Maranto and McShane, *President Obama and Education Reform,* 66–67; Lipman, *The New Political Economy of Urban Education,* especially chapters 1–3.

68. And in fact, Obama was the speaker for the inaugural meeting of DFER, who recommended Duncan over Darling-Hammond for secretary of education. Ravitch, *Reign of Error,* 26.

69. Dale Russakoff, *The Prize: Who's in Charge of America's Schools?* (Boston: Houghton Mifflin Harcourt), 2015.

70. Maranto and McShane, *President Obama and Education Reform,* 93–97; "The Teachers' Unions' Last Stand," *New York Times,* May 17, 2010.

71. Barack Obama, State of the Union Address, 2010, https://obamawhitehouse.archives.gov/the-press-office/remarks-president-state-union-address. Italics added by author.

CHAPTER 9. THINGS FALL APART

1. Andrew Kersten, *The Battle for Wisconsin: Scott Walker and the Attack on the Progressive Tradition* (New York: W. W. Norton, 2011).

2. Mertz, "Growing Realignment," chapter 9.

3. Patrick Marley and Lee Berquist, "Barrett, Walker Stick to Game Plans in Final Debate," *Milwaukee Journal Sentinel,* Oct. 29, 2010.

4. Katherine Cramer, *The Politics of Resentment: Rural Consciousness in Wisconsin and the Rise of Scott Walker* (Chicago: University of Chicago Press, 2016), chapter 5.

5. Marc Levine, "Race and Male Employment in the Wake of the Great Recession: Black Male Employment Rates in Milwaukee and the Nation's Largest Metro Areas 2010," UW-Milwaukee Center for Economic Development, Working Paper, 2012. African American turnout declined from 73.1 percent (higher than the state's overall turnout) in 2008 to 46.3 percent in 2010 (lower than the state's overall turnout of 49.7 percent). Wisconsin Elections Commission, "General Election Voter Registration and Absentee Statistics 1984–2016," https://elections.wi.gov/elections-voting/statistics/turnout; Andra Gillespie and Tyson-King Meadows, "Black Turnout and the 2014 Midterms," *Joint Center for Political and Economic Studies,* Oct. 29, 2014, 1–5, https://jointcenter.org/wp-content/uploads/2019/11/Joint-Center-2014-Black-Turnout-10-29-14_0.pdf.

6. Judis, *The Populist Explosion,* 53–59.

7. Jane Mayer, *Dark Money: The Hidden History of the Billionaires behind the Rise of the Radical Right* (New York: Doubleday, 2016).

8. I discuss much of this in my essay, "Walker's Wisconsin and the Future of the United States," in *Labor in the Time of Trump,* ed. Jasmine Kerrissey et al. (Ithaca, NY: Cornell University Press, 2019), 69–86.

9. Jeffrey Keefe, "Are Wisconsin Public Employees Over-compensated?" Economic Policy Institute, February 10, 2011, https://www.epi.org/press/news_from_epi_epi_study_finds_wisconsin_public-sector_workers_under-compens/.

10. Dave Umhoefer, "Recall Candidate Kathleen Falk Says Governor Scott Walker Enacted the 'Biggest Cuts to Education in Our State's History,'" *Politifact,* Feb. 19, 2012.

11. Valerie Strauss, "How Gov. Walker Tried to Quietly Change the Mission of the University of Wisconsin," *Washington Post,* Feb. 5, 2015.

12. Jon Shelton, "The Factory that Ate Wisconsin," *Dissent* 65 (4): 99–103.

13. Amanda Terkel and John Celock, "Ohio Issue 2: Controversial Anti-Union Law Defeated by Voters," *Huffington Post,* Nov. 8, 2011, https://www.huffpost.com/entry/ohio-issue-2-_n_1083100.

14. Sean Sullivan, "The Michigan Right-to-Work Battle, Explained," *Washington Post,* Dec. 10, 2012, https://www.washingtonpost.com/news/the-fix/wp/2012/12/10/the-michigan-right-to-work-battle-explained/. Melissa Daniels, "Pennsylvania's Public School Staffing at 10-year Low," *Pittsburgh Tribune,* Aug. 14, 2014," https://archive.triblive.com/news/pennsylvania/pennsylvanias-public-school-staffing-at-10-year-low/. On the right-to-work laws efforts to target teacher unions, see Jack Schneider and Jennifer Berkshire, *A Wolf at the Schoolhouse Door: The Dismantling of Public Education and the Future of School* (New York: The New Press, 2020), 53.

15. Sam Sanders, "The Surprising Legacy of Occupy Wall Street in 2020," *All Things Considered,* Jan. 23, 2020, https://www.npr.org/2020/01/23/799004281/the-surprising-legacy-of-occupy-wall-street-in-2020.

16. For more on this, see Jon Shelton, "Teacher Unionism in America: Lessons from the Past for Defending and Deepening Democracy," *American Educator* 42 (spring 2018): 30–40.

17. Joanne Barkan, "Firing Line: The Grand Coalition against Teachers," in *Public Education under Siege,* ed. Katz and Rose, 40.

18. Chicago Teachers Union, *The Schools Chicago's Students Deserve: Research-Based Proposals to Strengthen Elementary and Secondary Education in the Chicago Public Schools* (Chicago: Chicago Teachers Union, 2012), www.ctunet.com/blog/text/SCSD_Report-02-16-2012-1.pdf, quotation on p. 14.

19. Micah Uetricht, *Strike for America: Chicago Teachers against Austerity* (London: Verso, 2014), 2.

20. Tracy Jan, "Obama Campaign Attacks Romney's Record As Bain Capital Executive," *Boston.com*, May 14, 2012, https://www.boston.com/uncategorized/noprimarytag match/2012/05/14/obama-campaign-attacks-romneys-record-as-bain-capital-executive.

21. "Romney on '47 Percent': I Was 'Completely Wrong,'" *CNBC*, Oct. 5, 2012, https://www.cnbc.com/id/49299714.

22. "Full text: Obama's 2015 State of the Union Address," *USA Today*, Jan. 20, 2015, https://www.usatoday.com/story/news/politics/2015/01/20/full-text-obama-2015-state-of-the-union/22064089/.

23. "Full text: Obama's 2015 State of the Union Address."

24. Clotfelter, *Unequal Colleges in the Age of Disparity*, 98. Only about 28 percent was composed of Pell grants, while tax benefits made up the other 12 percent.

25. *A Test of Leadership*, 4.

26. "Remarks by the President on College Affordability—Buffalo, NY," Aug. 22, 2013, https://obamawhitehouse.archives.gov/the-press-office/2013/08/22/remarks-president-college-affordability-buffalo-ny.

27. See the website, https://collegescorecard.ed.gov/.

28. Jamie Dimon and Marlene Seltzer, "Closing the Skills Gap," *Politico Magazine*, Jan. 5, 2014, https://www.politico.com/magazine/story/2014/01/closing-the-skills-gap-101478#.UzgKOPldWT8.

29. Halah Touryalai, "Jamie Dimon Gets $20 Million for His Worst Year as CEO, Why the Big Raise?" *Forbes*, Jan. 24, 2014, https://www.forbes.com/sites/halahtouryalai/2014/01/24/jamie-dimon-gets-20-million-for-his-worst-year-as-ceo-why-the-big-raise/?sh=3f3b325b1869.

30. Paul Krugman, "Job Skills and Zombies," *New York Times*, Mar. 20, 2014.

31. "Remarks by the President and Vice President at Bill Signing of the Workforce Innovation and Opportunity Act," Jul. 22, 2014, https://obamawhitehouse.archives.gov/the-press-office/2014/07/22/remarks-president-and-vice-president-bill-signing-workforce-innovation-a.

32. "Transcript of Hillary Clinton's Campaign Launch Speech," *TIME*, Jun. 13, 2015, https://time.com/3920332/transcript-full-text-hillary-clinton-campaign-launch/.

33. Kaufman, *The Fall of Wisconsin*, 184; Michael Memoli, "Hillary Clinton Once Called TPP the 'Gold Standard,'" *Los Angeles Times*, Sep. 26, 2016, https://www.latimes.com/politics/la-na-pol-trade-tpp-20160926-snap-story.html.

34. Robert Scott and Elizabeth Glass, "Trade Deficits with TPP Countries Cost More than 2 Million U.S. Jobs in 2015," EPI briefing paper, Mar. 3, 2016, https://www.epi.org/publication/trans-pacific-partnership-currency-manipulation-trade-and-jobs/.

35. Bernie Sanders, *Our Revolution: A Future to Believe In* (New York: Thomas Dunne Books, 2016), 292–93.

36. Sanders, *Our Revolution*, 42–47; Bernie Sanders, "America Must End High-Stakes Testing, Finally Invest in Public Education," *USA Today*, Jan. 8, 2020, https://www.usatoday.com/story/opinion/2020/01/08/bernie-sanders-education-no-child-left-behind-testing-column/2827348001/.

37. Sen. Bernie Sanders Announcement Speech, Burlington, VT, May 26, 2015, http://www.p2016.org/sanders/sanders052615sp.html.

38. Sanders, *Our Revolution*, 354.

39. Robert Reich, *Saving Capitalism: For the Many, Not the Few* (New York: Vintage Books, 2016), especially 89–96, 115–32, 203–10.

40. Matt Karp, "Bernie Sanders's Five Year War," *Jacobin*, Aug. 28, 2020, https://www.jacobinmag.com/2020/08/bernie-sanders-five-year-war.

41. Kaufman, *Fall of Wisconsin,* 180–89.

42. Donald Trump, Presidential Announcement Address, June 16, 2015, https://time.com/3923128/donald-trump-announcement-speech/.

43. Trump, Presidential Announcement Address.

44. Hannah Fraser-Chanpong, "Hillary Clinton Apologizes for Saying She'd Put Coal 'Out of Business,'" *CBS News,* May 2, 2016, https://www.cbsnews.com/news/hillary-clinton-apologizes-for-saying-shed-put-coal-out-of-business/.

45. Katie Reilly, "Read Hillary Clinton's 'Basket of Deplorables' Remarks about Donald Trump Supporters," *TIME,* Sep. 10, 2016, https://time.com/4486502/hillary-clinton-basket-of-deplorables-transcript/.

46. Matthew Yglesias, "Donald Trump and the Indiana Carrier Factory, Explained," *Vox.com,* Dec. 1, 2016, https://www.vox.com/policy-and-politics/2016/12/1/13804918/donald-trump-carrier.

47. Roper Center for Public Research, "How Groups Voted in 2008," "How Groups Voted in 2012," and "How Groups Voted in 2016," https://ropercenter.cornell.edu/how-groups-voted-2008; https://ropercenter.cornell.edu/how-groups-voted-2012; https://ropercenter.cornell.edu/how-groups-voted-2016.

48. Sarah Jaffe, "Whose Class Is It Anyway? The 'White Working Class' and the Myth of Trump," in *Labor in the Time of Trump,* ed. Kerrissey et al., 88–95.

49. Geoffrey Skelley, "Just How Many Obama 2012-Trump 2016 Voters Were There?" *Sabato's Crystal Ball,* Jun. 1, 2017, https://centerforpolitics.org/crystalball/articles/just-how-many-obama-2012-trump-2016-voters-were-there/.

50. Yamiche Alcindor, "Some Who Saw Change in Obama Find It Now in Donald Trump," *New York Times,* Nov. 2, 2016, https://www.nytimes.com/2016/11/03/us/politics/obama-donald-trump-voting.html.

51. Florida, *The Rise of the Creative Class,* 281.

EPILOGUE

1. Emma Kerr, "See High School Graduation Rates by State," *US News and World Report,* Apr. 28, 2021, https://www.usnews.com/education/best-high-schools/articles/see-high-school-graduation-rates-by-state; National Center for Education Statistics, "Fast Facts," https://nces.ed.gov/fastfacts/display.asp?id=27.

2. Scott Horsley, "After 2 Years, Trump Tax Cuts Have Failed to Deliver on GOP's Promises," *NPR,* Dec. 20, 2019, https://www.npr.org/2019/12/20/789540931/2-years-later-trump-tax-cuts-have-failed-to-deliver-on-gops-promises; Anne Marie Knott, "Why the Tax Cuts and Jobs Act (TCJA) Led to Buybacks Rather Than Investment," *Forbes,* Feb. 21, 2019, https://www.forbes.com/sites/annemarieknott/2019/02/21/why-the-tax-cuts-and-jobs-act-tcja led-to-buybacks-rather-than-investment/?sh=d90530c37fbc.

3. On DeVos and the privatization movement she represents, see Schneider and Berkshire, *A Wolf at the Schoolhouse Door.*

4. See, for example, Peter Greene, "Judge Rejects Betsy DeVos Plan to Send Federal Funds to Private Schools," *Forbes,* Aug. 22, 2020, https://www.forbes.com/sites/petergreene/2020/08/22/judge-rejects-betsy-devos-plan-to-send-federal-funds-to-private-schools/?sh=ac90ba923295.

5. Ben Popken, "Why Trump Killed TPP—And Why It Matters to You," *ABC-News,* Jan. 23, 2017, https://www.nbcnews.com/business/economy/why-trump-killed-tpp-why-it-matters-you-n710781.

6. Richard Trumka, "USMCA is a Huge Win for Working People," *CNN.com,* Dec. 20, 2019, https://www.cnn.com/2019/12/20/opinions/usmca-huge-win-labor-rights-trumka/index.html.

7. John Judis, *The Nationalist Revival: Trade, Immigration, and the Revolt against Globalization* (New York: Columbia Global Reports, 2018), 70–71.

8. Shelton, "The Factory That Ate Wisconsin."

9. Josh Dzieza, "Wisconsin Report Confirms Foxconn's So-Called LCD Factory Isn't Real," *The Verge*, Oct. 21, 2020, https://www.theverge.com/2020/10/21/21526765/foxconn-lcd-factory-not-real-confirmation-wisconsin-report-exclusive.

10. Jon Shelton, "Red State Teacher Strikes and the Roots of Teacher Militancy," *Labor and Working-Class History Association*, Newsletter 2018, 6–9; Elizabeth Catte, Emily Hilliard, and Jessica Salfia, eds., *55 Strong: Inside the West Virginia Teachers' Strike* (Cleveland, OH: Belt Publishing, 2018); Eric Blanc, *Red State Revolt: The Teachers' Strikes and Working-Class Politics* (London: Verso, 2019).

11. Dylan Matthews, "4 Big Questions about Job Guarantees," *Vox.com*, Apr. 27, 2018, https://www.vox.com/2018/4/27/17281676/job-guarantee-design-bad-jobs-labor-market-federal-reserve.

12. "The Freedom Dividend," *Yang2020*, https://www.yang2020.com/policies/the-freedom-dividend/.

13. Madeline Will, "The New Flavor of Teacher Strike: More Than Just Pay Raises," *Education Week*, Jan. 25, 2019, https://www.edweek.org/ew/articles/2019/01/25/the-new-flavor-of-teacher-strike-more.html.

14. Jon Shelton, "There Is Now Way Forward without Organized Workers," *Jacobin*, Nov. 7, 2019, https://jacobinmag.com/2019/11/ctu-strike-chicago-teachers-union-public-schools-organized-labor.

15. Kalyn Belsha, "Chicago Teacher Union Leaders Back Sanders, Becoming Latest to Offer Personal Endorsements As Unions Tread Carefully," *Chalkbeat*, Mar. 4, 2020, https://www.chalkbeat.org/2020/3/4/21178699/chicago-teachers-union-leaders-back-sanders-becoming-latest-to-offer-personal-endorsements-as-unions.

16. Glenn Thrush, "'Accelerate the Endgame': Obama's Role in Wrapping Up the Primary," *New York Times*, Apr. 14, 2020, https://www.nytimes.com/2020/04/14/us/politics/obama-biden-democratic-primary.html?auth=login-email&login=email.

17. Chris Riotta, "Biden Sparks Outrage after Suggesting Black People Don't Know How to Raise Children: 'Put the Record Player on at Night,'" *Independent*, Sep. 13, 2019, https://www.independent.co.uk/news/world/americas/us-politics/joe-biden-black-parents-record-player-slavery-criminal-justice-debates-2020-speech-a9104346.html; Alexandra Kelley, "Biden Tells Coal Miners to 'Learn to Code,'" *The Hill*, Dec. 31, 2019, https://thehill.com/changing-america/enrichment/education/476391-biden-tells-coal-miners-to-learn-to-code.

18. Karp, "Bernie Sanders's Five-Year War"; Clotfelter, *Unequal Colleges in the Age of Disparity*, 213–19.

19. For a conservative version of this argument, see Oren Cass, *The Once and Future Worker: A Vision for the Renewal of Work in America* (New York: Encounter Books, 2018).

20. Lisa Lerer, "Joe from Scranton Didn't Win Back the Working Class," *New York Times*, Dec. 5, 2020, https://www.nytimes.com/2020/12/05/us/politics/biden-blue-collar-voters.html; Craig Gilbert, "If WOW Counties Were Ever a Political Bloc, They Are No Longer," *Milwaukee Journal Sentinel*, Nov. 22, 2020; Anya van Wagtendonk, "Milwaukee's Black Turnout Down in 2020," *Urban Milwaukee*, Nov. 13, 2020, https://urbanmilwaukee.com/2020/11/13/milwaukees-black-turnout-down-in-2020/.

21. Ford Fessenden, Lazaro Gamio, and Rich Harris, "Even in Defeat, Trump Found New Supporters across the Country," *New York Times*, Nov. 16, 2020, https://www.nytimes.com/interactive/2020/11/16/us/politics/election-turnout.html.

22. Mindy Isser, "Are Trump Voters a Lost Cause?" *In These Times,* Jan. 2021, 15; Matt Karp, "The Politics of a Second Gilded Age," *Jacobin,* Feb. 17, 2021, https://www.jacobin mag.com/2021/02/the-politics-of-a-second-gilded-age.

23. Ryan Nicol, "Impact Politics Leaders Tout 2020 Success, Including Backing Flori- da's Minimum Wage Increase," *Floridapolitics.com,* Dec. 10, 2020, https://floridapolitics. com/archives/388088-impact-politics-2020-success.

Index

Abel, I. W., 90
Action for Excellence, 107
ACTWU (Amalgamated Clothing and Textile Workers Union), 90
Affordable Care Act of 2010 (ACA), 183
African Americans: 2020 election and, 210; access to education for, 21–22, 52; Clinton and, 6; Freedom Budget and, 70–72; Full Employment Act and, 45; GI Bill and, 43, 136; Great Society reforms and, 62; job-training programs and, 84; Kerner Commission and, 72–75; knowledge economy and, 156; manufacturing sector and, 70; mathematics education and, 152; NAFTA and, 150; National Assessment of Educational Progress and, 106; New Deal programs and, 38; Reconstruction Era and, 27; slavery and, 23–28; standardized testing and, 170; voucher programs and, 133–35; welfare reform and, 155–56; in Wisconsin, 188
Alexander, Lamar, 125, 126, 129, 168
Allen, Danielle, ix, 5, 195
Allen-Bradley Company, 134
Amalgamated Association of Iron and Steel Workers, 28
Amalgamated Clothing and Textile Workers Union (ACTWU), 90
American Council of Education (ACE), 40
American Defense Education Act of 1982, 117–18
American Farm Bureau, 46
American Federation of Labor (AFL), 46, 72, 87, 94, 98, 150
American Federation of Teachers (AFT), 96–97, 98, 100, 157–61, 170
American Legion, 39–40
American Legislative Exchange Council (ALEC), 190
American Motors Company (AMC), 150
American Railway Union, 28
American Recovery and Reinvestment Act of 2009 (ARRA), 183, 184
Americans for Democratic Action, 90
America's Choice: High Skills or Low Wages, 143–44

Anderson, John, 101
A. Philip Randolph Institute, 70
Apple Computers, 128, 180
Arkansas Education Association, 140
Arkansas Science and Technology Development Authority, 140
Association of Land Grant Colleges, 40

Babbitt, Bruce, 120
Bailey, Keith, 171
Baisinger, Grace, 97
Baran, Paul, 224n46
Barkan, Joanne, 192
Barnard, Henry, 217n17
Bascom, John, 13, 176
Beadie, Nancy, 3
Becker, Gary, 10, 39, 55–57, 85, 102, 125, 143, 160, 177, 205; *Human Capital*, 55, 68, 145–46
Bell, Daniel, 79, 84, 167, 203; *The Coming of Post-Industrial Society*, 76–77, 83, 99, 124, 143, 164, 226n7
Bell, Terrel, 7, 9, 97, 103, 104–8
Bennett, Marion, 41
Bennett, William, 103, 112–15, 130, 131–32, 134
Bezos, Jeff, 10, 143
Biden, Joe: 2020 election, 7, 209–10; Crime Bill of 1994 and, 163; on Humphrey, 91–92; Workforce Innovation and Opportunity Act of 2014 and, 196
Blacks. *See* African Americans
Bloom, Allan: *The Closing of the American Mind*, 113
Blue-Ribbon Commission on 21st Century Jobs (Wisconsin), 174–76
Blue-Ribbon Task Force on Educational Excellence (NEA), 108
Boeing, 177
Booker, Cory, 184, 208
Bowen, Howard, 84
Brademas, John, 96
Bradley, Bill, 115
Bradley Foundation, 134
Briggs and Stratton Corporation, 109–10
Brock, Bill, 143

R.J. Nabisco, 129
Rockefeller, Nelson, 83
Romney, Mitt, 193
Roosevelt, Franklin D.: GI Bill and, 35, 39–43;
    Second Bill of Rights and, 1–2, 36, 37–39,
    48. *See also* New Deal
Rothenberg, Randall, 115–16, 161, 215n10,
    227n16
Rubin, Robert, 163
Rush, Benjamin, 17–18, 22
Rustin, Bayard, 2, 58, 62, 69–72, 205, 225n60
Ryor, John, 96, 97–98

Samuel, Howard, 143
*San Antonio Independent School District v.
    Rodriguez* (1973), 81–82
Sandel, Michael, 5, 188, 237n85
Sanders, Bernie, 7, 9, 189, 191, 197–99, 203,
    206, 209
School-to-Work Opportunities Act of 1994,
    148, 154
Schultz, George, 85
Schultz, Theodore, 10, 39, 55–56, 59, 85, 143,
    205
Schultze, Charles, 92
Second Bill of Rights, 1–2, 36, 37–39, 48
segregation, 52, 70, 81–82. *See also*
    desegregation
Self, Robert, 163
Seltzer, Marlene, 195
Service Employees International Union
    (SEIU), 151
Servicemen's Readjustment Act of 1944. *See*
    GI Bill
Sessions, Jeff, 207
Shanker, Albert, 88, 96–97, 98, 107, 157, 192
Sheil, Bernard, 45
Sherman, William Tecumseh, 27
Silber, John, 112
skills gap, 195–96
slavery, 15–16, 23–28
Smith, Adam, 142–43
Smith-Hughes Act of 1917, 31
Smith-Lever Act of 1914, 218n40
Snyder, Rick, 190, 191
social democracy: breadwinner model of, 194;
    Clinton and, 145–46, 148–49, 155, 161–62;
    defined, 10; education myth and, 2–3, 7, 98,
    157; founding of America and, 15–18; Great
    Society and, 4–5, 58–59, 65, 71–75; human
    capital and, x, 8; Humphrey-Hawkins Act
    and, 78, 86–95; need for recommitment
    to, ix, 204–10; neo-liberalism and, 115–16,
    118–20; New Deal and, 4, 35–38, 42–44, 47,

53–54; Obama and, 183, 185, 193; populist
    movements and, 28–29; Reagan and, 102–3,
    109, 122; Sanders and, 189, 191, 197–98;
    school voucher programs and, 135
Social Security Act of 1935, 14, 38, 44, 59
Southern Christian Leadership Council
    (SCLC), 90
Southern Regional Education Board, 152
Spellings, Margaret, 177
Spellings Commission, 178–79, 194, 241n41
Stein, David, 230n76
Stein, Judith, 228n45, 231n2
Steinhardt, Michael, 236n47
STEM, 180
Stevens, Thaddeus, 217n17
Summers, Larry, 183
Sweeney, John, 151
Sweezy, Paul, 224n46

Taft-Hartley Act of 1947, 87, 93–94, 162
Tappan, Henry, 23
tax credits for college tuition, 162–63
Tax Cuts and Jobs Act of 2017, 207
Tea Party, 189
*A Test of Leadership: Charting the Future of
    U.S. Higher Education*, 178–79
Thomas, Clarence, 112
Thompson, Tommy, 123, 133–34, 139, 156,
    168–70, 174, 176, 187
Tillerson, Rex, 207
*Time for Results: The Governors 1991 Report on
    Education*, 125–26
Tlaib, Rashida, 208
Torrijos, Omar, 111
Total Quality Management (TQM), 139, 158
Towner, Horace Mann, 33
Trans-Pacific Partnership (TPP), 6, 194, 197,
    202, 208
Treaty of Detroit (1950), 47–48
Truman, Harry, 4, 9, 36, 46, 50–52
Trumka, Richard, 208
Trump, Donald, 207–8; 2016 election, 7, 8, 11,
    189, 199–202; 2020 election, 8, 11, 209–10
Tsongas, Paul, 115, 118, 145
Twentieth Century Fund, 107

Udall, Morris, 86
unemployment insurance, 14, 42, 48
Union for Democratic Action, 46
unions. *See* labor unions
United Auto Workers (UAW), 47, 72
United Farm Workers, 72
United Teachers of Los Angeles (UTLA), 209
University of California, 65, 177